MUSIC TECHNIQUES
IN THERAPY, COUNSELING
AND SPECIAL EDUCATION

D1568972

JAYNE STANDLEY
RMT-BC, Ph.D
FLORIDA STATE UNIVERSITY

Publisher's Note

Several Competencies in this book call for the selection, duplication and distribution of song sheets to student groups. These activities are subject to international copyright laws and written permission to reprint must be obtained from copyright owners prior to any duplication and distribution of copyrighted material.

MUSIC TECHNIQUES IN THERAPY, COUNSELING, AND SPECIAL EDUCATION

Jayne M. Standley

Library of Congress Cataloging in Publication data

Standley, Jayne M.
   Music techniques in therapy, counseling, and special education /
Jayne M. Standley.
     p. cm.
   Includes bibliographical references.
   ISBN 0-918812-64-X : $18.95
   1. Music therapy—instruction and study. 2. Special education—
Activity programs. 3. Music as recreation. I. Title.
ML3920.S746 1991
615.8'5154—dc20
                                        91-30003
                                           CIP
                                          MN

DEDICATION

To the students whose endeavors to acquire the skills of a music therapist have resulted in such memorable group labs ... and to Cliff Madsen whose teaching, scholarship, and guidance have benefitted so many in the field of music therapy.

TABLE OF CONTENTS

PREFACE

The purpose of this book is to provide a systematic, hierarchical approach to the development of group leadership skills for music activities which are intended to function in an educational, therapeutic, or recreational capacity. The book does not, however, deal with the teaching of music as subject matter. Rather, it is intended to be a synthesis and clinical application of research in music and the acquisition of therapy skills. The contents utilize existing knowledge in the field, borrowing liberally from the many persons who have contributed across time to its accumulation.

Over one hundred music activities are included, covering a variety of client groups ranging in age from infants to the elderly and incorporating major disability labels used in the allied health fields. Current therapeutic/counseling techniques documented in the literature are emphasized. The activities are designed for use in actual practical experiences or with simulated client/student groups and include opportunities for the development of music performance skills and/or for the systematic use of recorded music.

All student activities are fully planned and explained with the group objectives and procedures given for implementation. They are also sequenced in hierarchical order on a variety of issues: from simple to complex skill acquisition, from single to multiple objectives to be accomplished, and from complete delineation of "how to" information to leader independence in determining how the session should be designed and implemented.

Further, the book is based on a philosophy of leader accountability for the group's response in the session. It stresses the establishment of *a priori* objectives, the use of documented techniques, and the collection of data for evaluating results. It is also designed for personalized skill development. To facilitate this, activities are indexed by population, technique and group objective. These indices allow selection of an appropriate activity to meet an individual student's particular needs.

Extensive bibliographies by type of education/therapeutic environment are provided as is a resource list of recorded music titles for use in group discussion sessions. These are intended to help students access existing literature and music repertoire as they become independent in planning and designing therapy sessions for specific client groups.

The inherent philosophy of this book is that clinical expertise is heightened by awareness of the available research literature in the field and the ability to transfer its findings to applied situations.

> Research, in the broadest definition, is a way of thinking, a state of mind. . . The research attitude represents an objective view of the world, and the finished product is a person who is informed and has the ability to think, that is to analyze, criticize, make transfers, and choose alternatives in the light of all possible evidence.[1]

Activities from Level 2 onward include research and group discussion questions to facilitate the practice of analysis and generalization of information so that the best future alternatives for therapeutic intervention might be chosen and implemented.

---

[1] Madsen, C.K.: Research and music therapy: The necessity for transfer. *JMT*, 1979, **23**(2), pp. 50-55.

PART I:

CONTENT AND ORGANIZATION

PART I: CONTENT AND ORGANIZATION

INTRODUCTION

Persons who counsel or teach act upon their own value systems by making many choices for others; among these choices are: determination of another's problem, deciding what to teach to promote its resolution, and selection of the most appropriate techniques to use in this endeavor. Many such persons identify professionally with the value system of a particular theoretical approach (as in the Montessori or Springhill educational methods or the Psychoanalytic, Reality Therapy, or Humanistic Psychology approaches to therapy, to name but a few). Others prefer an eclectic label usually implying adherence to values (or techniques) borrowed from many approaches on the premise that "if it works, use it."

Whatever the value system or theoretical premise underlying the individual's choices, at the level of interacting with the student/client a technique is utilized. There seem to be an unlimited number of theories or explanations of approaches that have evolved over time, but a finite number of techniques identified to accomplish the therapeutic/educational goal. Many techniques, such as role-playing, focusing of attention, or teaching incompatible responses seem to be shared or advocated by different approaches. Each system uses virtually the same procedure but interprets differently why it is used and what it is supposed to accomplish.

The actual procedures used with the client or student to implement the selected values are referred to here as techniques. This book is primarily concerned with the skills to lead a group and with a variety of therapeutic/educational *techniques* combined with music. It teaches these techniques through the opportunity to demonstrate the skills of planning, implementing and evaluating results. It also teaches values to the extent these *techniques* are discussed *contextually* at the conclusion of the demonstrated activity. That is, values become apparent as the discussion is guided toward identifying any implied choices inherent in a task and/or comparisons made between therapeutic/educational approaches.

The underlying premise of all activities included here is that the leader accepts responsibility for the group's response in the session. This establishes a direct relationship between session outcome and the calibre of skill demonstrated and allows the individual to determine personal effectiveness as a leader. Session outcome is, of course, relative to both adequate planning and the ability to adapt quickly to the realities of the interaction. A group of hyperactive children may certainly be more active than normal children, but if the leader fails to control the activity level enough to accomplish at least a portion of the session objective, then the leader has failed to demonstrate a skill. To rationalize by saying the children were *too* hyperactive for the assigned task would be to abdicate leader responsibility. If a session objective does not match the group's level, then the leader may adapt the planned objective and/or control the children's activity level. The premise of this book for the above example is that the more skillful the leader, the calmer and more on-task the children are and the greater the proportion of session objectives are achieved.

This text begins where development of the skill in writing a first lesson or session plan ends. Any such plan must subsequently be implemented with skills other than writing and in reality be immediately adapted to group interaction as it actually occurs. This ability to adapt immediately in response to a group's reactions is a necessary and critical teaching/therapy skill that can be learned only by practice. The skill development may be equivalent to learning to play a musical instrument. One does not become a group violinist solely by watching or listening to another play. Neither does one become a virtuoso by reading information on how to play, by writing plans for skillful violin playing, by listening to lectures on same or by providing correct answers to test questions about violin techniques. One learns to play the violin through many methods including long hours of actually attempting to play the violin. Similarly, a variety of opportunities to practice teaching/therapy leadership skills would seem to provide the experiential component necessary for development of these requisite abilities. This collection of activities is organized to maximize such development across many diverse clinical situations.

TEXT DESIGN

Both a competency based training program and a collection of indexed music treatment plans, this book is intended for many uses, including: instructors of future music therapists or other group leaders who wish to use music; students seeking assistance with planning activities for *practicum* or internship settings; internship directors/*practicum* supervisors who wish to assign client objectives which can be independently implemented; or practicing therapists who desire a resource for a variety of music applications to diverse therapeutic problems.

More than 100 activities or tasks designed to develop competencies in using music to change behavior whether for therapeutic, educational, or recreational reasons are included. They are arranged hierarchically for skill acquisition, from simple to more complex across three dimensions: music skills, group leadership objectives, and the decision-making skills necessary to plan and analyze effect of group interactions. They are comprehensive across group populations with respect to age and label and across current techniques in the allied health fields. They are further designed to acquaint users with the extensive body of research in music and behavior through implementation of documented techniques, discussion of research results and their transfer to applied situations, and provision of extensive bibliographic references. The activities reflect a philosophical bias of accountability, i.e., the leader is responsible for the *results* of the group interaction whether by commission or omission.

The development of skills for leading music activities includes the leader's music performance abilities which determine the quality of the musical aspects of the group interaction, such as singing, accompanying and conducting and the skill to teach others, usually nonmusicians, to perform in group music activities such as choruses, instrumental ensembles, or dance troupes. This text systematically develops musical repertoire while requiring greater musical competence of the leader in the areas of singing, playing and moving and in adapting such activities to meet the needs of the specific group, whether disabled or diverse in ability, preference and/or motivation.

For persons not desiring to develop the music performance skills necessary for leading groups in active music participation, tasks are designed to teach the application of recorded music repertoire to health-related objectives and to teach the leadership skills for directing group listening or discussion about music. Some tasks teach the use of selected music as a background for other group techniques to be developed by the leader, such as progressive relaxation, guided imagery, or the stimulation of group conversation.

The group leadership objectives progress solely from a consideration of the leader's abilities to the accountability for the group's response in the session and from a single music objective to simultaneous music, group, and individual group member objectives. The tasks are divided into four levels of competency achievement with skills accumulating across levels.

Students learn primarily by leading a group through one of these activities as assigned. Client groups can be real or simulated by peers, as in *practicum* assignments or internship sessions. Progress in community *practica* can be assessed and coordinated with additional activities and techniques learned in the classroom through simulation.

Students also learn vicariously by being participants in group sessions, observing the leader's techniques, and discussing intent, accomplishment, group response, and alternative methods and procedures.

Assessment is accomplished through skill checklists included in the manual which gradually become more comprehensive in content. Each task has a recommended *minimum* criterion score on a specific checklist and instructors may, of course, have higher or different criteria for grade differentiation. It is recommended that all sessions be videotaped for subsequent analysis. The student can self-evaluate and compare impressions with those of the instructor.[1] More advanced students can improve observation skills by completing checklists on peers and learn to give constructive feedback.[2] The checklist functions to assess progress while also identifying crucial desired skills and specific skill deficits which become future goals for the individual.

Competency Levels

The activities for competency development are divided into 5 levels, each cumulative and requiring increasingly difficult demonstration of skills and abilities.[3][4][5] Level 1 isolates the development of the leader's music skills and begins with a stated music objective and complete preparation and implementation guidelines. Initially, at this level only musical skill, group response to the leader, and accomplishment of the music objective are evaluated. Later activities at this level add evaluation of music repertoire and personal attributes of the leader, i.e., posture, nervous habits, facial expression, etc.

Level 2 moves beyond the music activity to add accountability for achieving a single nonmusic group objective. Activities at this level are evaluated for the leader's music skill, the leader's personal attributes and ability to demonstrate the basic skills necessary for conducting the specified activity, while also evaluating the effectiveness of the leader to assure the group's accomplishment of the *a priori* objective. Level 2 introduces labeled populations or client groups with a specific problem to be alleviated by the music session. Again, at this level complete session planning and preparation activities are provided.

Level 3 continues the application of music to specific problems of diverse populations while increasing the leader's accountability for the quality of music performance and the presentation and accomplishment of the nonmusic group objective. By the completion of this level, the group leader has been responsible for multiple nonmusic group objectives, has evaluated each objective through collection of group data, and has begun independently making choices about certain aspects of session preparation and planning.

Level 4 is designed to teach the leader to attend to individual problems or objectives within the group while simultaneously directing a music activity and teaching nonmusic group objectives. Leaders also become independent at this level in planning and preparing for the session. Activities here require more sustained periods of time in order for the multiple objectives and tasks to be incorporated.

Level 5 provides an opportunity for the spontaneous demonstration of comprehensive competencies learned and allows the assessment of overall skill development and repertoire depth. The student is given a set of specific session demographics, and with only five minutes of preparation time is expected to conduct a viable therapeutic interaction. This is intended to be analogous to the real clinical world where one's spontaneity is often tested.

---

[1] Greenfield, D.G.: Evaluation of music therapy practicum competencies: comparison of self and instructor rating of videotapes. *JMT*, 1978, **15**(1), pp. 15-20
[2] Prickett, C.A..: The effect of self-monitoring on positive comments given by music therapy students coaching peers. *JMT,* 1987, **24**(2), pp, 54-75.
[3] Alley, J.M.: Competency based evaluation of a music therapy curriculum. *JMT*, 1978, **15**(1), pp. 9-14.
[4] Alley, J.M.: The effect of self-analysis of videotapes on selected competencies of music therapy majors. *JMT,* 1980, **17**, pp. 113-132.
[5] Andersen, J.L.: The effect of feedback versus no feedback on music therapy competencies. *JMT*, 1982, **19**(3), pp. 130-140.

Throughout all levels, each task includes specified assessment and criteria for skill development. Beginning with Level 2, a list of discussion questions is also provided to facilitate generalization or transfer of concepts and techniques demonstrated. These questions are designed to provide information from the research literature, to stimulate thought regarding application to practical situations, to facilitate comparison of demonstrated group reactions with literature reports, and to transmit application of demonstrated cause-effect relationships to other group situations. Research instrumental in the development of these questions, the activities, and the values expressed herein is cited in the Bibliography section at the end of this text.

An outline follows which provides a concise review of the various areas of hierarchical skill development across levels:

Level 1 Tasks:

OBJECTIVES:
      Leader: Music Skills
      Group: Participation
TYPE OF MUSIC:
      Active music participation
POPULATION:
      Peers
LEADER DECISIONS:
      Selection of music according to criteria
EVALUATION:
      Music skill of leader
      Group responses
      Personal attributes of leader (later tasks)

Level 2 Activities:

OBJECTIVES:
      Leader: Music skills
               Teach group objective
      Group: Nonmusic objective, either health, educational or recreational context
TYPE OF MUSIC:
      Active music participation
      Music listening/discussion
      Music as background for other techniques
POPULATION:
      Groups with disability labels
LEADER DECISIONS:
      Selection of music according to criteria
EVALUATION:
      Music skills of leader
      General leadership skills of leader
      Personal attributes of leader
      Group responses

Level 3 Activities:

OBJECTIVES:
      Leader: Music skills
               Teach multiple nonmusic group objectives
      Group: Multiple nonmusic objectives

TYPE OF MUSIC:
  Active music participation
  Music listening/discussion
  Music as background for other techniques
POPULATION:
  Groups with disability labels
LEADER DECISIONS:
  Selection of music
  Preparation of activities
  Selection of data collection method
EVALUATION:
  Music skills of leader
  General leadership skills of leader
  Personal attributes of leader
  Group responses
  Proportion of group objective achieved according to collected data

Level 4 Activities:

OBJECTIVES:
  Leader: Music skills
           Teach nonmusic group objective
           Teach multiple, diverse, individual, nonmusic group objectives
  Group: Group nonmusic objective
           Individual nonmusic objectives
TYPE OF MUSIC:
  Active music participation
  Group music listening/discussion
  Music as background for other techniques
POPULATION:
  Groups with disability labels, diverse in age, severity, or type of label
LEADER DECISIONS:
  Specification of problem and procedures
  Selection of music
  Selection of techniques
  Preparation activities
  Selection of data collection method
EVALUATION:
  Music skills of leader
  General leadership skills of leader
  Personal attributes of leader
  Group responses
  Proportion of group objective achieved according to collected data
  Degree of individual objectives achieved according to collected data

Level 5 Task:

Conduct a music activity according to specifications received 5 minutes prior to implementation and demonstrate comprehensive music leadership, therapeutic, and/or educational competence.

Individualized Skill Development

The hierarchical arrangement of tasks in this text permits systematic development and accumulation of competencies while also allowing for diversity in student entry level and rate of acquisition. It is designed for highly individualized instruction based on personal assessment of each student, *a priori* objectives for skill development, consequated task assignment, ongoing evaluation of results, and continuous development through repetition of the process across levels.

For the purpose of this text, the adjectives teaching and therapy are used interchangeably to describe group leadership skills. To the extent that a therapeutic group objective and treatment plan are identified *a priori* and responsibility taken by the leader for their accomplishment, then the process of leading the group through an activity to achieve the stated objective seems to require relatively the same skills as those of a group music activity to teach subject matter. Since the group objective and planning/implementation procedures are specified in each activity, the skills to be developed and demonstrated are generic to many professions. Whether the student aspires to become a music therapist, music educator, or other professional using music activities (special educator, social worker, counselor, psychologist, psychiatrist, etc.) the exercises in this text teach the basic requisite skills and are carefully indexed so that objectives specific to the intended profession may be selected and skills demonstrated in context.[1] This text does not teach the writing of objectives *per se* since these are preselected. However, specific objectives in observable, measurable terms are modeled as is content from a variety of educational/therapeutic approaches.

Music Selection

In many activities, all procedural specifications are given for implementation except the specific piece of music to be used. Selection of appropriate music is a basic skill to be demonstrated in every activity. In each case the selection should be age appropriate for the identified population, as well as from the group's preferred category or type of music. Major issues to be considered when selecting music include the following:

1. Individual client preference seems to be the most important variable for assuring the desired effect of music. Research shows there is no music that is always perceived as sedative or stimulative by everyone. Rather, each individual's preference and past associations will most directly determine his/her response to music.

2. The difficulty of learning new music can be reduced and controlled through careful selection of lyrics, melody, and/or accompaniment. Repetitive words, rhythms, notes, and chords greatly simplify the learning task.

3. Both musical selections and accompanying activities must be age appropriate to function as intended. For instance, many elderly persons resent being given the type of rhythm instruments usually identified with children. Some dances, too, may be identified with children, e.g., "The Hokey Pokey," and may be insulting to older groups.

4. Music meant to facilitate memory must repetitiously pair a melody or melodic phrase with the discrete information to be remembered and must change as the content to be remembered changes. For instance, the same tune used repeatedly to teach 10 different names will probably not function to aid memory.

Use of Skills Checklist

The checklist of music group leadership skills included and used throughout the book was developed from a comprehensive review of research in music to change behavior. There was particular reliance upon items from the following data collection forms: The Behavior Checklist

---

[1]   Lathom, W.B.: Survey of current functions of a music therapist. *JMT*, 1982, **19**(1), pp. 2-27.

developed by Furman[1] for assessing guitar-accompanied song leading, the Music Conductor Observation Form developed by Madsen and Yarbrough,[2] the behavioral rating form for assessing *practicum* skills of music therapy students developed by Hanser and Furman,[3] and the Music Therapy Competency Observation form developed by Alley.[4] Additional items were drawn from the list of Essential Competencies for the Practice of Music Therapy[5] and from the competency list developed by Braswell, Decuir and Maranto.[6]

The initial version of the checklist used herein was field tested by observing two videotapes of each of 19 advanced music therapy students conducting song leading activities with their peers and a year later with children aged 4-5 years. (Scores on the 100 point checklist ranged in the song with peers from 13-78 with an average score of 49.3 and in the song with children a year later from 31-93 with an average score of 77.5) These 38 checklist evaluations were compared with two other analyses previously completed on the same teaching interactions.

Following this comparison the checklist was revised with items added, omitted, or rearranged to reflect comprehensively the primacy and frequency of competencies observed and cited. Additionally, items were reweighted for scoring, some on the basis of documented relationship in the research between competencies and effect on clients, some on the basis of frequency of inclusion in other published observation forms, and some on the field test comparison.

The final version of the 100 point checklist includes 93 items divided horizontally on the form into four major sections: Personal Skills (20 points), General Leadership Skills (40 points), Music Skills (20 points), and Client Responses (20 points). The first three sections list observable therapist skills while the final section includes observable client responses. Client responses were included and weighted to balance the therapist proficiency score thereby establishing a relationship between competency evaluation and client achievement and appropriate behavior.

A basal score in each category functions to weight that section in relationship to the overall test. This is intended to differentiate the special skills that therapists using music demonstrate across all populations and to differentiate music to meet a specific objective from other music interactions with handicapped persons.

The 93 items are further divided vertically into three columns: **Deficiencies** – behaviors or skills of the leader that are omitted, are performed poorly, or are undesirable to the extent that they interfere with the effectiveness of the session (N = 37); **Skills meeting minimum criteria** – behaviors deemed essential and basic to every music group activity (N = 30); and **Skills above minimum criteria** – behaviors that indicate more sophisticated group leadership abilities (N = 26). The final checklist is included in three versions: Checklist 1 – music skills only, for evaluation of initial Level 1 competencies; Checklist 2 – music and personal skills for later Level 1 competencies; and Checklist 3 – the full checklist for evaluating competencies on Levels 2 through 5.

---

[1] Furman, C.E.: Behavior checklists and videotapes versus standard instructor feedback in the development of a music teaching competency. In: C.K. Madsen and C.A. Prickett (eds.): *Applications of Research in Music Behavior.* Tuscaloosa, AL: The University of Alabama Press, 1987, pp. 73-98.

[2] Madsen, C.K., Yarbrough, C.: *Competency-Based Music Education.* Englewood Cliffs, NJ: Prentice-Hall, Inc., 1980.

[3] Hanser, S.B., Furman, C.E.: The effect of videotaped feedback vs. field-based feedback on the development of applied clinical skills. *JMT,* 1980, **17**, pp. 103-112.

[4] Alley, J.M.: The effect of videotape analysis on music therapy competencies: An observation of simulated and clinical activities. *JMT,* 1982, **19**(3), pp. 141-160.

[5] Bruscia, K.E., Hesser, B., Boxill, E.H.: Essential competencies for the practice of music therapy. *Music Therapy,* 1981, **1**(1), pp. 43-49.

[6] Braswell, C., Decuir, A., Maranto, C.D.: Ratings of entry level skills by music therapy clinicians, educators, and interns. *JMT,* 1980, **17**(3), pp. 133-147.

Scoring

Each student's music session is observed for those therapist skills meeting minimum criteria as listed in the center column, and a check is placed by all skills demonstrated. When a minimum criteria competency is *not observed* in a subset of any category on the form, then that item is left blank indicating skill omitted or marked NA (not applicable to this session, as in "sings, plays correct in tune pitches" in a session involving only exercising to a record or tape). If a minimum skill item is left blank due to the perception that a skill was omitted, then the deficiencies column immediately to the left of that subset is utilized. Any overt deficiencies noted may be checked there for specific feedback to the leader.

When minimum criteria *are* observed and checked in a subject of any category, then the right column is considered. Any additional skills meeting *above minimum criteria* are checked there.

Section 3.0, Music Skills, provides space for recording those music skills utilized in the sessions observed. These items are not included in scoring since therapists use a wide variety of music activities often in creative or unique ways. The number of music skills or type of skill used (live vs. recorded music) is sometimes less important than the quality of the skill and how it is incorporated into the therapeutic objective. It is considered important, however, to record what music skill was being analyzed in the overall checklist. This allows for comparison across the spectrum of music skills for one individual or for assessment of progress in development of a specific music skill.

The Checklist is scored according to the chart in Table 1.

TABLE I: SCORING CHART FOR MT GROUP ACTIVITY LEADERSHIP SKILLS
CHECKLIST

All skills meeting minimum criteria and above minimum criteria count 1 point each, except where noted on the form. Deficiencies count -1 each, except where noted on the form. Skills left blank or marked NA receive 0 points. Be sure to add the basal score* for each category in the category total.

Category	Minimum Criteria Points	Extra Points Above Minimum Criteria	Category Total
1.0 Personal Skills			
1.1 Posture/Stance/ Proximity/Body Language	2	2	
1.2 Speaking Voice	2	2	
1.3 Facial Expression	1	2	
1.4 Eye Contact	2	3	
*Basal Score: 4	7	9	20
2.0 General Leadership Skills			
2.1 Session Planning	4	3	
2.2 Session Preparation	4	1	
2.3 Session Implementation	6	4	
2.4 Session Evaluation	3	3	
*Basal Score: 12	17	11	40
3.0 Music Skills			
*Basal Score: 8	7	5	20
(All music skills utilized are checked but not included in scoring)			
4.0 Client Response			
*Basal Score: 8	6	6	20
(In this category all deficiencies count –2 each, all minimum criteria count +3 and all above minimum criteria count +2)			

Criteria

Each task includes a specified checklist score to meet criteria for the assignment as a guide for the student and for the instructor. (It is recommended that these criteria not be rigidly adhered to but used primarily to establish a reasonable goal.) The criteria scores were set according to results of field testing across 5 groups of persons with varying experience and expertise.[1] Table 2 shows average scores for these groups by skill column: deficiencies, minimum criteria, and above minimum criteria. These scores seem to indicate that the checklist as constructed discriminates expertise and experience primarily through increased scores in the above minimum criteria column: M = 24.5 for RMT-BC's and 18.9 for MT Pre-Interns as compared with mean scores of 2.6, 1.9, and 2.2 for the other three groups.

---

[1] Standley, J.M.: Use of a checklist to assess music therapy group activity leadership skills. Annual Conference, NAMT, Inc., Chicago, 1986.

TABLE 2: AVERAGE GROUP SCORES BY SKILL COLUMNS

	DEFICIENCIES	MINIMUM CRITERIA	ABOVE MINIMUM CRITERIA
RMT-BC	0.0	34.5	24.5
(N = 13)			
MT PRE-INTERNS	1.4	32.5	18.9
(N = 25)			
ME PRE-INTERNS	3.9	24.9	2.6
(N = 25)			
FRESHMEN MUSIC MAJORS	5.1	22.8	1.9
(N = 25)			
MT SENIORS-BASELINE	8.1	21.5	2.2
(N= 25)			
N = 113			

Field test scores for each group were also tallied across subcategories and for the assessment and as a whole. These results are shown in Table 3. It can be seen that the professional music therapists (RMT-BC) scored an average of 91.1 points, the MT Pre-Interns an average of 81.0 points, the music education Pre-Interns and Freshmen scored 55.4 and 51.6 points, respectively, and the MT Seniors on the baseline task scored 46.4 points. The MT Seniors Baseline group received the lowest score in almost all categories, even rating lower than Freshmen in all areas except client responses. It is felt that this was probably due to the difficulty of the assigned leadership task for this group to use an accompanying instrument. In comparison, no other individuals in groups untrained in music therapy (Freshmen or ME Pre-Interns) elected to use an accompaniment. Otherwise, scores decreased as experience and professional preparation in music therapy decreased.

TABLE 3: AVERAGE GROUP SCORES BY CATEGORY

	PERSONAL SKILLS	GENERAL LEADERSHIP SKILLS	MUSIC SKILLS	CLIENT RESPONSES	TOTAL
RMT-BC	17.7	37.7	16.1	19.5	91.1*
(N = 13)					
MT PRE-INTERNS	16.6	31.3	15.7	17.4	81.0*
(N - 25)					
ME PRE-INTERNS	9.4	19.3	14.2	12.5	55.4
(N = 25)					
FRESHMEN MUSIC MAJORS	8.2	17.9	14.2	10.7	51.6
(N = 25)					
MT SENIORS-BASELINE	6.5	16.3	11.3	12.6	46.4
(N = 25)					

N = 113, DF = 4, μ < .001

*Indicates significance from groups without asterisk

Ongoing Evaluation

A Student Progress Form (page 15) is included to assist in evaluating long-term progress for individuals across assignments and skill levels. It is cumulative with entries made after each checklist assessment of an assignment. A copy can be maintained by the student for recording self-evaluation with a second copy maintained by the instructor for course evaluation. Student-instructor conferences to set future objectives and select the next assignment also allow the form to function as a contract between the student and teacher.

Since the tasks are assigned individually and any combination may occur on a given class day, a Class Assignment Form is provided to help the instructor structure the class agenda (page 16). Each task has a recommended time limit to assist the instructor in determining how many interactions to schedule for each class meeting. The form can be replicated and completed for each planned class meeting.

Implementation Procedures

This text is a mechanism for diverse entry levels and rates of acquisition of competencies; for generalization or specialization by population, disability area, or field of endeavor; and for the use of live music or recorded music. Its use can coordinate skill development in simulation with skills developed in actual *practica* or internship settings. It is designed for highly individualized instruction within group and classroom situations.

The following procedures for use with groups of students are recommended:

1. Initial leadership opportunities should be as nonthreatening as possible and designed to *desensitize* the student to being in front of the group and to being videotaped.

Some techniques for desensitizing group members to being the leader are: the instructor can start a well-known song and have each class member take a turn leading it, with the music continuing as each one stands in place and leads; each person may be given multiple opportunities to stand up and lead a predetermined activity without interruption for feedback which may come at the end of the class and be given to the group, not the individual; everyone may lead the same song, but change it musically in some way. When students begin leading the group without hesitation, they are ready for their first individualized objective. If music skills need to be improved, then objectives at Level 1 would be appropriate. If students are accomplished at functional music skills, then repertoire might be developed through later Level 1 tasks. If students are accomplished in both areas, then Level 2 tasks may be the best starting place.

2. From the outset the class should be taught to be cooperative and supportive of peers in the leadership role.

This training is crucial for later group sessions when difficult client responses may be simulated. If leaders do not feel comraderie and support from their peers prior to dealing with the pressure of being the leader for clients with difficult to control behaviors, then "revenge" may become the *modus operandi*. Group members may become very inappropriate clients for subsequent leaders who gave them difficulty in prior simulations. If this happens, the group will become chaotic, uncontrolled and no longer simulating the specific type of student/client behavior desired.

The following rules are important to teach prior to allowing students to assume the leadership role with individualized objectives:

*   Attendance will be required of all students at all class meetings, whether or not they are presenting, so that a group will exist for each leader and so that everyone will feel a commitment to **effectively** role-play the desired client behavior.

*   Each leader will prepare to the best of his/her ability in order to maximize opportunities to learn, realizing that every leadership opportunity will be evaluated.

*   The group will cooperate with the leader at all times unless instructed by the teacher to simulate specific, contrary behavior.

*   If client groups are simulated, their behavior will be role-played exactly as instructed.

*   Only those students instructed to role-play client behavior will do so.

*   All persons role-playing client behavior will respond positively to correct techniques implemented by the leader to deal with the problem.

*   Students will make only positive comments about the leader. Any negative comments will be made and controlled by the teacher.

3.   All leadership opportunities will be evaluated.

Informal evaluation can be used to identify personal assets and deficits, skills demonstrated and not demonstrated. Formal evaluation can be systematic, like counting a specific event or using one of the three checklists provided (pages 17-22). Evaluating from a videotape is more objective than one's memory and allows both the instructor and student to evaluate at different times. To videotape simulations and *practica* at least two VCR units are necessary, one for taping and one for playback/evaluation. The taping one may be checked out by students trained in its use for taping outside the classroom. The VCR for playback should be centrally located and always available for use, and when earphones are used, can be placed in a common area like a library or study room.

4.   Leadership objectives should be assigned individually and mutually agreed upon in conference between the instructor and student.

The Student Progress Form may be completed after each conference and a copy maintained by the student and the instructor. The conference should be delayed until the previous simulation has been evaluated by both the student and instructor.

5.   Objectives should challenge an individual to develop a new skill but not be so difficult as to intimidate or lead to failure.

Activities are indexed according to population, techniques, and student objectives and classified according to level from simple (Level 1) to complex (Level 4). A Class Assignment Form (page 16) completed for each class meeting will help the instructor remember each student's assigned objective.

6.   The instructional process remains the same across multiple simulations, though the student's objectives change.

The process for the leader is:
- a)   receive assignment
- b)   prepare to best of ability
- c)   present in class and be videotaped (a videotape of a *practicum* interaction can also be a presentation)
- d)   review tape and evaluate according to instructions
- e)   confer with instructor about presentation and identify future objective (indexes may be used to find best activity for objective selected)
- f)   repeat process

The process for the group is:
- a)   participate in presentation as instructed
- b)   respond to all directions and techniques implemented
- c)   give positive feedback to leader
- d)   discuss session with teacher for transfer of observations, demonstrations, techniques, etc.

The process for the class instructor:
- a)   assess student on previous assignment using appropriate checklist by watching videotape or observing live and recording results on Student Progress Form
- b)   meet with student in an individual conference after student has self-evaluated and determine student's awareness of assets and deficits
- c)   select next leadership objective
- d)   select activity for next assignment by using indexes

  e) make any special assignments for individual to personalize the objectives of the activity

  f) record assignment and date due on Class Assignment Form

7. As students become more sophisticated and reach Competency Levels 3 and 4, they will be required to make more decisions about how the session should be structured and will also need to acquire some of their own information about techniques and client groups.

Bibliographies containing music articles by client group are included to assist with this endeavor. Students can be taught to know and utilize the literature in the field when planning sessions. This can be especially emphasized during the discussions for transfer following each presentation.

8. Decisions regarding selection of music for client discussion groups are crucial.

This task is facilitated by a resource list in the Appendix. Music titles are organized by general discussion topic. Students must decide, however, how the music fits the objective of the group. For instance, Willie Nelson's "Whiskey River" is listed under the topic Substance Abuse. Under the philosophy of this text, it would be considered a *lack* of skill for a leader to let the group discussion use the lyrics of this song to *justify* substance abuse instead of identifying its negative consequences since justifying deviant behavior is rarely a therapeutic objective.

9. When competencies are acquired they should remain a part of the person's repertoire, and become retrievable with little preparation.

The greater the repertoire, the more adaptable and skillful the group leader. Level 5 is provided as an opportunity for spontaneous demonstration of skill level. It is a synthesizing task that allows a person to assess comprehensively his/her development.

10. The instructor and students should note that *nonreligious* music is stressed, particularly at the beginning of the manual.

Secular music is stressed for several important reasons. The objective is to increase nonreligious repertoire and to sensitize students to the fact that music from *their* religious background *may not* be appropriate for every client in a group with which they might work. Once sensitized, the student might later select appropriate religious music from a client's faith to meet a therapeutic objective, i.e., as in counseling a terminally ill person with a strong reliance on religious belief. Initially, however, the manual directs the student to secular literature. There is also an initial emphasis on *peer age level* and *interest* that moves to other ages and music preferences.

STUDENT PROGRESS FORM

Student Name

| | | Future Objectives | Music Used | Skill Assets | Skill Deficits |

Checklist Scores					
	Total				
	Client Response				
	Group Leadership				
	Personal				
	Music				

Assignment:
Clients
Objective

LEVEL 1
1.0
2
3
4
5
6

LEVEL 1
2.0
2
3
4
5
6

LEVEL 1
3.0
2
3
4
5
6

LEVEL 1
4.0
2
3
4
5
6

CLASS ASSIGNMENT FORM

Date: _____

<u>Presentation Order</u>

1. Student Name _____
    Objective # _____ Time Limit _____
    Objective _____
    Special Assignments _____
    _____
    Evaluation _____
    _____

2. Student Name _____
    Objective # _____ Time Limit _____
    Objective _____
    Special Assignments _____
    _____
    Evaluation _____
    _____

3. Student Name _____
    Objective # _____ Time Limit _____
    Objective _____
    Special Assignments _____
    _____
    Evaluation _____
    _____

4. Student Name _____
    Objective # _____ Time Limit _____
    Objective _____
    Special Assignments _____
    _____
    Evaluation _____
    _____

5. Student Name _____
    Objective # _____ Time Limit _____
    Objective _____
    Special Assignments _____
    _____
    Evaluation _____
    _____

6. Student Name _____
    Objective # _____ Time Limit _____
    Objective _____
    Special Assignments _____
    _____
    Evaluation _____
    _____

NAME _____ CLIENTS _____

DATE _____ OBJECTIVE _____

CHECKLIST 1: MUSIC SKILLS

3.0 MUSIC SKILLS	DEFICIENCIES	SKILLS MEETING MINIMUM CRITERIA	SKILLS ABOVE MINIMUM CRITERIA

Check all used:
___ Voice
___ Autoharp
___ Guitar
___ Piano
___ Rhythm Implements
___ Movement: Dance
             Exercise
             Clapping
             Motions
___ Recorded music
	___ Mistakes in voice or accompaniment
	___ Difficulty in starting/ continuing music
	___ Lack of conducting cues for group participation
	___ Uncontrolled variations in beat/tempo/pitch
	___ Motor activities not matched to music, not sequenced, too easy or difficult
	___ Music not related to objective or ability level of clients
		___ Sings, plays correct in tune pitches
		___ Music uninterrupted by mistakes
		___ Cues group participation in music/motor activities
		___ Uses steady beat, appropriate dynamics and tempo
		___ Demonstrates motor tasks adequately
		___ Music related to objective and ability level (+2)
			___ Uses original music or creative adaptation
			___ Music skill at exceptional, artistic level (+2)
			___ Music is obviously enjoyable to participants/audience (+2)

BASAL: 8	− ___ SUBTOTAL	+ ___ SUBTOTAL	+ ___ SUBTOTAL = ___ MUSIC TOTAL
4.0 GROUP RESPONSES			
	___ Clients withdrawn, off-task, nonparticipatory (−2) ___ Objectives not achieved by at least 80% of group (−2) ___ High level of inappropriate behavior (psychotic, repetitive, negative, disruptive) (−2)	___ Clients on-task/participatory 80% of session (+3) ___ Objective achieved by 80% group (+3)	___ Primary objective achieved by all, secondary objective achieved by many (+2) ___ Client on-task/participation above 80% (+2) ___ Clients obviously enjoyed session (+2)
BASAL: 8	− ___ SUBTOTAL	+ ___ SUBTOTAL	+ ___ SUBTOTAL = ___ GROUP TOTAL
		OVERALL SCORE _____ (Add Music and Group Totals)	

Note: Instructions for use on p. 9

NAME _____ CLIENTS _____

DATE _____ OBJECTIVE _____

CHECKLIST 2: MUSIC AND PERSONAL SKILLS

1.0 PERSONAL SKILLS	DEFICIENCIES	SKILLS MEETING MINIMUM CRITERIA	SKILLS ABOVE MINIMUM CRITERIA
1.1 Posture/Stance/ Proximity/Body Language	___ Chronic slump or restless pacing ___ Repetitive touching of body, clothes, glasses (tic) ___ Physical barriers between leader and clients or distance too great	___ Stands or sits with prox– imity and posture appropriate to activity and clients ___ Exhibits no distracting mannerisms	___ Systematically varies, posture stance, proximity to enhance client interaction ___ Uses above for contingent approval
1.2 Speaking Voice	___ Unnecessary words/ sounds (ah, OK, you know); stuttering, hesitations ___ Speed too slow or fast for comprehension ___ Pitch distracting – too high, sing–song, irritating ___ Voice volume inaudible or uncomfortably loud	___ Uses appropriate speech patterns ___ Uses comfortable voice volume, speed and pitch	___ Systematically varies voice to enhance client interaction ___ Uses voice for contingent approval
1.3 Facial Expression	___ Expression incongruent with verbalizations or lesson objective ___ Expression chronically unpleasant or disapproving (more than 20%)	___ Has expression generally pleasant or congruent with objective, activity, client, verbalizations	___ Systematically varies expression to enhance client interaction ___ Uses expression for contingent approval
1.4 Eye Contact	___ Eye contact reduced or distracted by activity, materials, client placement ___ Failure to scan, look at entire group	___ Maintains eye contact across entire group throughout activity (+2)	___ Varies eye contact to enhance client interaction ___ Uses eye contact for contingent approval ___ Demonstrates high frequency of responses to client behavior
BASAL: 4	⁻ ___ SUBTOTAL	⁺ ___ SUBTOTAL	⁺ ___ SUBTOTAL
			= ___ PERSONAL TOTAL

3.0 MUSIC SKILLS

Check all used:			

___ Voice
 ___ Autoharp
 ___ Guitar
 ___ Piano
 ___ Rhythm Implements
 ___ Movement: Dance
          Exercise
          Clapping
          Motions
 ___ Recorded music
	___ Mistakes in voice or accompaniment
	 ___ Difficulty in starting/ continuing music
	 ___ Lack of conducting cues for group participation
	 ___ Uncontrolled variations in beat/tempo/pitch
	 ___ Motor activities not matched to music, not sequenced, too easy or difficult
	 ___ Music not related to objective or ability level of clients
		___ Sings, plays correct in tune pitches
		 ___ Music uninterrupted by mistakes
		 ___ Cues group participation in music/motor activities
		 ___ Uses steady beat, appropriate dynamics and tempo
		 ___ Demonstrates motor tasks adequately
		 ___ Music related to objective and ability level (+2)
			___ Uses original music or creative adaptation
			 ___ Music skill at exceptional, artistic level (+2)
			 ___ Music is obviously enjoyable to participants/audience (+2)

BASAL: 8	⁻ ___ SUBTOTAL	⁺ ___ SUBTOTAL	⁺ ___ SUBTOTAL
			= ___ MUSIC TOTAL

CHECKLIST 2: MUSIC AND PERSONAL SKILLS (continued)

4.0 GROUP RESPONSES	DEFICIENCIES	SKILLS MEETING MINIMUM CRITERIA	SKILLS ABOVE MINIMUM CRITERIA
	___ Clients withdrawn, off-task, nonparticipatory (–2) ___ Objectives not achieved by at least 80% of group (–2) ___ High level of inappropriate behavior (psychotic, repetitive, negative, disruptive) (–2)	___ Clients on-task/participatory 80% of session (+3) ___ Objective achieved by 80% group (+3)	___ Primary objective achieved by all, secondary objective achieved by many (+2) ___ Client on-task/participation above 80% (+2) ___ Clients obviously enjoyed session (+2)
BASAL: 8	– ___ SUBTOTAL	+ ___ SUBTOTAL	+ ___ SUBTOTAL
			= ___ GROUP TOTAL
		OVERALL SCORE _____ (Add Music and Group Totals)	

Note: Instructions for use p. 9

NAME _____ CLIENTS _____

DATE _____ OBJECTIVE _____

CHECKLIST 3: COMPREHENSIVE LEADERSHIP SKILLS

1.0 PERSONAL SKILLS	DEFICIENCIES	SKILLS MEETING MINIMUM CRITERIA	SKILLS ABOVE MINIMUM CRITERIA
1.1 Posture/Stance/ Proximity/Body Language	___ Chronic slump or restless pacing ___ Repetitive touching of body, clothes, glasses (tic) ___ Physical barriers between leader and clients or distance too great	___ Stands or sits with prox- imity and posture appropriate to activity and clients ___ Exhibits no distracting mannerisms	___ Systematically varies, posture stance, proximity to enhance client interaction ___ Uses above for contingent approval
1.2 Speaking Voice	___ Unnecessary words/ sounds (ah, OK, you know); stuttering, hesitations ___ Speed too slow or fast for comprehension ___ Pitch distracting – too high, sing-song, irritating ___ Voice volume inaudible or uncomfortably loud	___ Uses appropriate speech patterns ___ Uses comfortable voice volume, speed and pitch	___ Systematically varies voice to enhance client interaction ___ Uses voice for contingent approval
1.3 Facial Expression	___ Expression incongruent with verbalizations or lesson objective ___ Expression chronically unpleasant or disapproving (more than 20%)	___ Has expression generally pleasant or congruent with objective, activity, client, verbalizations	___ Systematically varies expression to enhance client interaction ___ Uses expression for contingent approval
1.4 Eye Contact	___ Eye contact reduced or distracted by activity, materials, client placement ___ Failure to scan, look at entire group	___ Maintains eye contact across entire group throughout activity (+2)	___ Varies eye contact to enhance client interaction ___ Uses eye contact for contingent approval ___ Demonstrates high frequency of responses to client behavior
BASAL: 4	⁻ ___ SUBTOTAL	⁺ ___ SUBTOTAL	⁺ ___ SUBTOTAL
			= ___ PERSONAL TOTAL

CHECKLIST 3: COMPREHENSIVE LEADERSHIP SKILLS (continued)

2.0 GENERAL LEADERSHIP SKILLS	DEFICIENCIES	SKILLS MEETING MINIMUM CRITERIA	SKILLS ABOVE MINIMUM CRITERIA
2.1 Session Planning	___ Objective not observable ___ Objective above or below client level or not related to identified needs ___ Uses appropriate materials ___ Objective too lengthy or brief for allotted time	___ Demonstrates specific objective ___ Task matches client level and needs ___ Plan fits allotted time	___ Uses task analysis ___ Uses successive approximations ___ Uses criteria related contingencies
2.2 Session Preparation	___ Room setup not adapted to activity ___ Extraneous items present hazard, barrier or distractor ___ Materials require further preparation before use which interrupts activity ___ Clients not in logical/ appropriate position for activity	___ Sets up room for activity ___ Clears extraneous items from area ___ Has materials ready for immediate use ___ Places clients appropriately for activity	___ Room setup and client placement arranged to achieve maximum class benefit, i.e., for peer tutors, peer modeling
2.3 Session Implementation	___ Lesson plan implemented without regard to client responses ___ Poor directions (not specific or sequenced, too lengthy) ___ Lack of cues/feedback ___ Pacing too slow or fast ___ Activity interrupted or diverted from original task	___ Adapts activity to client response (+2) ___ Uses appropriate directions ___ Uses appropriate cuing and feedback ___ Uses appropriate pacing ___ Uses time effectively	___ Gives contingent feedback ___ Demonstrates consistent directions and feedback ___ Shapes primary and secondary client objective ___ Maintains 4:1 positive ratio of feedback
2.4 Session Evaluation	___ No client criteria evident ___ No client data collected ___ No correction of problems encountered in session	___ Client criteria evident ___ Client data collected ___ Attempted to correct problems in session	___ Individualized client criteria ___ Collected client data on more than one objective ___ Resolved all problems satisfactorily during session
BASAL: 4	− ___ SUBTOTAL	+ ___ SUBTOTAL	+ ___ SUBTOTAL = ___ TOTAL

CHECKLIST 3: COMPREHENSIVE LEADERSHIP SKILLS (concluded)

3.0 MUSIC SKILLS	DEFICIENCIES	SKILLS MEETING MINIMUM CRITERIA	SKILLS ABOVE MINIMUM CRITERIA

Check all used:
___ Voice
___ Autoharp
___ Guitar
___ Piano
___ Rhythm Implements
___ Movement: Dance
           Exercise
           Clapping
           Motions
___ Recorded music
	___ Mistakes in voice or accompaniment
	___ Difficulty in starting/ continuing music
	___ Lack of conducting cues for group participation
	___ Uncontrolled variations in beat/tempo/pitch
	___ Motor activities not matched to music, not sequenced, too easy or difficult
	___ Music not related to objective or ability level of clients
		___ Sings, plays correct in tune pitches
		___ Music uninterrupted by mistakes
		___ Cues group participation in music/motor activities
		___ Uses steady beat, appropriate dynamics and tempo
		___ Demonstrates motor tasks adequately
		___ Music related to objective and ability level (+2)
			___ Uses original music or creative adaptation
			___ Music skill at exceptional, artistic level (+2)
			___ Music is obviously enjoyable to participants/audience (+2)

BASAL: 8	− ___ SUBTOTAL	+ ___ SUBTOTAL	+ ___ SUBTOTAL
			= ___ MUSIC TOTAL

4.0 GROUP RESPONSES			
	___ Clients withdrawn, off-task, nonparticipatory (−2) ___ Objectives not achieved by at least 80% of group (−2) ___ High level of inappropriate behavior (psychotic, repetitive, negative, disruptive) (−2)	___ Clients on-task/participatory 80% of session (+3) ___ Objective achieved by 80% group (+3)	___ Primary objective achieved by all, secondary objective achieved by many (+2) ___ Client on-task/participation above 80% (+2) ___ Clients obviously enjoyed session (+2)
BASAL: 8	− ___ SUBTOTAL	+ ___ SUBTOTAL	+ ___ SUBTOTAL
			= ___ GROUP TOTAL
		OVERALL SCORE _____ (Add category totals)	

Note: Instructions for use p. 9

PART II:

COMPETENCY ACTIVITIES

PART II: COMPETENCY ACTIVITIES

LEVEL 1 COMPETENCIES

Tasks at this level are designed to:

a) *desensitize* individuals to being in front of a group, to being videotaped, and to having their leadership skills evaluated;

b) assess and improve *personal skills* in the leadership role;

c) teach basic music leadership skills for the activities of *singing, dancing, exercising to music, and playing rhythms*;

d) improve *accompanying* skills;

e) increase *accompanying repertoire* for sing-alongs;

f) sensitize group leaders to the necessity for continuously monitoring members and *adapting instruction* to group's responses;

g) introduce the basic instructional techniques of: *Chaining*
    Modeling
    Cuing
    Correcting
    Approving
    Task analyzing
    Scanning
    Fading
    Signing to music
    Collecting data;

h) teach appropriate *simulation protocol* to group members, i.e., participation, cooperation, and active verbal support for colleagues as they perform.

OBJECTIVE 1.01

Lead group in singing a well-known, unaccompanied song.

Group: Peers

Procedure:

PREPARATION:
1. Select a well-known, *nonreligious* song.
2. Practice and memorize.

IMPLEMENTATION:
1. State title of song.
2. Give starting pitch.
3. Cue group to begin.
4. Sing along from memory without pause through entire song.
5. Use facial features to encourage participation.
6. Scan group continuously to assess who is singing and enjoying the music.
7. At end of activity write down names of people most on-task to music. Give to instructor at individual conference to document scanning skill.

Note: The objective is to *lead* the song with musical/conducting/facial cues and little or no talking.

Music Specifications:

1. Well-known, *nonreligious* song, *appropriate to peer level and interest.*
2. Song should have at least two verses and chorus (or 12 lines).

Recommended Time Limit: Usually 1–2 minutes

Criteria For Objective:

Checklist 1: Music Score   12
              Client Response Score   13
Music Selection as specified
Implementation in allotted time

Note: Repeat this objective with different songs until criteria are met on Checklist 1.

Techniques Included: *Songleading*
                         Scanning

OBJECTIVE 1.02

Accompany with most advanced technique of which you are capable on guitar, autoharp, or keyboard and lead group in singing a *well-known* song.

Group: Peers

Procedure:

PREPARATION:
1. Select a well-known, *nonreligious* song.
2. Practice and memorize accompaniment.

IMPLEMENTATION:
1. State title of song.
2. Play introduction and/or give starting pitch.
3. Cue group to begin.
4. Sing along and play from memory without pause through entire song.
5. Use facial features or verbal praise during music to encourage participation.
6. Scan group continuously to assess who is singing and enjoying the music.
7. At end of activity write down names of people most on-task to music. Give to instructor at individual conference to document scanning skill.

Note: The objective is to *lead* the song with musical/conducting/facial cues and little or no talking.

Music Specifications:
1. Well-known, *nonreligious* song, appropriate to peer level and interest.
2. Song should include at least I, IV, and V^7 chords.
3. Song should have at least two verses and chorus (or 12 lines).
4. Use most advanced accompaniment techniques of which you are capable on guitar, autoharp, or keyboard.

Recommended Time Limit: Usually 1–2 minutes

Criteria For Objective:

Checklist 1:	Music Score	12
	Client Response Score	13
Music Selection as specified		
Implementation in allotted time		

Note: Repeat this objective with different songs until criteria are met on Checklist 1.

Techniques Included: *Songleading*
Accompanying
Scanning

OBJECTIVE 1.03

Accompany with most advanced technique of which you are capable on guitar, autoharp, or keyboard and teach group to sing a *new* song.

Group: Peers

Procedure:

PREPARATION:
1. Select a *nonreligious* song that is probably *unknown* by peers.
2. Practice and memorize accompaniment.
3. Practice giving starting pitch, singing, and accompanying each line, then chaining lines together.

IMPLEMENTATION:
1. Sing one verse of song with accompaniment for group.
2. Make eye contact with all members and assess those who appear to be listening. If members appear bored, change something you are doing, i.e., talk more softly, speed up pacing, move closer to group, etc.
3. Tell group that you will sing one line while they listen and then they will sing along with you.
4. Say, "Listen" and sing the first line.
5. Give starting pitch, cue group entry and lead them in singing first line.
6. Repeat Steps 4 and 5 until 80% of group are accurate.
7. Nonverbally encourage singing, participation, eye contact, etc.
8. Sing first line with group, say "Listen" and continue singing second line.
9. Say, "Sing," give starting pitch and entry cue and lead group in singing second line.
10. Repeat singing second line until 80% group are accurate. Continue scanning group to assess accuracy, enjoyment, and participation.
11. Say, "Beginning," give starting pitch, first word of song, and entry cue, lead group in singing lines 1 and 2 together. Repeat until accurate.
12. Teach each subsequent line using this *chaining procedure* until entire song is learned. Correct any musical inaccuracies by singing correctly for group followed by their repeating your *modeling*.
13. Encourage participation, eye contact, enjoyment, etc., throughout teaching phase.

Note: The objective of the above technique is to teach quickly and efficiently while maintaining a high level of group interest and musical accuracy. Little or no talking should be required and occasions of stopping the flow of music should be reduced to a minimum.

Music Specifications:

1. Song should be appropriate to peer level and interest but probably new to majority of group.
2. Song should include at least I, IV, and V^7 and one additional chord.
3. Song should have at least two verses and chorus (or 12 lines).
4. Use most advanced accompaniment techniques of which you are capable on guitar, autoharp, or keyboard.

Recommended Time Limit: Approximately 5 minutes

Criteria For Objective:

Checklist 1: Personal Skill Score   9
                      Music Score   12
                      Client Response Score   13
         Music Selection as specified
         Implementation in allotted time

Techniques Included: *Songleading*
                                    Accompanying
                                    Scanning
                                    Chaining
                                    Modeling

OBJECTIVE 1.04

Select the instrument (guitar, autoharp, or keyboard) on which you consider your skill to be *second best* and accompany and teach a *new* song to group.

Group: Peers

Procedure:

PREPARATION:
1. Select a *nonreligious* song that is probably *unknown* by peers.
2. Practice and memorize accompaniment.
3. Practice giving starting pitch, singing, and accompanying each line, then chaining lines together.

IMPLEMENTATION:
1. Sing one verse of song with accompaniment for group.
2. Make eye contact with all members and assess those who appear to be listening. If members appear off-task, change something you are doing, i.e., talk more softly, speed up pacing, move closer to group, etc.
3. Tell group that you will sing one line while they listen and then they will sing along with you.
4. Say, "Listen" and sing the first line.
5. Give starting pitch, cue group entry and lead them in singing first line.
6. Repeat Steps 4 and 5 until 80% of group are accurate.
7. Nonverbally encourage singing, participation, eye contact, on-task, etc.
8. Sing first line with group, say "Listen" and continue singing second line.
9. Say, "Sing," give starting pitch and entry cue and lead group in singing second line.
10. Repeat singing second line until 80% of group are accurate. Continue scanning group to assess accuracy, enjoyment, and participation.
11. Say, "Beginning," give starting pitch, first word of song, and entry cue, lead group in singing lines 1 and 2 together. Repeat until accurate.
12. Teach each subsequent line using this *chaining procedure* until entire song is learned. Correct any musical inaccuracies by singing correctly for group followed by their repeating your *modeling*.
13. Encourage participation, eye contact, enjoyment, etc. throughout teaching phase.

Note: The objective of the above technique is to teach quickly and efficiently while maintaining a high level of group interest and musical accuracy. Little or no talking should be required and occasions of stopping the flow of music should be reduced to a minimum.

Music Specifications:

1. Song should be appropriate to peer level and interest but probably new to majority of group.
2. Song should include at least I, IV, and V^7 and one additional chord.
3. Song should have at least two verses and chorus (or 12 lines).
4. Use most advanced accompaniment techniques of which you are capable on *second best instrument* (guitar, autoharp, or keyboard).

Recommended Time Limit: Approximately 5 minutes

Criteria For Objective:

Checklist 2: Personal Skill Score 9
Music Score 12
Client Response Score 13
Music Selection as specified
Implementation in allotted time

Techniques Included: *Songleading*
Accompanying
Scanning
Chaining
Modeling

OBJECTIVE 1.05

Teach group to accompany a well-known song on autoharp.

Group: Peers

Procedure:

PREPARATION:
1. Select a well-known, *nonreligious* song.
2. *Practice* and *memorize* autoharp chord changes for accompaniment.
3. Practice teaching procedure in implementation, especially Step 14.
4. Acquire enough autoharps for group and place on floor in front of chairs prior to beginning activity.

IMPLEMENTATION:
1. State task in one sentence.
2. Instruct group to pick up autoharps but not to play them.
3. Quickly and briefly *approve* specific individuals as they follow instructions.
4. Show the group correct position of autoharp on lap. Scan group *correcting* any who require it.
5. Direct group to place left hand on the three buttons needed for song by specifying each finger and button name (or color) in sequence. Scan group *correcting* any who require it.
6. Direct group to press finger 1 on button _____ (name or color) and to reach right hand across and strum once across all strings *modeling* these steps as you say them. *Correct* anyone who made an error.
7. Say, "Listen" and demonstrate four strums on this chord in rhythm of song while nodding head in rhythm.
8. Say, "Press button _____ and strum four times in rhythm with me, ready, begin," and use strum hand for entry cue.
9. Approve those who are correct and who stop after four strums, etc. Repeat if there were errors.
10. Say, "This time we will strum four times on button _____ then four times on button _____. I will cue you when to change fingers. Press button _____ and strum four times in rhythm with me, ready, begin." Use head and strum arm for entry cue. As group begins strum four, say "Change to button _____" and use head and arm to cue to maintain the rhythm of the next four strums. *Praise* those who are correct. Repeat and *correct* if there were errors. Encourage those who are trying, watching, listening, following directions, making music, etc.
11. Use procedure in Step 10 to direct group in strumming four times each on the three chords of song while maintaining rhythm.
12. Use *cuing* procedure described in Step 10 to strum chords in the sequence used in the song.
13. Repeat Step 12 at tempo appropriate to song.
14. Tell group that you will sing while they accompany and that you will *cue* changes. Say, "Press button _____, ready, begin," and give head and arm entry cue while beginning to sing song. *Cue* each chord change.
15. Ask group to sing along. Use all *cuing* procedures for beginning, maintaining rhythm, and chord changes.
16. Encourage participation, following specific directions, singing, correct chord changes, accurate rhythm, stopping, etc.

Note: All approval should be *age appropriate*.

The technique described above is a systematic *task analysis* of how to teach someone to play the autoharp and accompany a well-known song.

Note: If there are not enough autoharps for each person in the group to have one, have those persons without an autoharp simulate one by practicing the same procedures on their lap. Transfer autoharps after Steps 6, 7, 10, 12, 14. Persons without autoharps should continue to practice each step in simulation.

Music Specifications:

1. Well-known, *nonreligious* song should be appropriate to peer level.
2. Song requires *only* I, IV, and V^7 chords.
3. Song should have at least two verses and chorus (or 12 lines).

Recommended Time Limit: Approximately 5–7 minutes

Criteria For Objective:

Checklist 2: Personal Skill Score   9
Music Score   13
Client Response Score   13

Techniques Included: *Songleading*
Teaching from task analysis
Cuing
Modeling
Approving
Correcting

OBJECTIVE 1.06

Compose a "hello" song appropriate for group age and interest level. Teach the song to group and accompany it.

Group: Peers

Procedure:

PREPARATION:
1. Compose a "hello" song of at least four lines with original melody and prepare an accompaniment.
2. Practice and memorize song.
3. Practice teaching procedure below which is called *chaining*.

IMPLEMENTATION:
1. Sing one verse of song for group.
2. Make eye contact with all members and assess those who appear to be listening.
3. Tell group that you will sing one line while they listen and then they will sing along with you.
4. Say, "Listen" and sing first line.
5. Give starting pitch, cue group entry and lead them in singing first line.
6. Repeat steps 4 and 5 until 80% of group are accurate.
7. Nonverbally encourage singing, participation, eye contact, on-task, etc.
8. Sing first line with group, say "Listen" and continue singing second line.
9. Say, "Sing," give starting pitch and entry cue and lead group in singing second line.
10. Repeat singing second line until 80% group are accurate. Continue scanning group to assess accuracy, enjoyment, and participation.
11. Say, "Beginning," give starting pitch, first word of song, and entry cue, lead group in singing lines 1 and 2 together. Repeat until accurate.
12. Teach each subsequent line using this *chaining procedure* until entire song is learned. Correct any musical inaccuracies by singing correctly for group followed by their repeating your *modeling*.
13. Encourage participation, eye contact, enjoyment, etc. throughout teaching phase.

Music Specifications:

1. Compose a song that *functions* to *greet* and that contains at least four lines, has an original melody and accompaniment.
2. Song uses at least I, IV, V^7 chord changes.
3. Song is appropriate to group age, interests, and vocal range.
4. Use most advanced accompanying techniques on guitar, autoharp, or keyboard.

Recommended Time Limit: Approximately 5 minutes

Criteria For Objective:

Checklist 2: Personal Skill Score   9
             Music Score   14
             Client Response Score   14
     Music selection as specified
     Implementation in allotted time

Techniques Included: *Composing*   *Chaining*
                          Songleading   *Modeling*
                          Accompanying   *Scanning*

OBJECTIVE 1.07

Compose a "good-bye" song appropriate for group age and interest level. Teach the song to group and accompany it.

Group: Peers

Procedure:

PREPARATION:
1. Compose a "good-bye" song of at least four lines with original melody and prepare an accompaniment.
2. Practice and memorize song.
3. Practice teaching procedure below which is called *chaining*.

IMPLEMENTATION:
1. Sing one verse of song for group.
2. Make eye contact with all members and assess those who appear to be listening.
3. Tell group that you will sing one line while they listen and then they will sing along with you.
4. Say, "Listen" and sing first line.
5. Give starting pitch, cue group entry and lead them in singing first line.
6. Repeat steps 4 and 5 until 80% of group are accurate.
7. Nonverbally encourage singing, participation, eye contact, on-task, etc.
8. Sing first line with group, say "Listen" and continue singing second line.
9. Say, "Sing," give starting pitch and entry cue and lead group in singing second line.
10. Repeat singing second line until 80% group are accurate. Continue scanning group to assess accuracy, enjoyment, and participation.
11. Say, "Beginning," give starting pitch, first word of song, and entry cue, lead group in singing lines 1 and 2 together. Repeat until accurate.
12. Teach each subsequent line using this *chaining procedure* until entire song is learned. Correct any musical inaccuracies by singing correctly for group followed by their repeating your *modeling*.
13. Encourage participation, eye contact, enjoyment, etc. throughout teaching phase.

Music Specifications:

1. Compose song that *functions* to *end* a group session and that contains at least four lines, has an original melody and accompaniment.
2. Song uses at least I, IV, V^7 chord changes.
3. Song is appropriate to group age, interests, and vocal range.
4. Use most advanced accompanying techniques on guitar, autoharp, or keyboard.

Recommended Time Limit: Approximately 5 minutes

Criteria For Objective:

Checklist 2: Personal Skill Score	9	
Music Score	14	
Client Response Score	14	
Music selection as specified		
Implementation in allotted time		

Techniques Included: *Composing*   *Chaining*
Songleading   *Modeling*
Accompanying   *Scanning*

OBJECTIVE 1.08

Teach a new round to group.

Group: Peers

Procedure:

PREPARATION:
1. Select a simple round of four lines.
2. Practice teaching it according to *chaining* procedures described in Objective 1.03.
3. Practice Step 4 below with a friend to be sure you can sing the second part.

IMPLEMENTATION:
1. Teach song according to *chaining* procedure.
2. After song is learned, encourage and *cue* group to sing it loudly. *Fade* your participation (singing along) mid-way and cue group to continue. *Approve* group for singing without you.
3. Direct group to sing song without you. *Cue* entry and drop out, *cue* group to continue.
4. Say, "Again," cue entry and at appropriate place begin singing *softly* second part of round by yourself while using *cue* for group to continue. Use facial features to encourage continuation. If group successfully continues, *approve* them and go to Step 5. If group stops, tell them their task is to continue when you come in and repeat Step 4 singing *very softly* and exaggerating continuation *cue*.
5. Label this a "round" and say "This time I am going to pick a couple of people to help me. Every one else will *continue*." Give starting *cue* to group. At appropriate point in song, move to two people on one side of group, look at them intently, say "Sing," give only these two an entry *cue* and begin singing second part. If unsuccessful, *correct* and repeat. If successful, continue procedure enlarging Group 2 until it is one half of total group.

Note: All approval should be age appropriate.

Music Specifications:
1. Use new round probably not known to majority of group.
2. Round has *only* four lines.

Recommended Time Limit: Approximately 5–7 minutes

Criteria For Objective:

Checklist 2: Personal Skill Score   9
                      Music Score   15
                      Client Response Score   14
Music selection as specified
Implementation in allotted time
Approval is age appropriate

Techniques Included: *Chaining*
                                        Cuing
                                        Fading
                                        Approving
                                        Correcting

OBJECTIVE 1.09

Teach a rhythm reading task of at least sixteen measures.

Group: Peers

Procedure:

PREPARATION:
1. Select sixteen written measures of rhythm and prepare poster large enough for entire group to read.
2. Practice playing rhythm accurately while maintaining a steady beat.
3. Assess the most difficult measures which might be problematical to learn and plan how to correct them.
4. Select kitchen implements for creation of a rhythm band: pots, pan lids, strainers, glasses or bottles of water, silverware, alarm clock, etc.

IMPLEMENTATION:
1. Hand out instruments and show people how to play them.
2. Teach rhythm two measures at a time using *modeling* and *chaining* (Objective 1.03). Scan group to assess persons having difficulty. Correct any inaccuracies.
3. When entire rhythm is learned, divide group into parts letting each part begin on a different measure. Direct group and cue entry and accurate rhythms.
4. Encourage on-task, following directions, accuracy, enjoyment, etc.
5. Maintain efficient teaching and reduce necessity for talking, stopping.

Music Specifications:

1. Example should have sixteen written measures of rhythm including rests and at least three different note values. Do not make rhythms so difficult that task cannot be learned in allotted time.

Recommended Time Limit: Approximately 7–10 minutes

Criteria For Objective:

Checklist 2: Personal Skill Score   9
               Music Score   15
               Client Response Score   14
Music selection as specified
Implementation in allotted time

Techniques Included: *Group Leadership–Rhythm Ensemble*
                                 Chaining
                                 Cuing
                                 Modeling

OBJECTIVE 1.10

Teach sign language to a simple well-known song.[1]

Group: Peers

Procedure:

PREPARATION:
1. Select song and signs for major words in song. (See Specifications below.) Choreograph signs.
2. Practice and memorize song and signs.
*3. Videotape self signing to music and assess choreography and difficulty. Revise signing task to improve smoothness and rhythmic accuracy.

IMPLEMENTATION:
1. Lead group through song according to Objective 1.01.
2. Use *modeling* and *chaining* to teach signs.
3. *Cue* rhythmic accuracy of signs.

Music Specifications:

1. Choose a well-known, *nonreligious* song of four lines with highly repetitious words.
2. Use at least six *different* signs.

Recommended Time Limit: 10 minutes

Criteria For Objective:

Checklist 2: Personal Skill Score   9
                Music Score   15
                Client Response Score   14
Music selection as specified
Implementation in allotted time

Techniques Included: *Songleading*
                         Chaining
                         Modeling
                         Cuing
                         Signing to Music

* Optional step

---

[1] Riekehof, L.L.: *The Joy of Signing.* Springfield, MO: Gospel Publishing House, 1978.

OBJECTIVE 1.11

Teach eight different exercises (no more than eight repetitions each) *synchronized* to music.

Group: Peers

Procedure:

PREPARATION:
1. Select exercises that fit peer group age and level of physical ability.
2. Select recorded music with probable appeal to group and strong beat. Synchronize exercises so that they fit rhythmically and are not too strenuous to complete. (No more than eight repetitions each)
3. Practice and memorize routine.

IMPLEMENTATION:
1. Teach each of the eight exercises with verbal *cue* to identify each. (Use *modeling* and *correction*.) Ensure that each exercise is practiced at tempo of recorded music to be used.
2. Turn on music and lead group through routine using *cuing*. Scan continuously to assess errors or non-participation.
3. Encourage participation, enjoyment, rhythmic accuracy.

Music Specifications:
1. Recorded music of at least 64 measures, strong beat (as in disco music) at tempo appropriate to physical abilities of group and of interest to them.

Recommended Time Limit: 5–7 minutes

Criteria For Objective:

Checklist 2: Personal Skill Score 9
Music Score 15
Client Response Score 14
Music selection as specified
Implementation in allotted time

Techniques Included: *Group Leadership–Exercise*
Cuing
Scanning

OBJECTIVE 1.12

Teach a simple dance of at least ten different sequential steps.

Group: Peers

Procedure:

PREPARATION:
1. Select dance steps and music, *synchronize* steps with music and design *cues* for each step. Use *chaining* procedure to teach routine. (See Objective 1.03 for chaining procedure and adapt to dance task.)
2. Practice and *memorize* dance and *chaining* routine.
3. Design *data collection* form that allows recording of number of persons making an error in each of the dance steps in performance. Compute the percentage of overall error using formula:

$$\frac{\text{Total \# of errors on all steps}}{\text{\# of people in group x \# of dance steps}} = \% \text{ of error}$$

IMPLEMENTATION:
1. Teach a dance using *cuing*, *chaining*, and *correction*. *Scan* group continuously to assess those who require assistance. *Correct.*
2. Encourage participation, enjoyment, rhythmic accuracy.
3. Ensure that tempo of dance matches that of recording during practice.
4. Turn on music and perform dance.
5. Have colleague who has been pretrained *collect data* on percent of group errors during performance for *evaluating* teaching effectiveness.

Music Specifications:

1. Recorded song, moderate tempo, obvious beat of probable interest to peers.

Recommended Time Limit: 10 minutes

Criteria For Objective:

Checklist 2: Personal Skill Score   9
            Music Score   15
            Client Response Score   14
Music selection as specified
Implementation in allotted time
80% accuracy of group on total dance

Techniques Included: *Group Leadership–Dance*
                        Cuing
                        Chaining
                        Evaluating/Data

OBJECTIVE 1.13

Conduct a group sing-along.

Group: Peers

Procedure:

PREPARATION:
1. Select ten well-known, *nonreligious* songs and prepare a song sheet containing the words of at least one verse and chorus of each. Obtain enough copies for group.
2. Practice and *memorize* accompaniment for all ten.

IMPLEMENTATION:
1. Hand out song sheets while stating you will conduct a sing-along.
2. Ask group which song they would like to sing first. Determine if there is consensus for songs suggested. If not, lead group in negotiating until consensus is achieved.
3. Sing any three songs selected by group for which there is consensus.
4. Accompany each, *cuing* entry and using facial and verbal encouragement for participation.
5. Scan group continuously to assess participation, enjoyment, etc.

Music Specifications:

1. Choose ten well-known songs appropriate for peer group with words on song sheets, multiple copies for group.
2. Accompany with most advanced techniques in guitar, autoharp, or keyboard.

Recommended Time Limit: 7–10 minutes

Criteria For Objective:

Checklist 2: Personal Skill Score   9
                Music Score   15
                Client Response Score   14
Music selection as specified
Implementation in allotted time
Extra credit for use of more than one accompanying instrument

Techniques Included: *Songleading*
                               Accompanying
                               Repertoire

LEVEL 2 COMPETENCIES

Tasks at this level are designed to:

a)   help students maintain and improve *personal skills* in the leadership role;

b)   teach students to adapt music activities to the needs of various *client groups* while maintaining basic music leadership skills. The basic goal is to teach students to use music to achieve a nonmusic group objective for peers (Objectives 2.01 - 2.12) and for a variety of simulated client groups (Objectives 2.14 - 2.62), including:

> Retarded Persons
> Visually Impaired Persons
> Emotionally Disturbed Persons
> Hearing Impaired Persons
> Cerebral Palsied Persons
> Learning Disabled Persons
> Delinquent Adolescents
> Geriatric Persons
> Developmentally Disabled Infants
> Child Abusers
> Parents of Handicapped Children
> Medical Patients
> Persons Under Stress
> Psychiatric Patients
> Families in Counseling
> Terminally Ill Persons
> Epileptic Persons
> Pregnant Women

Note: See Index on page 162 for specific activity objectives by Population;

c)   teach students to *design procedures* to achieve the desired group objectives and to evaluate their effectiveness;

d)   teach *simulation protocol* for role-playing client groups, including controlled, specified deviant behavior and compliance responses to leader attempts to deal with them;

e)   promote transfer of ideas, techniques, materials, and skills to other situations for generalized learning;

f)   increase awareness of research literature and its clinical applications.

OBJECTIVE 2.01

Use music to maintain group eye contact with you. Note: Instructor will assign two or three members of group to look away occasionally.

Group: Peers

Procedure:

PREPARATION:
1. Select a well-known, *nonreligious* song.
2. Practice and memorize song and accompaniment.
3. Practice stopping and starting randomly throughout song.
4. Develop *data collection* form for assessing eye contact.

IMPLEMENTATION:
1. Direct group in singing song while accompanying them.
2. Use starting pitch and *cuing* for entry.
3. Start singing when eye contact is established. *Scan* group continuously to monitor eye contact.
4. *Stop* singing when eye contact is lost with any one person. *Begin* again as soon as that person looks at you.
5. Do not use cues such as "Look at me" or "Watch me" to maintain eye contact, only stopping and starting music.
6. Give only directions about singing.
7. Use facial features and pointing to encourage participation, starting, stopping and *eye contact*.
8. Continue procedure and song until music is uninterrupted and eye contact is 100%.
9. Have colleague *collect data* on eye contact to evaluate your technique.

Music Specifications:
1. Select well-known song which contains at least two verses and chorus (or 12 lines), I, IV, V^7 chords and at least two additional chords.
2. Accompany on guitar, autoharp, or keyboard.

Recommended Time Limit: 5 minutes

Criteria For Objective:

Checklist 3: Minimum Scores
Personal Skills	10
General Leadership Skills	29
Music Skills	15
Client Responses	14
Total	68

Percentage of group eye contact in last verse of song = 95%

Techniques Included: *Songleading*
Maintaining Eye Contact
Scanning
Evaluating/Data

Discussion for Transfer:

1. Research shows music interruption can extinguish inappropriate behavior. Did it in this situation?
2. Typical music rehearsal techniques can be very negative if there is frequent stopping. How can a group leader restructure a music rehearsal to enhance pleasure and reduce negative feedback?
3. Why is eye contact important between leader and group? How does this importance vary with different types of groups?
4. How was eye contact evaluated? Discuss alternative ways to evaluate eye contact.

OBJECTIVE 2.02

Eliminate talking in the group. Note: Instructor will assign two or three people to occasionally speak out inappropriately.

Group: Peers

Procedure:

PREPARATION:
1. Select adult action song. *Memorize* song and motions and practice them.
2. Practice stopping and starting song at random places in order to *approve* participation, and *responses incompatible* with talking.
3. Practice a variety of verbal statements which specifically *approve* participation and which are appropriate for adults.
4. Develop *data collection* sheet to assess talking/minute.

IMPLEMENTATION:
1. Lead group in adult action song.
2. *Scan* continuously to assess participation and talking.
3. *Approve* persons for participating who are *not* talking.
4. If talking occurs, immediately select person who is not talking and who is closest to the talker and *approve* for participating.
5. As soon as talker stops talking and *begins participating, approve* that individual.
6. Continue until talking ceases and participation is 100%.
7. Ask colleague to *collect data* on talking to *evaluate* effectiveness of your technique.

Music Specifications:
1. Select adult action song which will allow enough repetitions to fill five minutes.

Recommended Time Limit: 5 minutes

Criteria For Objective:

Checklist 3: Minimum scores in each category
Overall minimum score = 70
Percentage of no talking in last repetition = 95%

Techniques Included: *Songleading*
Scanning
Approving an Incompatible Response
Evaluating/Data

Discussion for Transfer:
1. How did the selected music activity *function* in this situation? What aspects of the music vs. the actions vs. the leader skills most affected this situation?
2. Discuss the data collection form utilized. How else can talking in a group be evaluated?
3. What are the benefits of identifying a response that is incompatible with one you, the leader, deem inappropriate?

OBJECTIVE 2.03

Use music to teach appropriate peer touching. Increase touching 25% over baseline taken five minutes prior to beginning of session.

Group: Peers

Procedure:

PREPARATION:
1. Specifically define "appropriate peer touching" by observing colleagues prior to planning session.
2. Select music activity that is *structured* to elicit touching.
3. Select and practice music.
4. Practice verbal statements that specifically *approve* touching without using that word.
5. Develop data collection form to assess touching.

IMPLEMENTATION:
1. Lead selected activity and *scan* continuously to identify touching.
2. *Approve* all appropriate touching without using the word "touch."
3. Ask colleague to observe and record touching.

Music Specifications:
1. Select music activity of appropriate length that requires frequent touching.

Recommended Time Limit: 5–7 minutes

Criteria For Objective:

Checklist 3: Minimum scores in each category
                   Overall minimum score = 70
Increase touching 25% over baseline

Techniques Included: *Structuring Music to Elicit Specific Response*
                                        Scanning
                                        Approving
                                        Evaluating/Data

Discussion for Transfer:
1. What is appropriate touching and how does it vary within different types of groups?
2. How did selected music activity *function* in this situation? What aspects of the music vs. the actions vs. the leader skills most affected this situation?
3. Was group aware touching was being taught?
4. How else can touching, physical proximity, body language be evaluated?

OBJECTIVE 2.04

Use music to create 100% on-task defined as:
a) all group members consistently maintaining eye contact and
b) no talking.

Note: Instructor will assign two or three people to look away and talk occasionally.

Group: Peers

Procedure:

PREPARATION:
1. Select music of interest to peers.
2. Design and coordinate rhythmic activities with music. Practice these in "follow the leader" format to structure looking and paying attention.
3. Develop data collection form to *evaluate* on-task.

IMPLEMENTATION:
1. Direct adult rhythm activity in "follow the leader" format.
2. Approve *incompatible responses* at least every 20 seconds, including: looking, following leader, participating, watching, etc.
3. Ask colleague to collect data on on-task/minute.

Music Specifications:

1. Use recorded music of interest to peers and appropriate for "follow the leader" rhythm activity.

Recommended Time Limit: 5 minutes

Criteria For Objective:

Checklist 3: Minimum scores in each category
Overall minimum score = 70
Percentage of group on-task in last minute of session = 90%

Techniques Included: *Approving Incompatible Response*
Evaluating/Data

Discussion for Transfer:

1. How does approving an incompatible response affect inappropriate behavior? How frequently does such approval need to be given? How does this approval rate vary across client populations?

OBJECTIVE 2.05

Use music to teach an academic task. Compose a song to teach the meaning of the ten words listed below:

Dithyramb	Plinth
Gibbous	Speedwell
Hong	Tebbad
Monodont	Torose
Orach	Zoril

Group: Peers

Procedure:

PREPARATION:
1. Compose song, plan accompaniment, practice and memorize both.
2. Practice *chaining* procedure.
3. Develop form for vocabulary post test.

IMPLEMENTATION:
1. Use *chaining* and *cuing* to teach song to group while accompanying.
2. Give paper/pencil post test to *evaluate* vocabulary learned.
3. Encourage participating and *remembering the words to the song*.

Music Specifications:

1. Compose song to teach meaning of ten words above. Melody may be original or adapted from existing song.
2. Accompany on guitar, autoharp, or keyboard using most advanced techniques.

Recommended Time Limit: 10 minutes

Criteria For Objective:

Checklist 3: Minimum scores in each category
               Overall minimum score = 70
Group accuracy on test = 90% or above

Techniques Included: *Composing*
                         Songleading
                         Chaining
                         Cuing
                         Evaluating/Data

Discussion for Transfer:

1. Research shows music can teach academic information. Did it in this case? How did the music function: reduce boredom of repetition, convey the information, enhance memory?
2. How difficult was this task for the group? How much information can be learned by different types of groups in a specified period of time? specified number of repetitions? using the same melody?
3. Were *chaining* and *cuing* effective techniques to teach this particular information?
4. How else can academic learning be evaluated?

OBJECTIVE 2.06

Use music to teach paired responses listed below:

ba–mto	pru–coz
gen–ti	frl–haj
ov–ler	sim–qyv

Group: Peers

Procedure:

PREPARATION:
1. Compose a song that uses melody and words to pair the nonsense syllables above.
2. Practice accompaniment.
3. Practice and memorize song and accompaniment.
4. Practice *chaining* technique.
5. Prepare post test form.

IMPLEMENTATION:
1. Use *chaining* and *cuing* to teach song.
2. After song is learned, *fade* cues and your singing and have group supply the second half of each pair of syllables.
3. Encourage group for participation and remembering pairings.
4. Use paper/pencil post test by presenting *half* of each paired response in random order having students identify *other half* of the paired response.

Music Specifications:
1. Compose song to teach the paired nonsense syllables above.
2. Accompany on guitar, autoharp, or keyboard.

Recommended Time Limit: 10 minutes

Criteria For Objective:

Checklist 3: Minimum scores in each category
Overall minimum score = 70
90% group accuracy on post test

Techniques Included: *Composing*
Chaining
Cuing
Fading
Evaluating/Data

Discussion for Transfer:
1. How difficult was this task? Is learning a paired relationship easier or more difficult than learning a series of facts?
2. How might paired relationships/associations be used in therapy? How might music facilitate such objectives?
3. If group members had difficulty with this memory task, for what other attributes might they have been approved.

OBJECTIVE 2.07

Use music to teach pronunciation of the three words listed below:

> Yttrium
> Opisthognathous
> Gastroenteritis

Group: Peers

Procedure:

PREPARATION:
1. Use dictionary to ascertain correct pronunciation.
2. Compose music that emphasizes and teaches *correct* pronunciation.
3. Prepare accompaniment.
4. Practice and memorize song and accompaniment.
5. Practice *chaining* techniques.
6. Develop *individual* test procedure.

IMPLEMENTATION:
1. Use *chaining* and *cuing* to teach song.
2. After song is learned, use *fading* of cues and require group to sing and pronounce words alone.
3. Encourage participation and *remembering* the pronunciation.
4. No modeling or repetitive practice concerning the correct pronunciations may be used other than that in musical teaching techniques.
5. Use individual post test to *evaluate* song's effectiveness.

Music Specifications:
1. Compose song that emphasizes correct pronunciation of three words.
2. Prepare accompaniment on guitar, autoharp, or keyboard.

Recommended Time Limit: 10 minutes

Criteria For Objective:

Checklist 3: Minimum scores in each category
                    Overall minimum score = 72
80% group accuracy on test

Techniques Included: *Composing*
                                  Chaining
                                  Cuing
                                  Fading
                                  Evaluating/Data

Discussion for Transfer:
1. Did music function to teach pronunciations? Was singing the word easier than *saying* the word?
2. Is an individual test procedure more threatening than a group one?
3. How difficult or easy was it to discriminate the correct pronunciation while singing?

OBJECTIVE 2.08

Use music to teach foreign language vocabulary.

Group: Peers

Procedure:

PREPARATION:
1. Select at least ten words from a foreign language that are used in greeting someone.
2. Set these words and their definitions to music.
3. Practice and memorize words, music, and accompaniment.
4. Have group role-play meeting someone who is from the country of the language selected and use vocabulary learned.
5. Develop *evaluation* form to assess correct usage and pronunciation.

IMPLEMENTATION:
1. Use *chaining* and *cuing* to teach song.
2. After song is learned, *fade* cues and require group to sing and pronounce words alone.
3. Encourage participation and *remembering* the pronunciation.
4. No modeling or repetitive practice concerning the correct pronunciations may be used other than that in musical teaching techniques.
5. Use individual post test to *evaluate* song's effectiveness.

Music Specifications:

1. Compose song that teaches words, meaning, and pronunciation.
2. Accompany on guitar, autoharp, or keyboard.

Recommended Time Limit: 15 minutes

Criteria For Objective:
Checklist 3: Minimum scores in each category
Overall minimum score = 72
80% group accuracy on evaluation form

Techniques Included: *Composing*
Chaining
Cuing
Fading
Evaluating/Data

Discussion for Transfer:

1. Did music function to teach foreign vocabulary?
2. Could clients use the vocabulary in conversation? Is this a different task from singing? How could the singing skill be adapted to transfer the vocabulary to a conversational skill?

OBJECTIVE 2.09

Use music to teach relaxation.

Group: Peers

Procedure:

PREPARATION:
1. Prepare relaxation routine using alternating tension/relaxation of parts of body from feet up to head (4 minutes) followed by focused attention task such as imagining floating through space, lying in sun on the beach, etc. (4 minutes).
2. Select appropriate music and tape selected segments onto one uninterrupted tape that is synchronized with #1 above.
3. Develop form for recording pulse pre and post test.

IMPLEMENTATION:
1. Take group pulse rate pre and post test to *evaluate* techniques.
2. Direct group to lie on floor in relaxed position and close eyes. Reduce light in room as much as possible.
3. Turn on music at moderate volume and slowly reduce the *background level*.
4. Direct planned relaxation routine.
5. Speak in calm, smooth, relaxed style.
6. Encourage "thinking relaxed thoughts" and relaxed body language. Do not call participants by name since you wish them to focus on music and relaxation content.

Music Specifications:
1. Recorded music played at low enough volume to allow you to easily be heard over it (*background level*), which is instrumental (nonverbal) and probably perceived by peers as "quiet" music.
2. Uninterrupted tape prepared and synchronized as specified.
3. Use of tape recorder that provides quality playback for size of room and setting.

Recommended Time Limit: 15 minutes

Criteria For Objective:

Reduction in individual pulse rates of 5%
Checklist 3: Minimum scores in each category
　　　　　　Overall minimum score = 72

Techniques Included: *Synchronized Activity to Background Music*
　　　　　　　　　　　　Directing Relaxation Routine (Differentiating tension/relaxation and
　　　　　　　　　　　　　　　　　　　　　　focused attention)
　　　　　　　　　　　　Evaluating/Data

Discussion for Transfer:
1. Why might selected music not have enhanced relaxation?
2. Why might directions to think specific thoughts (focused attention or imagining) not enhance relaxation?
3. What was the function of the tension/relaxation routine as a form of enhanced body awareness or biofeedback?
4. What was the range of pulse rates and their increase or decrease? What relationship would there be to the pulses of various client groups?
5. What effect did speaking voice and leadership style have on the group's response?
6. Contrast types of relaxation procedures and their applicability to clinical situations.

OBJECTIVE 2.10

Use music to teach group two action steps to deal with disappointment in their lives.

Group: Peers

Procedure:

PREPARATION:
1. Select and specify action steps focusing on potentially positive outcomes of situation, i.e., extinguishing blame, anger, grief; thought stopping; perceiving situation as growth opportunity; putting situation in perspective by identifying far worse problems in life; etc.
2. Select or compose music to introduce the concepts in the selected steps.
3. Practice and memorize music if it is to be performed or acquire recording and quality playback equipment.
4. Prepare a slip of paper for each participant that contains a disappointing situation that might possibly be encountered by peers.

IMPLEMENTATION:
1. Direct people to read slips of paper and assume the role.
2. Perform or play recorded music.
3. Have brief discussion about disappointment and how it is possible to learn to deal with it. State that the task is to practice some possible techniques (2 minutes).
4. Pair participants and have each quickly describe their disappointment to others.
5. Describe selected Action Step 1 and give an example.
6. Direct pairs to help each other apply this step to their own situation by eliciting options and consequences, being supportive and helping each other reach closure on selected option.
7. Repeat steps 5 and 6 for Action Step 2.
8. Play music again and lead entire group in discussion about how their perception of the problem might have changed.

Music Specifications:

1. Music to be performed or played that conveys concepts of the action steps selected. [See Discography by Counseling Topic (p. 155) for possible titles.]

Recommended Time Limit: 15 minutes

Criteria For Objective:

Checklist 3: Minimum scores in each category
Overall minimum score = 72

Techniques Included: *Role-Playing*
Teaching Action Steps

Discussion for Transfer:

1. Research shows that music can establish or change an emotion. Did it in this situation? Did it function to *motivate* taking the action step? If so, when–at the beginning or end of session?
2. What specific behaviors did participants use to support, motivate, etc. each other?
3. Do these behaviors differ from "simply telling a person what to do to solve the problem?"

OBJECTIVE 2.11

Shape a unanimous group decision within a 10 minute time limit.

Group: Peers

Procedure:

PREPARATION:
1. Select six songs of equal difficulty, familiarity, popularity, etc. Memorize songs and accompaniment.
2. Prepare list of songs.

IMPLEMENTATION:
1. Tell group that the objective is to select one song to sing from this list but that the decision must be unanimous. Note: Instructor will select one of the songs before the session and leader must shape group to select that one.
2. Open floor for suggestions. Elicit disagreement or alternate suggestions following all songs named *except* the one desired. Elicit agreement or positive reactions to the suggestion of that song.
3. Continue eliciting discussion until majority of group seems to be responding positively to desired song, then vote. Do not allow group to vote until consensus seems apparent.
4. Sing unanimously selected song whether it is the desired one or not.

Music Specifications:
1. Six songs of equal difficulty, familiarity, popularity, etc. Accompaniment on guitar, autoharp, or keyboard.

Recommended Time Limit: 10 minutes

Criteria For Objective:

Checklist 3: Minimum scores in each category
Overall minimum score = 72

Techniques Included: *Shaping a Group Discussion*
Accompanying

Discussion for Transfer:
1. Was group aware they were being shaped to a predetermined point?
2. How is shaping a group discussion or decision to a predetermined point different from *leading* an open-ended discussion? When is this appropriate/inappropriate for the group leader? How does this relate to the concept of directive/indirective/therapy techniques?
3. How might participation in this activity in either the leader or group member role benefit other types of groups?

OBJECTIVE 2.12

Use music to introduce the topic of drugs/alcohol then lead group discussion about the use of drugs or alcohol which results in formulation of guidelines.

Group: Peers

Procedure:

PREPARATION:
1. Select music with specified content. If to be performed, practice and memorize it. If recorded music, acquire quality playback equipment.
2. Formulate five basic guidelines that would probably be acceptable to peers–memorize them.
3. Review shaping techniques in Objective 2.11 Implementation and plan how to apply them to this task.

IMPLEMENTATION:
1. Perform or play recorded music.
2. Introduce topic and elicit group discussion about how it relates to them.
3. Shape the group to formulate the predetermined five guidelines for advice to peers about use of drugs and alcohol.
4. Encourage every member of group to participate using verbal or nonverbal techniques.

Music Specifications:

1. Music that conveys concepts about use of drugs/alcohol that are included in the guidelines to be formulated.

Recommended Time Limit: 15 minutes

Criteria For Objective:

Checklist 3: Minimum scores in each category
Overall minimum score = 72

Techniques Included: *Leading a Group Discussion*
Shaping a Group Discussion

Discussion for Transfer:

1. Was group aware they were being shaped to formulate predetermined guidelines?
2. Why might a therapist *not* wish to let a group have an *open-ended* discussion about guidelines for substances that are commonly abused?
3. How might participation in this activity in either the leader or group member role benefit other types of groups?
4. How would guidelines differ for various groups?
5. Did selected music convey desired concepts? Does some music encourage "inappropriate" substance use? If so, what music does? Should this music be censored with certain groups? If so, which ones?

OBJECTIVE 2.13

Teach class how to handle a *grand mal* epileptic seizure that protects and assists clients while *eliminating stigmatic reactions* of bystanders.

Group: Peers

Procedure:

PREPARATION:
1. Contact the local Epilepsy Association for literature on this topic.
2. Practice techniques with a friend. Also consult instructor to insure you have learned them correctly.

IMPLEMENTATION:
1. Teach class appropriate action techniques for before, during, and after an epileptic seizure.
2. Demonstrate crowd control techniques, and define action steps to reduce stigmatic reactions of bystanders.
3. Have class pair up and role-play being epileptic and being the assistant; then, have them reverse roles.
4. Maintain serious demeanor.
5. Immediately extinguish any laughing by approving persons treating the situation seriously.

Music Specifications:

1. None

Recommended Time Limit: 15 minutes

Criteria For Objective:

Checklist 3: Minimum scores in each category
Overall minimum score = 72

Techniques Included: *Handling Seizures*

Discussion for Transfer:
1. In what situation might group members be expected to handle a seizure?
2. What stigma does our society attach to seizures? How can this be reduced, generally, and specifically, when confronted by a seizure?
3. Discuss types of seizures and when and to whom referral of an observed seizure should be made.

OBJECTIVE 2.14

Use music and relaxation to teach persons with epilepsy how to monitor their fatigue/tension level in order to reduce the potential of seizures.

Group: Persons with epilepsy

Procedure:

PREPARATION:
1. Review Objective 2.09 tension/relaxation procedures. Review information about epilepsy, effect of tension/fatigue on seizure frequency, and types of auras that may precede or signal seizure onset.
2. Plan relaxation routine that emphasizes awareness and contrasts of biological signs of tension/fatigue vs. relaxation—muscle tension, fatigue or pain, pulse rate, breathing, etc.
3. Select music and prepare uninterrupted tape synchronized to routine.

IMPLEMENTATION:
1. Tell group they are role-playing persons with epilepsy.
2. Conduct relaxation activity to music as per objective 2.09.
3. Have group sit up, then practice achieving immediate relaxed state in response to music being turned on. After five repetitions of this, have group achieve immediate relaxed state while imagining the music.
4. Lead group discussion about effects of tension/fatigue on seizure frequency and use of aura as signal to immediately implement relaxed state.

Music Specifications:
1. Recorded music played at low enough volume to allow you to easily speak over it (*background level*), which is instrumental (nonverbal) and probably perceived by peers as quiet music.
2. Uninterrupted tape prepared and synchronized as specified.
3. Use of tape recorder that provides quality playback for size of room and setting.

Recommended Time Limit: 15 minutes

Criteria For Objective:

Checklist 3: Minimum scores in each category
Overall minimum score = 72

Techniques Included: *Using Relaxation Techniques*

Discussion for Transfer:
1. Discuss different types of relaxation procedures (see Objective 2.09).
2. Discuss how achievement of "immediate relaxed state" might be evaluated other than through biofeedback.
3. Discuss how the music might facilitate #2 above and how many repetitions might be necessary to master the ability.

OBJECTIVE 2.15

Use music to teach the spelling concept "i before e except after c." Include five words that follow the rule and five words that are exceptions to the rule.

Group: Learning disabled fifth grade students

Procedure:

PREPARATION:
1. Compose song, plan accompaniment, practice and memorize it.
2. Practice *chaining* procedure.
3. Develop form for post test.

IMPLEMENTATION:
1. Use *chaining* and *cuing* to teach song to group while accompanying.
2. Give paper/pencil post test to *evaluate* spelling learned.
3. Encourage participating and *remembering the words to the song.*
4. Solicit individual responses for memory of rule and spelling of words.
5. Encourage singing the spelling of words to facilitate memory.

Music Specifications:

1. Compose song to teach objective above. Melody may be original or adapted from existing song.
2. Accompany on guitar, autoharp, or keyboard using most advanced techniques.

Recommended Time Limit: 10 minutes

Criteria For Objective:

Checklist 3: Minimum scores in each category
            Overall minimum score = 72
Group accuracy on spelling test = 90%

Techniques Included: *Composing*
                         Songleading
                         Chaining
                         Cuing
                         Evaluating/Data

Discussion for Transfer:

1. Research shows music can teach academic information. Did it in this case? How did the music function: reduce boredom of repetition, convey the information, enhance memory?
2. How difficult was this task for the group? How much information can be learned by different types of groups in a) a specified period of time, b) by a specified number of repetitions, and c) using the same melody?
3. Would this music be easily remembered to function as an ongoing memory aid across time for LD students with spelling problems?
4. How else can academic learning be evaluated?

OBJECTIVE 2.16

Use music to increase reading fluidity, comprehension, and pleasure in reading.

Group: Learning disabled third grade students

Procedure:

PREPARATION:
1. Select reading paragraph appropriate to age and ability level.
2. Compose song that replicates paragraph. Plan accompaniment, then practice and memorize it.
3. Prepare two charts for group reading: one that replicates selected paragraph and one that changes the paragraph by using the same words in different combinations.

IMPLEMENTATION:
1. Teach song paired with a pointing *cue* to each written word on the chart when sung. Begin with slow tempo. Approve watching and singing.
2. Increase tempo of song until it is as fast as desired reading speed for fluidity. After each sung line, have group read the line by speaking.
3. *Approve* reading smoothly and all pleasure responses.
4. Allow students to read individually while each one points to the words on the chart.
5. *Evaluate* results of activity by having group read second chart which rearranges the words.

Music Specifications:
1. Compose song to teach above objective. Melody may be original or adapted from existing song.
2. Accompany on guitar, autoharp, or keyboard using most advanced techniques.

Recommended Time Limit: 10 minutes

Criteria For Objective:
Checklist 3: Minimum scores in each category
Overall minimum score = 72

Techniques Included: *Composing*
Songleading
Cuing
Approving
Evaluating/Data

Discussion for Transfer:
1. Research shows music can teach academic information. Did it in this case?
2. How could this activity be adapted to increase reading speed?

OBJECTIVE 2.17

Teach a circle dance to 15-year-old EMR adolescents with emphasis on simple, clear, concise, specific directions. Use *chaining* and *cuing*.

Group: Educable mentally retarded adolescents aged 15 years

Procedure:

PREPARATION:
1. Select ten sequential steps for a circle dance.
2. Do a task analysis to determine most concise, descriptive direction, effective *cues* for each, and number of beats necessary to complete step. (Examples of task analysis: 1.05, 2.20)
3. Memorize task analysis.
4. Develop data collection form to *evaluate* direction following.

IMPLEMENTATION:
1. Teach dance using *chaining, cuing*, and *correcting*.
2. Scan continuously to determine persons needing additional *cues* and respond accordingly.

Music Specifications:
1. Recorded instrumental music appropriate for dance.

Recommended Time Limit: 15 minutes

Criteria For Objective:

Checklist 3: Minimum scores in each category
            Overall minimum score = 72
90% group directions followed

Techniques Included: *Chaining*
                        Cuing
                        Task Analysis
                        Evaluating/Data

Discussion for Transfer:
1. Discuss whether difficulty of dance matched probable EMR capabilities.
2. Discuss additional cues or ways to simplify further the dance and directions for those with lesser abilities.
3. If there was excessive talking in directing the activity, discuss and model ways of eliminating it.

OBJECTIVE 2.18

Therapist will teach choral performance skills to EMR adolescents, including song, stage entry, posture, smiling, bowing, exit.

Group: Educable mentally retarded adolescents aged 15 years

Procedure:

PREPARATION:
1. Plan systematic way to teach skills. Use *modeling, cuing,* and *fading.*
2. Select song that would probably be familiar to group.

IMPLEMENTATION:
1. Teach song and rehearse it to achieve most musical sound possible.
2. Teach performance skills. Use *chaining, cuing,* and *fading.*
3. Scan group for those needing assistance and for inappropriate behaviors that require correction. Use *approval* of an *incompatible response* for correcting. Note: Instructor will assign some persons to be inappropriate.
4. If some persons are exhibiting low affect, exaggerate bowing and smiling cues and teach high affect behaviors. If group is exhibiting hyperactivity, teach low affect behaviors.

Music Specifications:

1. Song consisting of one verse and chorus that would probably be familiar to group.

Recommended Time Limit: 15 minutes

Criteria For Objective:

Checklist 3: Minimum scores in each category
Overall minimum score = 72

Techniques Included: *Modeling*
Cuing
Fading
Approving Incompatible Response

Discussion for Transfer:

1. Discuss performance standards for music groups of handicapped persons and importance of social skills in audience perception. How can leader insure audiences admire rather than pity group?
2. Discuss benefit of the above skills taught to EMR persons in situations other than performance.
3. Discuss effect of *modeling* and *cuing* on the learning that occurred. Which was more effective? Did some people *need* both?

OBJECTIVE 2.19

Use a music activity to teach TMR adults manners appropriate for an adult social occasion.

Group: Trainable mentally retarded adults

Procedure:

PREPARATION:
1. Select three skills to be taught, i.e., shaking hands, introducing self, response to introduction, etc.
2. Do task analysis to determine all aspects of each behavior to be taught, i.e., physical proximity, intensity, speed, eye contact.
3. Plan *modeling* and *cuing* techniques to implement task analysis.
4. Compose music that teaches at least one of the three skills.
5. Develop form to *evaluate* social skills learned.

IMPLEMENTATION:
1. Teach the three skills using music, *modeling,* and *cuing*. Have each person practice with leader.
2. Pair group and have them practice with each other.
3. Scan group constantly to determine those needing additional help.
4. Approve all correct responses. Point out individual styles that are socially effective.
5. Correct inappropriate behaviors such as rocking, hugging, loud laughing, etc.
6. *Evaluate* group response.
7. Be sure that your responses to group are on *adult* level.

Music Specifications:
1. Music composed to teach a social skill as specified.

Recommended Time Limit: 15 minutes

Criteria For Objective:

Checklist 3: Minimum scores in each category
            Overall minimum score = 72
80% accuracy on evaluation form

Techniques Included: *Modeling*
                      Cuing
                      Evaluating/Data
                      Teaching Social Skills

Discussion for Transfer:

1. Discuss how skills can be taught systematically but with enough variability that learned responses do not seem stereotyped.
2. Discuss importance of treating impaired adults as adults even though interaction by necessity must be simplified.
3. Discuss other social skills that would be important to teach this group.

OBJECTIVE 2.20

Use color coding system to teach EMR children aged 10–12 years to play two chords on the guitar.

Group: Educable mentally retarded children aged 10–12 years

Procedure:

PREPARATION:
1. Prepare guitar with red dots (numbered 1, 2, 3) on frets for finger placement of C chord and numbered blue dots for G^7.
2. Practice teaching procedure in Implementation, especially Step 11.
3. Place guitars on floor in front on chairs prior to beginning.

IMPLEMENTATION:
1. State task in one sentence.
2. Instruct group to pick up guitars but not to play them.
3. Quickly and briefly *approve* specific individuals as they follow instructions.
4. Show the group correct position of guitar on lap. Scan group *correcting* any who require it.
5. Direct group to place left hand on the three red dots by specifying each finger and numbered dot in sequence. Scan group *correcting* any who require it.
6. Direct group to press all fingers on dots and to reach right hand across and strum once across all strings *modeling* these steps as you say them. *Correct* anyone who made an error.
7. Say, "Listen" and demonstrate four strums on this chord in rhythm of song while nodding head in rhythm.
8. Say, "Play and strum four times on this chord in rhythm with me. Ready, begin," and use strum hand for entry cue.
9. *Praise* those who are correct and who stop after four strums, etc. Repeat if there were errors.
10. Repeat Steps 5, 6, 7, 8, and 9 for blue dots.
11. Say, "This time we will strum four times on red, then four times on blue. I will *cue* you when to change fingers. Press red and strum four times in rhythm with me. Ready, begin." Use head and strum arm for entry *cue*. As group begins strum four, say, "Change to blue dots" and use head and arm as *cue* to maintain the rhythm of the next four strums. *Praise* those who are correct. Repeat and *correct* if there were errors. Encourage those who are trying, watching, listening, following directions, making music, etc.

The technique described above is a systematic *task analysis* of how to teach someone to play the guitar using a color-coded system.

Hint: If there are not enough guitars for each person in group to have one, have those persons without a guitar simulate one by practicing same procedures on their lap. Transfer guitars after Steps 9 and 10. Persons without guitars always continue to practice each step in simulation.

Music Specifications:
1. C and G^7 chords

Recommended Time Limit: Approximately 10 minutes

Criteria For Objective:

    Checklist 3: Minimum scores in each category
                       Overall minimum score = 72
    Music selection as specified
    Implementation in allotted time

Techniques Included: *Teaching From Task Analysis*
                               Cuing
                               Modeling
                               Approving
                               Correcting

Discussion for Transfer:

1.   Discuss the learning problem which a structured lesson plan with successive approximations might permit.
2.   Under what circumstances might such a plan need major revision?

OBJECTIVE 2.21

Use music to teach children to follow two-part directions.

Group: Trainable mentally retarded children aged 5 years

Procedure:

PREPARATION:
1. Select three two-part directions, i.e., "Pick up the toy and put it in the box."
2. Compose separate songs to teach each pair of directions.
3. Review *chaining* and *cuing* techniques.
4. Acquire any materials necessary for selected tasks.

IMPLEMENTATION:
1. Teach songs while modeling task.
2. *Guide* children through task individually while singing songs.
3. Sing a song and allow children to all perform task at same time. *Evaluate* those needing further assistance.
4. Approve following directions, waiting turn, sitting quietly, listening, etc.

Music Specifications:

1. Three short songs each composed to teach a two-part direction as specified.

Recommended Time Limit: 15 minutes

Criteria For Objective:

Checklist 3: Minimum scores in each category
Overall minimum score = 72

Techniques Included: *Composing*
Chaining
Cuing
Guided Assistance

Discussion for Transfer:

1. Discuss how the selected two-part directions varied in difficulty. Could three be learned by TMR groups in one session? What would realistic timeline be for this group to learn one of these tasks?
2. Discuss function of music. Was it effective in teaching skill? Would TMR children also need cues and guided assistance in addition to music?

OBJECTIVE 2.22

Use music to teach one aspect of the concept of honesty to TMR children.

Group: Trainable mentally retarded children aged 12 years

Procedure:

PREPARATION:
1. Define one specific aspect of honesty that is clearly differentiated from dishonesty, i.e., "take only your own objects."
2. Acquire any materials necessary.
3. Compose, practice, and memorize music.

IMPLEMENTATION:
1. Use *modeling* and music to teach specific concept selected.
2. *Approve* and *label* correct responses as "being honest."

Music Specifications:

1. Music composed to teach selected aspect of honesty.

Recommended Time Limit: 15 minutes

Criteria For Objective:

Checklist 3: Minimum scores in each category
Overall minimum score = 72

Techniques Included: *Composing*
Modeling
Approving

Discussion for Transfer:

1. Discuss various definitions of honesty and how these other honesty concepts might be simply taught.
2. Discuss learning problems of TMR children and realistic timelines for them to acquire ideas such as honesty, responsibility, etc. How many different examples would be needed before a concept is formed?
3. Was the music simple enough for TMR children aged 12?

OBJECTIVE 2.23

Use music to teach one language development task.

Group: Severely/profoundly retarded children aged 8 years

Procedure:

PREPARATION:
1. Select a language development task appropriate to the age and population.
2. Decide how to use music and prepare music.
3. Develop evaluation form.

IMPLEMENTATION:
1. Teach task using music and *cuing*.
2. *Approve* correct responses.

Music Specifications:
1. Student's choice

Recommended Time Limit: 15 minutes

Criteria For Objective:

Checklist 3: Minimum scores in each category
Overall minimum score = 72
80% group accuracy on evaluation form

Techniques Included: *Cuing*
Approving

Discussion for Transfer:
1. Discuss characteristics of the population and realistic language goals for them.
2. Discuss techniques demonstrated.
3. Was pacing of this demonstration matched to responses of the group? Was it too fast or too slow?

OBJECTIVE 2.24

Use music to teach one color.

Group: Severely/profoundly retarded children aged 6 years

Procedure:

PREPARATION:
1. Select a basic color to be taught.
2. Decide how to use music and prepare music.
3. Develop evaluation form.

IMPLEMENTATION:
1. Teach task using music and *cuing*.
2. *Approve* correct responses.

Music Specifications:

1. Student's choice

Recommended Time Limit: 15 minutes

Criteria For Objective:

Checklist 3: Minimum scores in each category
                 Overall minimum score = 72
80% group accuracy on evaluation form

Techniques Included: *Cuing*
                             Approving

Discussion for Transfer:

1. Discuss techniques demonstrated.
2. Discuss how the concept of color can be differentiated from the object, i.e., blue vs. blue crayon or blue paper.

OBJECTIVE 2.25

Use music to teach responses to three types of stimulation: one physical stimulus, one auditory stimulus, and one visual stimulus.

Group: Severely/profoundly retarded infants

Procedure:

PREPARATION:
1. Specify stimuli–physical (touch or guided movement); auditory (name of child); and visual (brightly colored balloon). Determine multiple responses desired (moving, smiling, vocalizing, visual tracking, head turning toward stimulator and/or source of sound). Plan stimulation routine designed to elicit these responses.
2. Select appropriate recorded music and synchronize it with routine.
3. Develop form to evaluate infant responses.

IMPLEMENTATION:
1. Pair group into stimulator/infant teams with "infants" lying on floor and "stimulators" sitting beside them.
2. Demonstrate each stimulation technique used in routine and identify desired responses. Demonstrate use of stroking, vocalizations to encourage desired responses.
3. Begin music and routine.
4. Move around group and encourage stimulators who are using appropriate techniques. Reverse roles and continue.
5. Use form to evaluate responses.

Music Specifications:

1. Student's choice

Recommended Time Limit: 15 minutes

Criteria For Objective:

Checklist 3: Minimum scores in each category
            Overall minimum score = 72
80% group response to stimuli

Techniques Included: *Infant Stimulation*
                         Evaluating

Discussion for Transfer:

1. Discuss characteristics of the group.
2. How did music function? Did it have a function for the infant as well as the stimulators?
3. How would general stimulation activities become more focused over time to evolve into a specific training task?
4. In what ways might music inappropriately stimulate physically handicapped persons? Discuss uninhibited primary reflexes, e.g., startle, and seizure activity.
5. Would talking to clients during this activity be desirable?

OBJECTIVE 2.26

Use music to teach body parts.

Group: Visually impaired children aged 4 years

Procedure:

PREPARATION:
1. Plan which body parts are to be taught and how music is to be used.
2. Plan a teaching strategy that avoids visual cues.
3. Acquire necessary materials.
4. Develop evaluation procedure.

IMPLEMENTATION:
1. Bring blindfolds for each group member to simulate visual impairment.
2. Teach task using *cuing* and *approving* with emphasis on specificity of verbal feedback.
3. Evaluate results.

Music Specifications:
1. Student's choice

Recommended Time Limit: 15 minutes

Criteria For Objective:

Checklist 3: Minimum scores in each category
                   Overall minimum score = 72
80% group accuracy on evaluation form

Techniques Included: *Cuing*
                                    Approving

Discussion for Transfer:
1. Discuss characteristics of the population and learning problems.
2. Discuss verbal vs. physical auditory *cuing*.
3. Discuss any techniques demonstrated.

OBJECTIVE 2.27

Use music to teach two grooming skills to visually impaired persons while reducing inappropriate, stereotyped behaviors.

Group: Visually impaired children aged 8 years. Note: Instructor will assign some persons to have inappropriate, stereotyped behaviors.

Procedure:

PREPARATION:
1. Specify two grooming skills that would be appropriate for this disability and age level.
2. Do *task analysis* to teach grooming skills, omitting visual cues while using verbal and physical *cuing*. (Task analysis example: 2.20)
3. Determine use of music. Prepare and memorize selected or composed music.
4. Develop evaluation procedure to determine whether grooming skills meet criteria.
5. Bring blindfolds for group.

IMPLEMENTATION:
1. Blindfold group.
2. Direct activity, *cuing* and *approving* correct responses and eliminating inappropriate, stereotyped behaviors by using *approval for incompatible responses.*
3. Evaluate grooming skills and reduction in inappropriate responses.

Music Specifications:
1. Student's choice

Recommended Time Limit: 15 minutes

Criteria For Objective:

Checklist 3: Minimum scores in each category
Overall minimum score = 72
80% group accuracy on evaluation form

Techniques Included: *Cuing*
Task Analysis
Approving Incompatible Responses

Discussion for Transfer:

1. Discuss inappropriate mannerisms of the visually impaired, e.g., rocking, finger pressing on eyes, inappropriate laughing, facial grimacing, constant smiling, etc. How might these best be monitored and eliminated? Would using the hands for sensory input be inappropriate?
2. How can visually impaired persons monitor their personal grooming and hygiene? Discuss issues of cleanliness, attractiveness, and changing styles.

OBJECTIVE 2.28

Use music to extinguish pity-seeking behaviors and "I can't do that" responses in recently visually impaired adults while teaching a mobility task.

Group: Visually impaired adults

Procedure:

PREPARATION:
1. Specify possible pity-seeking behaviors that recently impaired persons might develop.
2. Develop directions designed to eliminate as many "pity-seeking" behaviors as possible. Also, identify environmental cues that can help the person feel secure in movement across the room.
3. Select music that can be used to cue authoritative (rather than tentative) mobility from one point in room to another.
4. Develop *data collection* and evaluation procedures.
5. Acquire blindfolds for group.

IMPLEMENTATION:
1. Blindfold group.
2. Instruct group about desired movement using directions designed to eliminate "I can't do that" responses and *successive approximation* of movement across entire room.
3. Play selected music. Tell group you will stop music if mobility is too tentative or if danger is evident, i.e., walking into something.
4. Let each person practice individually.
5. Approve *specific* authoritative movements, like head-up, length of stride, etc.
6. Evaluate mobility.

Music Specifications:
1. Student's choice

Recommended Time Limit: 15 minutes

Criteria For Objective:

Checklist 3: Minimum scores in each category
Overall minimum score = 72
Increased mobility
Extinction of pity-seeking behaviors

Techniques Included: *Mobility Training*
Cuing
Evaluating/Data
Successive Approximation

Discussion for Transfer:
1. Research shows that discontinuing the music can function as feedback. Did it in this situation?
2. How could authoritative mobility discriminations become more discrete on the part of the VI group and the leader? What is the final goal? How is this determined?
3. What environmental cues were used? How many were present and simply needed to be identified as opposed to those added by the leader as an assistive device?

OBJECTIVE 2.29

Use music to reduce hyperactivity in a group of 8-year-old emotionally disturbed clients while increasing an incompatible response.

Group: Emotionally disturbed children aged 8 years

Procedure:

PREPARATION:
1. Select an *incompatible response* that reduces the probability of a wide range of hyperactive behaviors, i.e., sitting in chair with hands in lap reduces the probability of running around the room, hitting self or others, etc.
2. Plan music activity that requires selected *incompatible response.*
3. Develop form to assess reduction in hyperactivity.

IMPLEMENTATION:
1. Use *modeling* and *cuing* to get group engaged in selected *incompatible response.* As soon as everyone is responding appropriately, start music.
2. Stop music when any one in group deviates from selected response.
3. Approve correct responses frequently (about every 10-15 seconds).
4. Evaluate.

Music Specifications:
1. Student's choice

Recommended Time Limit: 15 minutes

Criteria For Objective:

Checklist 3: Minimum scores in each category
Overall minimum score = 72
Increased mobility
Demonstrated reduction in hyperactivity

Techniques Included: *Reducing Hyperactivity*
Modeling
Cuing
Approving
Teaching Incompatible Response

Discussion for Transfer:
1. Discuss characteristics of population and subsequent learning problems.
2. How can very frequent, specific approving become less frequent and more generalized? What is a realistic time for this to occur with this population?
3. How did the music function in this situation? What procedural changes would be necessary with real ED children?
4. What music activities would be more fun for these children than the inappropriate behaviors they usually engage in?

OBJECTIVE 2.30

Use music and approval/disapproval to teach on-task behavior defined as eye contact, no talking, and following directions.

Group: Emotionally disturbed adolescents

Procedure:

PREPARATION:
1. Select music activity that is structured to require the above on-task behavior.
2. Plan evaluation procedure to assess on-task behavior of groups and to count approvals and disapprovals of leader.

IMPLEMENTATION:
1. Use *approving* and *disapproving* in a 4:1 ratio while teaching music activity. Give feedback at least once per 15 seconds. Maintain 4:1 ratio.
2. After five minutes, eliminate approval/disapproval and continue music activity.
3. Evaluate.

Music Specifications:
1. Student's choice

Recommended Time Limit: 10 minutes

Criteria For Objective:

Checklist 3: Minimum scores in each category
             Overall minimum score = 72
Feedback given once per 15 seconds
Maintenance of 4:1 ratio of approval to disapproval

Techniques Included: *Approving/Disapproving in 4:1 Ratio*

Discussion for Transfer:
1. Research shows a 4:1 ratio of approval to disapproval is most effective in maintaining behavior. Discuss how the procedure functioned in this situation with emphasis on *contingent* approval/disapproval and frequency.
2. What happened in the second half of the activity? Were appropriate behaviors "learned" so that the music structure maintained them? Why or why not?
3. Were approval/disapproval statements appropriate for age level/sophistication of adolescents? If not, what revision would be necessary?
4. Was the group able to identify when approvals/disapprovals were *not* contingent? Do you think a *real* group of ED adolescents would identify this?

OBJECTIVE 2.31

Use music to teach rule following to 10-year-old emotionally disturbed children.

Group: Emotionally disturbed children aged 10 years

Procedure:

PREPARATION:
1. Delineate two appropriate, short rules, each stated positively.
2. Pair a physical cue with each rule.
3. Develop music activity that requires rule following.
4. Develop data collection and evaluation procedures.

IMPLEMENTATION:
1. Teach rules by stating each one and modeling and cuing appropriate responses.
2. Quickly approve persons following rules, *ignore* those not following rules, watch those being ignored for any attempts to begin following rules, then approve them immediately.
3. Conduct music activity approving rule following and ignoring rule breaking while watching for those breaking rules to be correct. Do not stop music. Keep going.

Music Specifications:
1. Student's choice

Recommended Time Limit: 15 minutes

Criteria For Objective:

Checklist 3: Minimum scores in each category
Overall minimum score = 72
80% rule following on evaluation form

Techniques Included: *Rule Following*
Ignoring

Discussion for Transfer:
1. Discuss the three elements of ignoring techniques:
   a) Ignore inappropriate behavior.
   b) Watch those being ignored to determine if they become correct.
   c) "Catch them being good" by immediately approving the previously ignored as soon as they become correct.
2. How does the music function when ignoring techniques are being used?
3. How does ignoring as taught in #1 above differ from "pretending it's not happening?"

OBJECTIVE 2.32

Teach signs to a well-known recorded song. (Reference: *The Joy Of Signing.* See 1.10)

Group: Hearing impaired students aged 8–12

Procedure:

PREPARATION:
1. Select song and signs for major words.
2. Practice and memorize signs for song and instructional direction and feedback.
*3. Video tape self signing to music and assess choreography and difficulty. Revise signing task to improve smoothness and rhythmic accuracy.

IMPLEMENTATION:
1. Use signs *paired with verbalizations* for all instructional information.
2. Lead group through song (without signs) according to Objective 1.01.
3. Use *modeling* and *chaining* to teach signs.
4. *Cue* rhythmic accuracy of signs.
*5. Videotape group signing and assess overall ensemble effect.

Music Specifications:
1. A well-known, *nonreligious*, recorded song with some repetitious words.
2. Use at least twenty *different* signs.

Recommended Time Limit: 10 minutes

Criteria For Objective:

Checklist 3: Minimum scores in each category
Overall minimum score = 72
Music selection as specified
Implementation in allotted time

Techniques Included: *Songleading*
Chaining
Modeling
Cuing
Signing to Music
Evaluating

Discussion for Transfer:
1. How rhythmically accurate were signs? Were all people signing in the same direction? How could choreography be improved? What cues are needed for rhythmic accuracy?
2. How could hearing impaired people be incorporated into a sign choir with hearing persons? What social objectives would be important with such a group?
3. Was the sign proficiency adequate for instructional purposes? How could this be improved?
4. What other types of clients might enjoy or benefit from signing to music?
5. Did the leader remember to talk while signing? Why is this important?

* Optional step

OBJECTIVE 2.33

Teach a rhythm reading task of at least sixteen measures.

Group: Hearing impaired students aged 12–15 years

Procedure:

PREPARATION:
1. Select sixteen written measures of simple rhythms and prepare poster large enough for entire group to read. (Use only half, quarter, and eighth notes and rests.)
2. Practice playing rhythms accurately while maintaining a steady beat.
3. Assess the most difficult measures which might be problematical to learn.
4. Select rhythm instruments or Orff instruments with best potential for resonance/vibration.
5. Pair each note value and rest value with a different physical manipulation of the instrument.
Example: q = strike; h = rub for 2 beats; g = hands apart for one beat.

IMPLEMENTATION:
1. Hand out instruments contingent upon appropriate social behavior and show people how to play them.
2. Teach rhythm two measures at a time using *modeling* and *chaining* (Objective 1.03). Scan group to assess persons having difficulty. Correct any inaccuracies.
3. When entire rhythm is learned, divide group into parts with each part to begin on a different measure. Direct and cue entry and accurate rhythms.
4. Encourage on-task, following directions, accuracy, enjoyment, etc.

Music Specifications:

1. Sixteen written measures of rhythm including rests and at least four different note values.

Recommended Time Limit: 7–10 minutes

Criteria For Objective:

Checklist 3: Minimum scores in each category
Overall minimum score = 72
Music selection as specified
Implementation in allotted time
Extra credit given for ability to use signs with teaching instructions

Techniques Included: *Group Leadership–Rhythm Ensemble*
Cuing
Chaining
Modeling

Discussion for Transfer:

1. How does a hearing impaired person learn the concept of duration of sound? How do the paired physical manipulations in this activity help teach that concept? After this concept is learned, could the hearing impaired person play varying rhythms without the paired physical manipulations?
2. Did the leader hand out instruments contingent upon social behavior or did they just go around the room in seated order? Why would the social contingency be important in a therapy group? If a social contingency was not used, model and practice this technique until it is mastered.

OBJECTIVE 2.34

Use music to teach an auditory discrimination task to hearing impaired children, i.e., sound vs. no sound or vocal vs. instrumental sound.

Group: Hearing impaired students aged 5 years

Procedure:

PREPARATION:
1. Select discrete auditory discrimination task and appropriate music.
2. Plan simple directions and learn signs for them.
3. Learn signs to approve correct responses.
4. Develop data collection and evaluation procedures.

IMPLEMENTATION:
1. Use signs paired with verbal directions to conduct music activity approving correct responses.
2. *Exaggerate* body language and facial expressions.

Music Specifications:
1. Student's choice

Recommended Time Limit: 15 minutes

Criteria For Objective:

Checklist 3: Minimum scores in each category
Overall minimum score = 72
80% group accuracy on evaluation form

Techniques Included: *Use of Signs*
Auditory Discrimination
Evaluating

Discussion for Transfer:
1. Discuss characteristics of the population and subsequent learning problems.
2. Discuss ways in which music can function with the hearing impaired.
3. Were the leader's facial cues and body language exaggerated enough to function well for HI clients?

OBJECTIVE 2.35

Use music to teach range of motion exercises appropriate for cerebral palsied children.

Group: Cerebral palsied children aged 10 years

Procedure:

PREPARATION:
1. Learn three range of motion exercises and their individual purposes.
2. Select music and synchronize it with exercises.
3. Develop evaluation procedure.

IMPLEMENTATION:
1. Pair up group in teams with one CP patient and one exerciser.
2. Conduct music activity and teach exercises.
3. Explain function of each exercise.
4. Emphasize client independence.
5. Switch roles in teams and repeat.
6. Evaluate.

Music Specifications:

1. Student's choice

Recommended Time Limit: 15 minutes

Criteria For Objective:

Checklist 3: Minimum scores in each category
Overall minimum score = 72

Techniques Included: *Range of Motion Exercises*
Evaluating

Discussion for Transfer:

1. Discuss characteristics of the population and necessity for physical therapy.
2. Discuss uninhibited primary reflexes and how they can be controlled through training. How can music be detrimental in this process? What musical adaptations can be made to avoid detrimental effects?

OBJECTIVE 2.36

Use music to teach group interaction.

Group: Cerebral palsied adults, moderately retarded

Procedure:

PREPARATION:
1. Specifically define "group interaction," i.e., asking question, listening, answering question, eliciting participation, etc.
2. Develop music activity to teach selected skills.
3. Develop evaluation procedure.

IMPLEMENTATION:
1. Place group in circle with leader outside. Move around circle to cue looking at others in group and verbalizations.
2. Conduct planned music activity. Be sure to teach group to talk to other members, not leader.
3. If spontaneous interactions begin, withdraw and let them develop. If they subside, move closer and being cuing.

Music Specifications:
1. Student's choice

Recommended Time Limit: 15 minutes

Criteria For Objective:

Checklist 3: Minimum scores in each category
Overall minimum score = 72
80% group interaction on evaluation form

Techniques Included: *Stimulating Group Interaction*
Evaluating

Discussion for Transfer:

1. Discuss special CP physical and verbal problems that tend to dissipate group interaction.
2. How can these problems be overcome through learning new techniques?
3. What problems could groups be given to solve that would stimulate interaction?

OBJECTIVE 2.37

Use music to teach concepts of reinforcement and positive feedback.

Group: Parents of retarded children. Note: Instructor will pair up group members and give them role-playing assignments to which leader should react.

Procedure:

PREPARATION:
1. Select simple concepts to teach, i.e., immediacy of feedback; contingencies, physical/verbal approval; modeling/cuing.
2. Select simple tasks that a retarded child might need to learn and select music to teach them, i.e., a color, the concept of up/down.
3. Develop evaluation procedure.

IMPLEMENTATION:
1. Introduce topic and use positive techniques to get parents involved in simulated training sessions.
2. Use *ignoring* techniques (see 2.31) with parents verbalizing negative statements about their child.
3. Encourage positive statements and commitment to training.

Music Specifications:
1. Student's choice

Recommended Time Limit: 15 minutes

Criteria For Objective:

Checklist 3: Minimum scores in each category
Overall minimum score = 72

Techniques Included: *Approving*
Ignoring
Evaluating

Discussion for Transfer:
1. Discuss problems of parents of handicapped children. How do these contribute to the high divorce rate in such families?
2. What is the role of the music therapist in parent training?
3. How did the music function in this situation? What other functions could it have?

OBJECTIVE 2.38

Lead a group discussion on appropriate parenting techniques for dealing with problems of handicapped children. Use music to introduce the topic.

Group: Parents of handicapped children

Procedure:

PREPARATION:
1. Select one problem to discuss.
2. Plan some role-playing situations to demonstrate the problem.
3. Select music to introduce topic.
4. Develop evaluation procedure.

IMPLEMENTATION:
1. Play music.
2. Lead group discussion.
3. Shape each person in group to participate without calling on them. Use eye contact, facial expression, body language, pausing, etc.
4. Set up role-playing situations to demonstrate ideas expressed. Note: Role-playing situations can be written and given to all members simultaneously rather than verbally explaining them sequentially to members one at a time.
5. Evaluate.

Music Specifications:
1. Student's choice

Recommended Time Limit: 15 minutes

Criteria For Objective:

Checklist 3: Minimum scores in each category
               Overall minimum score = 72
80% group accuracy on evaluation form

Techniques Included: *Leading Group Discussion*
                        Parenting Techniques
                        Role-Playing
                        Evaluating

Discussion for Transfer:

1. In a group discussion, it is often important for everyone to participate. What is the effect of nonparticipation in such a situation?
2. What techniques can a leader use to elicit and encourage participation?

OBJECTIVE 2.39

Use music to teach juvenile clients to accept responsibility for their actions.

Group: Adolescents with behavior problems

Procedure:

PREPARATION:
1. Select two or three action steps that demonstrate acceptance of responsibility, i.e., no excuses, attaching consequences to action, no blame, etc.
2. Select or compose song that expresses these concepts.
3. Plan some role-playing situations with incidents in which adolescents would have to accept responsibility for some action they had taken.
4. Develop evaluation plan.

IMPLEMENTATION:
1. Play music.
2. Lead group discussion.
3. Shape each person to participate (see 2.38).
4. Set up role-playing situations in pairs to practice action steps for accepting responsibility.
5. Lead evaluation discussion with group on degree of satisfaction with the assigned roles and problem resolutions.

Music Specifications:
1. Student's choice

Recommended Time Limit: 15 minutes

Criteria For Objective:

Checklist 3: Minimum scores in each category
Overall minimum score = 72

Techniques Included: *Leading Group Discussion*
Role-Playing
Evaluating

Discussion for Transfer:
1. Discuss actions demonstrating responsibility vs. verbalizations about same. How can verbalization contribute to the manipulative abilities of clients? Is this a potential problem with adolescents?
2. What special problems do adolescents have participating in a group discussion? What skills can a leader use to deal with these?
3. What was the function of music in this situation? How could it have been used earlier or later in the session? Was this music current and likely to be preferred by teenagers? How would a music therapist know the "in" music for any given period? Would this need to be updated weekly, monthly, annually?

OBJECTIVE 2.40

Teach a complex rhythmic activity to adolescents while reinforcing the rules.

Group: Adolescents with behavior problems

Procedure:

PREPARATION:
1.   Define three rules appropriate for adolescents with behavior problems.
2.   Plan a complex rhythmic activity using a highly structured format that requires rule following.
3.   Develop evaluation procedure.

IMPLEMENTATION:
1.   State rules quickly and simply and start enforcing them immediately.
2.   Conduct activity. Approve rule following frequently and equally to all three rules. Keep music activity going.
3.   Be sure approvals are appropriate to adolescents.
4.   Evaluate

Music Specifications:

1.   Student's choice

Recommended Time Limit: 15 minutes

Criteria For Objective:

Checklist 3: Minimum scores in each category
                Overall minimum score = 72
80% group rule following

Techniques Included: *Use of Rules*
                          Approving
                          Evaluating

Discussion for Transfer:

1.   Adolescents sometimes fail to respond to approval of adults. How can a leader deal with this problem?
2.   What was the function of music in this situation? How can continuing the music contribute to the interaction with problem students?
3.   Was the music of the type preferred by adolescents?

OBJECTIVE 2.41

Use a music activity to teach an adolescent group to *control* the emotion "anger."

Group: Adolescents with behavior problems

Procedure:

PREPARATION:
1. Specifically define anger and some action steps to control it, i.e. interruption, deep breathing, counting to ten, etc.
2. Develop an activity using music which requires the group to *control* anger, *not express it*.
3. Develop evaluation procedures.

IMPLEMENTATION:
1. Model your specific definition of anger and its control and shape group to imitate it in musical activity. Encourage *overcompensation* of anger control.
2. Lead a group discussion on how to deal with anger in one's lifestyle.
3. Evaluate.

Music Specifications:
1. Student's choice

Recommended Time Limit: 15 minutes

Criteria For Objective:
Checklist 3: Minimum scores in each category
Overall minimum score = 72

Techniques Included: *Controlling Anger*
Leading Group Discussion
Overcompensating
Evaluating

Discussion for Transfer:

1. What are the techniques of anger *control*? When should they be used? How is controlling anger different from expressing anger?
2. Persons with chronic anger control problems may benefit from learning *overcompensation* techniques. Discuss what these are and how they could be taught.

OBJECTIVE 2.42

Use music to teach adolescents two specifically defined techniques for establishing a nonsexual relationship with the opposite sex.

Group: Adolescents with behavior problems

Procedure:

PREPARATION:
1. Select two action steps for establishing a relationship, i.e., initiating friendliness, finding out about another person, listening attentively, etc.
2. Define parameters of a nonsexual relationship.
3. Select music that demonstrates these concepts.
4. Develop evaluation procedure.

IMPLEMENTATION:
1. Play music and introduce topic.
2. Teach the two techniques for establishing a relationship.
3. Use role-playing and keep the entire group participating.
4. Help each person work out one additional action step in this area and implement it.
5. Encourage commitment to try action step.
6. Evaluate.

Music Specifications:

1. Student's choice

Recommended Time Limit: 15 minutes

Criteria For Objective:

Checklist 3: Minimum scores in each category
Overall minimum score = 72

Techniques Included: *Establishing Relationships*
Role-Playing
Evaluating

Discussion for Transfer:

1. Why might adolescents need to be taught how to establish relationships? Why nonsexual relationships? Would this be a threatening or nonthreatening task for adolescents?
2. Was the music chosen likely to be captivating to teenagers?

OBJECTIVE 2.43

Use music to teach adolescents to resist peer pressure.

Group: Adolescents with behavior problems

Procedure:

PREPARATION:
1. Select action steps that adolescents could use to resist peer pressure (assertively saying "no," reversing pressure, leading rather than following, use of humor, etc.).
2. Prepare role-playing situations in which adolescents might encounter peer pressure: taking drugs, riding with intoxicated driver, shoplifting, etc.
3. Select music that expresses these concepts.

IMPLEMENTATION:
1. Play music.
2. Begin role-playing situations.
3. When pressure is resisted, encourage group to signal recognition of this by group designed cheer for team members. Approve creativity in dealing with those applying pressure.
4. Lead group discussion on "winning" at resisting peer pressure.

Music Specifications:
1. Student's choice

Recommended Time Limit: 15 minutes

Criteria For Objective:

Checklist 3: Minimum scores in each category
Overall minimum score = 72

Techniques Included: *Role-Playing*
Approving

Discussion for Transfer:

1. Discuss problems of resisting peer pressure. What are some techniques that might be effective?
2. Can teenagers be taught a *value* for resisting pressure? Why are action techniques probably more effective than lecturing techniques?
3. How could adolescents' propensity for group cohesiveness be used to help them resist inappropriate pressure?
4. Were music and group encouragement techniques age appropriate?

OBJECTIVE 2.44

Use music to teach three Reality-Orientation (RO) objectives.

Group: Geriatric clients

Procedure:

PREPARATION:
1. Select three RO objectives, i.e., day, time, place, current event, season, etc.
2. Compose a song or songs to teach each objective.
3. Review *cuing* techniques.
4. Prepare visual materials to facilitate objectives (clock, calender, newspaper, etc.).
5. Develop evaluation procedure.

IMPLEMENTATION:
1. Teach objectives through songs and paired visual materials.
2. Solicit *individual* feedback on selected objectives.
3. Approve remembering information.
4. Encourage spontaneous discussion of selected issues.
5. Evaluate.

Music Specifications:
1. A song or songs composed to teach three selected objectives.
2. Accompaniment on preferred instrument.

Recommended Time Limit: 15 minutes

Criteria For Objective:

Checklist 3: Minimum scores in each category
Overall minimum score = 72
80% group accuracy on evaluation form

Techniques Included: *Composing*
Cuing
Evaluating

Discussion for Transfer:
1. Discuss how the selected objectives varied in difficulty. Could three be learned by the group in one session? What would a realistic timeline be for such a group to learn one of these tasks? How many repetitions? Would responses vary from day to day? How did individual responses vary? What can a leader do about these individual differences?
2. Discuss the function of music. Was it effective in teaching a skill and was it age appropriate? Would geriatric clients also need cues in addition to music? Was the music appropriate for the age and probable preference of geriatric clients? What does the research show to be the music preference of older adults?

OBJECTIVE 2.45

Teach eight different exercises synchronized to music.

Group: Geriatric clients, some of whom are wheelchair bound

Procedure:

PREPARATION:
1. Select exercises that fit client age, level of physical ability and need to exercise all parts of the body.
2. Select recorded music with probable appeal to this group that has a strong beat, then synchronize the exercises so that they fit rhythmically and are in a sequence that is not too strenuous to complete.
3. Practice and memorize routine.
4. Develop evaluation procedure.

IMPLEMENTATION:
1. Teach each of the eight exercises with verbal *cue* to identify each. Use *modeling* and *correction*. Insure that each exercise is practiced at tempo of recorded music to be used.
2. Turn on music and lead group through routine using *cuing*. Scan continuously to assess errors or nonparticipation.
3. Encourage participation, enjoyment, rhythmic accuracy. Use physical proximity for encouragement.
4. Evaluate.

Music Specifications:
1. Recorded music of at least sixty four measures, strong beat (as in disco music) at tempo appropriate to physical abilities of group and of interest to them.

Recommended Time Limit: 5–7 minutes

Criteria For Objective:

Checklist 3: Minimum scores in each category
　　　　　　　Overall minimum score = 72
Music selection as specified
Implementation in allotted time

Techniques Included: *Group Leadership–Exercise*
　　　　　　　　　　　　Cuing
　　　　　　　　　　　　Scanning
　　　　　　　　　　　　Evaluating

Discussion for Transfer:
1. How can exercises be adapted to varying degrees of physical disabilities?
2. What music would best stimulate exercise participation with elderly clients?
3. How would the accoutrements of exercise function in such a group, i.e., sweat bands, jogging caps, stop watches, sweat shirts, etc.?
4. What precautions should the leader take in leading exercise groups with elderly persons?

OBJECTIVE 2.46

Use music to enhance social interaction.

Group: Geriatric clients

Procedure:

PREPARATION:
1. Specifically define "social interaction," i.e., asking question, listening, answering question, eliciting participation, looking at or smiling at another member, touching.
2. Develop music activity to teach selected skills.
3. Develop evaluation procedure.

IMPLEMENTATION:
1. Place group in circle with leader outside. Move around circle to cue looking at others in group and verbalizations.
2. Conduct planned activity. Be sure to teach group to interact with other members, not leader.
3. If spontaneous interactions begin, withdraw and let them develop. If they subside, move closer and being cuing.
4. Evaluate.

Music Specifications:
1. Student's choice

Recommended Time Limit: 15 minutes

Criteria For Objective:

Checklist 3: Minimum scores in each category
Overall minimum score = 72
80% group accuracy on evaluation form

Techniques Included: *Stimulating Group Interaction*
Evaluating
Cuing

Discussion for Transfer:
1. Discuss special geriatric problems that tend to dissipate group interaction.
2. How can these problems be overcome through learning new techniques?
3. What problems could groups be given to solve that would stimulate interaction?

OBJECTIVE 2.47

Assist geriatric clients to plan a musical performance that can be videotaped and sent to their families as a present.

Group: Geriatric clients

Procedure:

PREPARATION:
1. Select a music activity as warm-up for group.
2. Plan group discussion and feasible activities that might be suggested.

IMPLEMENTATION:
1. Conduct activity as warm-up.
2. Lead group discussion on topic.
3. Insure that everyone participates and has a definite role in plan.
4. Select one activity to begin practicing.

Music Specifications:

1. Student's choice

Recommended Time Limit: 15 minutes

Criteria For Objective:

Checklist 3: Minimum scores in each category
Overall minimum score = 72

Techniques Included: *Leading a Group Discussion*
Conducting Musical Warm-up

Discussion for Transfer:

1. Why might a videotape function as a very special gift to families? How could each individual be spotlighted?
2. Could an audiotape serve the same function if it were an individual vs. group tape?

OBJECTIVE 2.48

Use music to increase positive interactions between nursing home clients and their caretakers.

Group: Geriatric clients in nursing home

Procedure:

PREPARATION:
1. Select music that expresses appreciation for a special person.
2. Prepare "Appreciation Medals" for each client to award.

IMPLEMENTATION:
1. Sing song. Teach it if it is not already known.
2. Introduce topic of appreciating special people and use group discussion techniques to get clients involved in discussing positive staff interactions.
3. Help each person identify a staff member whom they sincerely appreciate.
4. Insure that a variety of staff are chosen by suggesting people at all administrative levels and in all different departments.
5. Lead group through facility, strolling and singing selected song while clients make awards to selected staff.

Music Specifications:
1. Student's choice

Recommended Time Limit: 15 minutes

Criteria For Objective:

Checklist 3: Minimum scores in each category
Overall minimum score = 72

Techniques Included: *Approving*
Leading Group Discussion
Songleading

Discussion for Transfer:
1. Discuss problems of nursing home clients and their relationship to caretakers.
2. What is the role of the music therapist in a nursing home? Should it include enhancing relationships with the staff?
3. How did the music function in this situation? What other functions could it have to enhance positive interactions?

OBJECTIVE 2.49

Teach presurgical patients the use of music listening and focused attention to deal with postoperative pain.

Group: Presurgical patients

Procedure:

PREPARATION:
1. Select music that is probably of interest to planned group.
2. Select short relaxation routine that moves quickly to focus attention on a musical element (listening for a particular instrument, counting crescendos, etc.).
3. Synchronize relaxation routine with music.
4. Develop evaluation procedure.

IMPLEMENTATION:
1. Play music and implement relaxation routine.
2. Teach focused attention task.
3. Help each person select their personal music for surgery.

Music Specifications:
1. Student's choice

Recommended Time Limit: 15 minutes

Criteria For Objective:

Checklist 3: Minimum scores in each category
Overall minimum score = 72

Techniques Included: *Focused Attention*
Music Leading
Evaluating

Discussion for Transfer:
1. Research shows that the individual patient's preferred music is probably the most effective in reducing pain. How can this be dealt with in a group situation?
2. Group members may develop their own focused attention task. What should the group leader do if this is reported?

OBJECTIVE 2.50

Use music and relaxation to teach stress reduction.

Group: General hospital patients with heart disease, high blood pressure, ulcers

Procedure:

PREPARATION:
1. Review Objective 2.09 tension/relaxation procedures. Review information about stress and its physiological effects.
2. Plan tension/relaxation routine that emphasizes awareness of biological signs of tension/stress vs. relaxation–muscle tension, fatigue or pain, pulse rate, breathing, etc.
3. Select music and prepare uninterrupted tape synchronized to routine.
4. Develop evaluation procedure.

IMPLEMENTATION:
1. Tell group they are role-playing persons with medical diagnoses related to stress.
2. Conduct relaxation activity to music as per Objective 2.09.
3. Have group sit up, then practice achieving immediate relaxed state in response to music being turned on. After five repetitions of this, have group achieve immediate relaxed state while imagining the music.
4. Lead group discussion about effects of tension/stress on medical problems and use of music to implement immediately relaxed state.
5. Evaluate.

Music Specifications:

1. Recorded music played at low enough volume to allow you to be heard easily over it (*background level*), which is instrumental (nonverbal) and probably perceived by group as "quiet music."
2. Uninterrupted tape prepared and synchronized as specified.
3. Use of tape recorder that provides quality playback for size of room and setting.

Recommended Time Limit: 15 minutes

Criteria For Objective:

Checklist 3: Minimum scores in each category
            Overall minimum score = 72

Techniques Included: *Using Relaxation Techniques*
                        Evaluating

Discussion for Transfer:

1. Discuss relaxation procedures in general (see Objective 2.09).
2. Discuss how achievement of "immediate relaxed state" might be evaluated other than through biofeedback.
3. Discuss how imagining the music might facilitate #2 above and how many repetitions might be necessary to master the ability.

OBJECTIVE 2.51

Use music to teach group to *control* anger with their spouses and children.

Group: Parents who abuse their children

Procedure:

PREPARATION:
1. Specifically define anger. Develop tension routine to help group identify physiological sensations that precede anger.
2. Select an anger control action step, i.e., leave room and implement relaxation routine, then make nonviolent plan to deal with problem, and music application.
3. Do *not* allow persons to engage in music behaviors that act out anger (like beating drums) since this is what you wish to inhibit.

IMPLEMENTATION:
1. Model your definition of anger and its control and shape group to imitate. Conduct music activity.
2. Role-play situations with children and let members practice control.
3. Lead a group discussion on how to control anger with one's children.
4. Evaluate.

Music Specifications:
1. Student's choice

Recommended Time Limit: 15 minutes

Criteria For Objective:

Checklist 3: Minimum scores in each category
Overall minimum score = 72

Techniques Included: *Anger Control*
Role-Playing
Evaluating

Discussion for Transfer:
1. How can people with anger control problems learn to censor violence when angry?
2. What might be a detrimental effect of substituting anger responses such as drum beating vs. child beating?

OBJECTIVE 2.52

Demonstrate "realistic life goals" by leading a group discussion on modification vs. realization of desirable life goals. Use music to introduce positive perspective on the topic.

Group: Terminally ill patients. Note: Instructor will assign nonparticipatory roles to some persons.

Procedure:

PREPARATION:
1. Select music as specified.
2. Plan ways to elicit discussion from members who might be angry.
3. Use empathetic listening–repeating what client said back to the individual.
4. Develop evaluation procedure.

IMPLEMENTATION:
1. Play music.
2. Lead group discussion–approve members for participation.
3. Elicit participation from everyone by demonstrating empathetic listening.
4. Try to shape discussion toward indicators of positive acceptance of terminal aspect of illness.
5. Evaluate.

Music Specifications:
1. Student's choice

Recommended Time Limit: 15 minutes

Criteria For Objective:

Checklist 3: Minimum scores in each category
Overall minimum score = 72

Techniques Included: *Leading Group Discussion*
Empathetic Listening
Evaluating

Discussion for Transfer:
1. What are the indicators that someone has accepted the reality of their death?
2. How can group members be taught by the leader to be supportive of each other?
3. How can a group leader accept all types of participation while shaping toward a specific goal? How does empathetic listening function in this situation?
4. What is "positive acceptance" of one's impending death?

OBJECTIVE 2.53

Use music to teach terminally ill clients one action step to deal with their diagnosis.

Group: Terminally ill patients

Procedure:

PREPARATION:
1. Select inspirational, *nonreligious* music as background for activity.

IMPLEMENTATION:
1. Play music.
2. Have group make a list of things they want to do.
3. Direct each person to select one thing from list that can be done today and make a commitment to it.
4. Elicit feedback about commitment.
5. Evaluate.

Music Specifications:

1. Student's choice

Recommended Time Limit: 15 minutes

Criteria For Objective:

Checklist 3: Minimum scores in each category
Overall minimum score = 72

Techniques Included: *Teaching Action Steps*
Evaluating

Discussion for Transfer:

1. Discuss protection of client privacy in group situations. Would this topic be an important one on which to maintain privacy?
2. How can commitment to a task be discerned and evaluated?

OBJECTIVE 2.54

Use music to enhance relationship between family members.

Group: Families with terminally ill member

Procedure:

PREPARATION:
1. Select two techniques for enhancing a family relationship, i.e., initiating closeness, finding out about another person's feelings, speaking openly, listening attentively.
2. Select music that incorporates or demonstrates these concepts.

IMPLEMENTATION:
1. Play music and introduce topic.
2. Teach the selected techniques for enhancing a relationship.
3. Break group into "families" and use role-playing to practice techniques. Keep the entire group participating.
4. Help each family work out one additional action step to implement these techniques at home.
5. Encourage commitment to try action step.
6. Evaluate.

Music Specifications:
1. Student's choice

Recommended Time Limit: 15 minutes

Criteria For Objective:

Checklist 3: Minimum scores in each category
Overall minimum score = 72

Techniques Included: *Establishing Relationships*
Role-Playing
Evaluating

Discussion for Transfer:
1. Why might families need to be taught how to enhance a relationship with a terminally ill member? Could this be a threatening task?
2. How did the music function in this activity? What are other ways music could be used with this objective?

OBJECTIVE 2.55

Use music to teach families of organ donors how to be positive about their decision and to deal with probable negative confrontations from others.

Group: Families of organ donors

Procedure:

PREPARATION:
1. Select inspirational music that promotes the concept of sharing the gift of life and that is *nonreligious*.
2. Review group discussion techniques in Objective 2.52.
3. Develop evaluation procedure.

IMPLEMENTATION:
1. Separate group into several family units.
2. Play music and lead discussion on positive aspects of the decision.
3. Have each family discuss among themselves the person most likely to feel negative about their decision.
4. Have each family role-play this person verbally confronting them on this topic.
5. Lead group discussion on most effective ways of handling such problems. Role-play these action steps.
6. Play music again and have members be supportive of each other's decision.
7. Evaluate.

Music Specifications:
1. Student's choice

Recommended Time Limit: 15 minutes

Criteria For Objective:

Checklist 3: Minimum scores in each category
Overall minimum score = 72

Techniques Included: *Leading Group Discussion–Empathy*
Role-Playing
Using Action Steps
Evaluating

Discussion for Transfer:
1. Next of kin must give permission for organ donation. What pressure does this place on the deciding individual with the rest of the family? Are such decisions usually unanimous?

OBJECTIVE 2.56

Develop a music activity dealing with identifying roles of family members in a group interaction.

Group: A family in distress. Note: Instructor will divide group into families and give them assignments to which you must react.

Procedure:

PREPARATION:
1. Identify possible roles of family members: authoritarian, dissenter, victim, facilitator, etc.
2. Collect a variety of rhythm instruments.
3. Select recorded music to be used with rhythmic activity.
4. Develop evaluation procedure.

IMPLEMENTATION:
1. Make available groups of instruments to each family.
2. Have groups select instruments and work out group coordinated accompaniment to music.
3. After playing accompaniment have family self-analyze their roles. Ask them if each likes the role he/she played. If not, repeat the activity by having the family design a new accompaniment while each person plays the role selected.
4. Lead discussion on how the family interaction changes as the roles change.
5. Evaluate.

Music Specifications:
1. Student's choice

Recommended Time Limit: 15 minutes

Criteria For Objective:

Checklist 3: Minimum scores in each category
Overall minimum score = 72

Techniques Included: *Leading Group Discussion*
Role Analysis
Evaluating

Discussion for Transfer:

1. What are the possible roles in family interactions? Which are beneficial and which are detrimental?
2. How could the family work toward permanently changing its interaction patterns?
3. What was the function of music in this situation?

OBJECTIVE 2.57

Develop a music activity to help family members enhance their positive interactions.

Group: A family in distress. Note: Instructor will divide group into families and give them assignments to which you must react.

Procedure:

PREPARATION:
1.   Write a short *simple* rap about family membership.
2.   Develop a data collection procedure to assess positive interactions.

IMPLEMENTATION:
1.   Teach group to rap using the Family Rap you wrote.
2.   Break groups into families to rehearse rap for performance. Move among groups and approve positive interactions.
3.   Have families perform. Stimulate enthusiastic applause from audience.
4.   Have each family write a new rap verse about themselves. Use form to observe interactions.
5.   Have families perform new verses in sequence interspersed with entire group doing rap chorus.
6.   Have families talk with each other about how they felt while interacting to plan the rap and make a plan to try interacting this way at home on a short (5 minute), preselected task.

Music Specifications:
1.   Rap as specified above.

Recommended Time Limit: 15 minutes

Criteria For Objective:

Checklist 3:   Minimum scores in each category
                     Overall minimum score = 72
80% positive family interactions

Techniques Included: *Rapping*
                                     Approving
                                     Composing
                                     Leading Group Discussion
                                     Evaluating/Data

Discussion for Transfer:

1.   What positive roles were observed in the family interactions?
2.   How could a family work toward permanently changing its interaction patterns?
3.   What was the function of music in this situation?

OBJECTIVE 2.58

Teach a square dance to group using more outgoing members as partners for more withdrawn members.

Group: Chronic psychiatric patients

Procedure:

PREPARATION:
1. Select ten sequential steps for a simple square dance.
2. Do a *task analysis* to determine most concise, descriptive directions, effective cues for each, and number of beats necessary to complete step.
3. Memorize task analysis.
4. Plan ways to cue *tutors* to stimulate participation in their partners.
5. Develop evaluation procedure.

IMPLEMENTATION:
1. Teach dance using *chaining, cuing*, and *correcting*.
2. Scan continuously to determine persons needing additional *cues* and respond accordingly.
3. Approve all spontaneous participation and spontaneous interactions between partners.
4. Evaluate.

Music Specifications:
1. Recorded music, instrumental, appropriate for dance.

Recommended Time Limit: 15 minutes

Criteria For Objective:

Checklist 3: Minimum scores in each category
Overall minimum score = 72
90% group directions followed

Techniques Included: *Chaining*
Cuing
Task Analysis
Peer Tutoring
Approving
Evaluating

Discussion for Transfer:
1. Discuss whether the difficulty of the dance matched probable group capabilities.
2. Discuss additional cues or ways to further stimulate participation and interaction.
3. Discuss behaviors that chronic patients might exhibit which would be socially inappropriate, i.e., rocking, not participating, dancing alone. How would the therapist handle these?

OBJECTIVE 2.59

Use music to teach social interaction in a chorus rehearsal.

Group: Chronic psychiatric patients

Procedure:

PREPARATION:
1. Specifically define appropriate "social interaction," i.e., asking question, listening, answering question, eliciting participation, etc.
2. Develop music activity in a choral structure to teach selected skills.
3. Develop evaluation procedure.

IMPLEMENTATION:
1. Place group in choral rehearsal format.
2. Conduct planned activity. Be sure to teach group to interact with other members, not leader.
3. If spontaneous interactions begin, withdraw and let them develop. If they subside, move closer and begin cuing.
4. Evaluate.

Music Specifications:
1. Student's choice

Recommended Time Limit: 15 minutes

Criteria For Objective:

Checklist 3: Minimum scores in each category
Overall minimum score = 72
90% group interaction

Techniques Included: *Stimulating Group Interaction*
Evaluating
Cuing

Discussion for Transfer:
1. Discuss special problems of chronic psychiatric patients that tend to reduce group interaction.
2. How can these problems be overcome through learning new techniques?
3. What problems could choral groups be given to solve that would stimulate interaction?
4. When would the music interfere with interaction? How could this be controlled?

OBJECTIVE 2.60

Use a music activity to facilitate reality-based verbalizations.

Group: Acute psychiatric patients. Note: Instructor will assign some group members to exhibit psychotic behavior.

Procedure:

PREPARATION:
1. Write a *simple* rap that incorporates facts about group and setting.
2. Plan evaluation procedure.

IMPLEMENTATION:
1. Teach group the *reality rap.*
2. Have group discuss the "here and now," the reality of where they are, with whom and for what reason.
3. Ignore hallucinatory, delusional, or nonfactual statements. Verify all reality statements.
4. Evaluate.

Music Specifications:

1. Rap as specified above.

Recommended Time Limit: 15 minutes

Criteria For Objective:

Checklist 3: Minimum scores in each category
Overall minimum score = 72
80% appropriate, reality-based group behavior

Techniques Included: *Leading Group Discussion*
Ignoring
Approving
Rapping

Discussion for Transfer:
1. What is the difference between hallucinations, delusions, paranoia, nonreality based thoughts or perceptions?
2. How can music function to stimulate awareness of the present reality? What music activities might stimulate nonreality based thought?

OBJECTIVE 2.61

Use music to teach group two realistic action steps to begin resolving a problem in their life.

Group: Acute psychiatric patients

Procedure:

PREPARATION:
1.   Select and specify action steps focusing on potentially positive outcomes of a situation while extinguishing blame, anger, grief, i.e., thought stopping, perceiving situation as growth opportunity, putting situation in perspective, making a decision and implementing it, etc.
2.   Select or compose music to introduce the concepts in the selected steps.
3.   Practice and memorize music if it is to be performed or acquire recording and quality playback equipment.

IMPLEMENTATION:
1.   Perform or play recorded music.
2.   Have brief discussion about disappointment and problems and how it is possible to learn to deal with them. State that the task is to practice some possible techniques.
3.   Describe selected action step 1 and give an example.
4.   Have group role-play and practice the technique in simulated problem situations.
5.   Have each person apply this step to their own situation by writing out a short plan.
6.   Repeat steps 3, 4 & 5 for Action Step 2.
7.   Play music again and lead group discussion on how the perception of the problem might have changed.
8.   Evaluate, using plans written by each person.

Music Specifications:

1.   Music to be performed or played that conveys concepts of the action steps selected.

Recommended Time Limit: 15 minutes

Criteria For Objective:

Checklist 3: Minimum scores in each category
Overall minimum score = 72

Techniques Included: *Role-Playing*
Teaching Action Steps
Evaluating

Discussion for Transfer:
1.   Research shows that music can affect mood. Did it in this situation? Did it function to *motivate* taking the action step? If so, when–at beginning or end of session?
2.   What specific behaviors did leader use to elicit, support, motivate, etc., the group?
3.   Do these behaviors differ from "simply telling a person what to do to solve the problem"?
4.   Fifteen minutes is too short a period of time in which to conduct this session in a real, clinical situation. If it were extended across an hour, how would it be conducted?

OBJECTIVE 2.62

Plan a facility-wide special occasion dance (for instance, Valentine's Day) with entry criteria to increase social skills.

Group: Chronic psychiatric patients

Procedure:

PREPARATION:
1. Determine minimum social criteria for dance entry that is slightly above that usually exhibited by client group. Consider dress code, attending with partner or guest, participation in dance preparation, etc.
2. Develop evaluation procedure.

IMPLEMENTATION:
1. Lead and focus group discussion to set entry criteria. Insure that predetermined criteria are included.
2. Play recorded dance music and help group practice (role-play) selected social skills.
3. Help group plan what to wear and how to organize preparations.
4. Evaluate.

Music Specifications:
1. Dance music preferred by client group.

Recommended Time Limit: 15 minutes

Criteria For Objective:

Checklist 3: Minimum scores in each category
Overall minimum score = 72

Techniques Included: *Leading Focused Group Discussion*
Teaching Social Skills
Role-Playing
Evaluating

Discussion for Transfer:
1. Discuss how social skills can be taught with music as a contingency.
2. Discuss importance of treating impaired adults as adults even though interaction by necessity might be simplified.
3. Discuss other social skills that would be important to teach this group.

LEVEL 3 COMPETENCIES

Tasks at this level are designed to:

a) maintain and improve students' musical, personal, and group leadership skills;

b) increase students' expertise in utilizing music to achieve primary therapeutic objectives with a variety of client groups, including:

Psychiatric Patients
Substance Abusers
Delinquent Adolescents
Families in Counseling
Cerebral Palsied Children
Suicidal Clients
Marital Counseling Clients
Geriatric Persons
Terminally Ill Persons
Stroke Victims
Developmentally Disabled Infants
Hearing Impaired Persons
Retarded Adults
Child Abusers
Emotionally Disturbed Children
Persons with Acute Stress
Agoraphobic Persons;

c) teach students to design and conduct music activities that meet multiple needs of a group by incorporating two or more group objectives while quantifying responses for evaluating effectiveness.

Note: Time limits are kept short (15–20 minutes) to facilitate multiple simulations in one class period. They are not realistic for true clinical situations and discussion of each simulation should center around appropriate opening and closing activities and pacing for these sessions. At some point, the instructor may wish to give each student an assigned time limit of 40–45 minutes to demonstrate such comprehensive leadership skills.

OBJECTIVE 3.01

Use music to teach assertiveness and anger control and the discrimination of when each is appropriate.

Group: Passive-aggressive persons

Procedure:

PREPARATION:
1. Specifically define at least two assertive behaviors to be taught.
2. Plan role-playing situations in which these behaviors can be demonstrated.
3. Determine anger control procedure to be taught.
4. Plan "spontaneous" transfer activity for end of session in which level of assertiveness can be measured.
5. Develop form to assess assertiveness.
6. Select or compose music.

IMPLEMENTATION:
1. Discuss traits of passive-aggressive reaction to problems. Use *negative modeling* to give examples.
2. Describe and demonstrate two assertive behaviors and anger control techniques.
3. Involve group in role-playing the demonstrated techniques. Alternate with negative modeling of passive-aggressive reaction to same situation.
4. Teach *discrimination* of when each behavior is appropriate.
5. Conduct transfer activity and evaluate assertiveness.
6. Use song at end to motivate people to try these techniques when encountering their next problem.

Music Specifications:
1. Student's choice

Recommended Time Limit: 15 minutes

Criteria For Objective:

Checklist 3: Minimum scores in each category
Overall minimum score = 75

Techniques Included: *Action Techniques for Anger Control*
Action Techniques for Assertiveness
Discrimination
Role-Playing
Negative Modeling
Evaluating/Data

Discussion for Transfer:

1. When does assertiveness become aggression? How can the leader assure that clients discriminate the difference?
2. In what situations would a passive-aggressive person have the most difficulty being assertive? Could these be structured as role-playing assignments?
3. How can the leader get feedback on how effectively the client applies these newly learned action steps when in the "real" world of his/her everyday environment?

OBJECTIVE 3.02

Use music to teach group to:

a) identify five of the most commonly abused drugs and symptoms of their abuse,
b) develop guidelines for reactions to suspected drug experimentation,
c) role-play responses recommended in guidelines.

Group: Parents of teenagers and middle school teachers

Procedure:

PREPARATION:
1. Determine five most widely abused drugs and get literature and information about them.
2. Develop *a priori* parent and teacher guidelines for responses to suspected abuse.
3. Develop role-playing situations.
4. Select or compose music.
5. Develop handout on drug issues for discussion between parents and children and develop a survey to assess success.

IMPLEMENTATION:
1. Teach information about drugs. Get immediate feedback from group on amount of information acquired.
2. Lead *focused* group discussion to develop a few, simple guidelines for responding to suspected abuse. (See 2.11 for techniques.)
3. Involve group in role-playing to practice the responses formulated by the group.
4. Teach selected or composed song at end to motivate people to remember drug information, symptoms, and preferred reactions to suspected abuse.
5. Hand out discussion topics and survey and give instructions on their return to you.

Music Specifications:
1. Student's choice

Recommended Time Limit: 15 minutes

Criteria For Objective:

Checklist 3: Minimum scores in each category
Overall minimum score = 75

Techniques Included: *Focused Group Discussion*
Role-Playing
Evaluating

Discussion for Transfer:
1. How can a parent or teacher's reaction to suspected drug abuse make the problem worse/better?
2. Why would it be a good idea to train parents and teachers together on this issue?
3. How would the discussion survey function or not function to get parents and teachers talking with their children about these issues?

OBJECTIVE 3.03

Use music to reduce inappropriate behavior in the lunchroom by letting disruptive students:
- a) formulate guidelines,
- b) select music,
- c) enforce the contingencies.

Group: Disruptive middle school students

Procedure:

PREPARATION:
1. Develop *a priori* guidelines.
2. Develop role-playing situations.
3. Select music that probably would be preferred by teenagers and acquire quality equipment for playback.
4. Develop form to assess accuracy of contingency enforcement.

IMPLEMENTATION:
1. Lead discussion on lunchroom problems.
2. Propose use of music and its contingent interruption to improve situation.
3. Let students select music (radio station, recordings).
4. *Focus* discussion to formulate guidelines for appropriate behavior and operation of the music contingency.
5. Involve students in role-playing to train them to enforce the guidelines.
6. *Approve* all instances of correct enforcement and indicators of commitment toward implementation.
7. Have students assess whether contingencies are enforced.

Music Specifications:
1. Student's choice

Recommended Time Limit: 15 minutes

Criteria For Objective:

Checklist 3: Minimum scores in each category
Overall minimum score = 75

Techniques Included: *Music Interruption*
Focused Group Discussion
Approving
Self-Evaluation/Data

Discussion for Transfer:
1. Research shows music interruption can function to decrease inappropriate behavior. How did it function in this situation?
2. Why would letting *disruptive* students set the guidelines function to improve lunchroom behavior?
3. How would self-evaluation of contingency enforcement function in this situation?
4. Research also shows that peer punishment is usually more severe than that of authority figures. How would focusing discussion toward *a priori* guidelines *prevent* them from being too strict?

OBJECTIVE 3.04

Use music activity to teach one selected aspect of improving family relationships.

Group: Families in distress

Procedure:

PREPARATION:
1. Specifically define the family issue which will be taught.
2. Develop a music activity to teach the issue.
3. Develop a data sheet to assess effect of activity.

IMPLEMENTATION:
1. Direct music activity.
2. Use role-playing and simulation for group to practice the appropriate behavior.
3. Shape positive verbalizations by the group and action steps directed toward dealing with the problem.

Music Specifications:

1. Student's choice

Recommended Time Limit: 15 minutes

Criteria For Objective:

Checklist 3: Minimum scores in each category
Overall minimum score = 75

Techniques Included: *Teaching an Interpersonal Skill*
Role-Playing
Evaluation

Discussion for Transfer:

1. What actions can be taken to improve relationships?
2. How can a music task be used to evaluate or assess the quantity and quality of a group's interactions?

OBJECTIVE 3.05

Use a regularly scheduled facility-wide dance as a reinforcer to encourage and teach reality-based, appropriate social behavior.

Group: Chronic psychiatric persons in mental health facility and staff

Procedure:

PREPARATION:
1. Plan entry criteria for dance (dress, hygiene, price of admission which might be a ticket earned in a therapy session that week).
2. Plan guidelines for dancing (must have partner and face them while dancing, no rocking, etc.).
3. Plan instructions for staff in attendance to monitor and reinforce appropriate behavior.
4. Plan dance music, refreshments, decorations.

IMPLEMENTATION:
1. Assign diagnoses to members of the group.
2. Implement entry criteria, cue staff to assist.
3. Begin dancing. Cue staff to assist in approving and maintaining guidelines.
4. Approve staff for assisting and clients for appropriate social behavior.
5. Evaluate effect of activity on appropriate social behavior.

Music Specifications:
1. Student's choice

Recommended Time Limit: 15 minutes

Criteria For Objective:

Checklist 3: Minimum scores in each category
Overall minimum score = 75

Techniques Included: *Using Music as a Reinforcer*
Cuing
Approving
Evaluation

Discussion for Transfer:

1. Why would staff traditionally believe that dealing with *problems* (emergencies, fights, seizures) was their only responsibility at a dance? How could this attitude be changed over time? What would be the payoff for staff to change this belief?
2. Why might a dance with no entry criteria or no restrictions on "appropriate" dancing actually allow mentally ill persons to practice their symptoms?
3. What is the responsibility of the leader to teach a facility how music can best be used in a treatment plan?

OBJECTIVE 3.06

Use music to teach depressed clients an action behavior to reduce the depression.

Group: Depressed patients in acute, short-term facility

Procedure:

PREPARATION:
1. Select several action steps to reduce depression that cover cognitive, emotional, and physiological issues.
2. Select a music activity to teach one or more (exercising to music, thought stopping through music listening, etc.).
3. Select music needed.
4. Develop form to assess effect of activity.

IMPLEMENTATION:
1. Teach the action step and when and how to use that action to reduce depression. Role-play implementation.
2. Have each client select one additional action step they could take to reduce depression.
3. Assess effectiveness of activity.

Music Specifications:
1. Student's choice

Recommended Time Limit: 20 minutes

Criteria For Objective:

Checklist 3: Minimum scores in each category
Overall minimum score = 75

Techniques Included: *Using Action Steps*
Role-Playing
Evaluating/Data

Discussion for Transfer:

1. Why would depressed persons need a plan of action that covered physiological, cognitive, and emotional issues? How could music be effectively incorporated into all of these areas?
2. Research shows that medication is most effective immediately in reducing depression, while counseling or therapy is more effective in maintaining stability across the long term. How would this activity as described maximize the effects long term and also immediately?

OBJECTIVE 3.07

Use music to teach two or three academic issues while shaping individualized social behaviors for each member.

Group: Cerebral palsied preschoolers

Procedure:

PREPARATION:
1. Select two or three academic tasks at the preschool level (colors, numbers, identifying letters, etc.). Select music for each.
2. Plan a different individual social behavior to be taught to each group member (waiting turn, speaking softly, keeping hands in lap, etc.).
3. Develop form to assess both academic and social behavior.

IMPLEMENTATION:
1. Assign roles to group with each having specific social problem.
2. Direct music activities and teach academic tasks while shaping individual social behaviors. *Cue* each member to use appropriate behavior and *approve* those who do.
4. Evaluate effect of activity on academic and social behaviors.

Music Specifications:
1. Student's choice

Recommended Time Limit: 20 minutes

Criteria For Objective:

Checklist 3: Minimum scores in each category
Overall minimum score = 75

Techniques Included: *Cuing*
Approving
Ignoring
Evaluating

Discussion for Transfer:

1. Why would the ability to individualize instruction be important for preschoolers, especially CP preschoolers?
2. Why would it be important to teach these children in a group setting vs. one to one? Is MT a good technique for grouping such clients?
3. How can a leader acquire the skill of attending to the needs of individuals while maintaining the teaching of a group task?

OBJECTIVE 3.08

Use music to teach client to establish a relationship with others in the group.

Group: Suicidal clients. Note: Instructor will assign some group members to simulate suicidal clients and some to be therapy assistants.

Procedure:

PREPARATION:
1.   Select activity and music to best help people establish a new relationship.
2.   Review procedures in Objective 2.11 on how to lead a focused group discussion.
3.   Develop means to assess effect of activity.

IMPLEMENTATION:
1.   Direct group in activity. Use supportive, approving techniques to help members initiate relationships.
2.   Lead focused group discussion to help members verbalize commitment to each other and group.
3.   Help members verbalize commitment to initiate a relationship outside the session. Help each develop a plan to accomplish this.
4.   Assess the effects of this session.

Music Specifications:
1.   Student's choice

Recommended Time Limit: 20 minutes

Criteria For Objective:

Checklist 3: Minimum scores in each category
Overall minimum score = 75

Techniques Included: *Teaching an Interpersonal Skill*
Leading Focused Group Discussion
Using Action Steps
Evaluating

Discussion for Transfer:

1.   Why might or might not commitment to a group help a suicidal person maintain stability from one week to the next?
2.   Why might initiating relationships be an initial goal for all members of such a group? Would this be the terminal goal for such clients?
3.   With whom should such clients try to establish a relationship?

OBJECTIVE 3.09

Lead a focused group discussion on the negative consequences of drug abuse with emphasis on harm to significant others.

Group: Substance abusers

Procedure:

PREPARATION:
1. Acquire and learn facts about substance abuse (incidence, amounts, frequency of typical abuse, age, etc.).
2. Select relevant music for use before, during, or after discussion.
3. Review procedures for focused group discussion (Objective 2.11).

IMPLEMENTATION:
1. Lead discussion and shape the group to focus on the assigned topic. Contribute facts about abuse as appropriate and use music at some point in the discussion. Have group monitor and eliminate denial responses.
2. Approve members of the group for participation by nonverbal means.
3. Insure that all members participate.
4. Evaluate your effectiveness as a leader.

Music Specifications:

1. Student's choice

Recommended Time Limit: 15 minutes

Criteria For Objective:

Checklist 3: Minimum scores in each category
             Overall minimum score = 75

Techniques Included: *Teaching an Interpersonal Skill*
                             Leading Focused Group Discussion
                             Using Action Steps
                             Evaluating

Discussion for Transfer:

1. What are the benefits of the group monitoring denial?
2. What was the effect on the discussion of the leader "dropping" specific facts about abuse? Should a therapist know such facts about the disorders with which they deal?

OBJECTIVE 3.10

Use music to help couples learn appropriate techniques for improved communication.

Group: Couples in marital counseling. Note: Instructor will assign a few class members to be resistive or hostile.

Procedure:

PREPARATION:
1. Define specific techniques of effective communication (initiating, responding, listening, giving feedback about what is heard).
2. Develop a music activity to teach the above. Select appropriate music.
3. Develop form to assess communication skills of each couple.

IMPLEMENTATION:
1. Divide class into couples.
2. Use music to teach basic guidelines/techniques for effective communication. Identify resistive and hostile members and shape them in more positive, participatory behaviors.
3. Give couples time during the class to practice communication skills in a variety of situations, e.g., expressing affection, solving a serious problem, etc.
4. Evaluate.

Music Specifications:
1. Student's choice

Recommended Time Limit: 20 minutes

Criteria For Objective:

Checklist 3: Minimum scores in each category
Overall minimum score = 75

Techniques Included: *Teaching an Interpersonal Skill*
Evaluating

Discussion for Transfer:
1. Are effective communication techniques situational (expression of affection vs. problem solving)? What communication skills are common to all interactions?
2. What is communication? What is the goal? How do you know if it is good or bad? If you have good communication, do you have a good relationship?

OBJECTIVE 3.11

Use music to improve gait and ambulation abilities.

Group: Stroke victims

Procedure:

PREPARATION:
1. Select music to match these three gait problems: 1) use of walker, 2) shuffling with minimal stride length at fast tempo, and 3) limping with one normal and one short stride due to one dysfunctional leg.
2. Plan instruction to correct stride with physical and verbal cues for each.
3. Develop form to assess improvement in stride.

IMPLEMENTATION:
1. Divide group into three diagnoses specified. Work with one group at a time while others evaluate and give positive feedback to their peers.
2. Use music, cues, and instructions about walking to regulate rhythm and stride for each group. Approve trying, continuing, and improved gait.
3. After each group begins to improve, cut off music volume for a few seconds and encourage clients to continue, then resume music. Continue intermittent interruption for longer periods of time.
4. Evaluate effectiveness of activity.

Music Specifications:
1. Music matched to three gait problems: 1) use of walker (3/4 time), 2) shuffling with minimal stride length (2/4 or 4/4 time), and 3) dysfunction of one leg in shortened stride on one side (2/4 or 4/4 time).

Recommended Time Limit: 20 minutes

Criteria For Objective:

Checklist 3: Minimum scores in each category
Overall minimum score = 75

Techniques Included: *Gait Training*
Approving
Intermittent Interruption of Music
Evaluating/Data

Discussion for Transfer:

1. Research shows music can be effective in regulating stride width, length, and rhythm. Was it applied to all these areas in this activity?
2. How can progress in all these areas be assessed?
3. How did interruption of music affect gait? How long could a person sustain good gait initially without the music to structure them? (Seconds or minutes?)

OBJECTIVE 3.12

Conduct range of motion exercises to music while teaching sign language for basic daily needs.

Group: Stroke victims

Procedure:

PREPARATION:
1. Learn range of motion exercises. Select music to fit them.
2. Learn at least five signs for basic needs (eat, drink, bed pan, sit up, etc.).
3. Plan range of motion routine that incorporates opportunity to teach signs and that is matched to music.
4. Develop means to assess use of signs.

IMPLEMENTATION:
1. Divide group into clients and therapists.
2. Start music and instruct therapists in conducting range of motion routine and use of signs. Physically demonstrate and verbally cue each exercise and sign. Give feedback to therapists
3. Evaluate clients' ability to use signs.

Music Specifications:
1. Music matched to range of motion/sign language routine.

Recommended Time Limit: 20 minutes

Criteria For Objective:

Checklist 3: Minimum scores in each category
Overall minimum score = 75

Techniques Included: *Range of Motion Exercises*
Sign Language
Evaluating

Discussion for Transfer:
1. Why might sign language instruction be necessary for stroke victims? Who would have to be trained in addition to the clients?
2. How can a person who daily conducts range of motion exercises with a client be sensitive to any motor rehabilitation that might be occurring?

OBJECTIVE 3.13

Use music to teach infant stimulation techniques to parents.

Group: Multiply handicapped infants and their parents

Procedure:

PREPARATION:
1. Plan music activities to stimulate the auditory, visual, and physical senses of infants. Plan verbal and nonverbal ways to approve infant responses.
2. Plan verbal and physical cues to prompt parents.
3. Develop measure of responses to stimuli in each category.

IMPLEMENTATION:
1. Divide class into infants and parents. Note: Simulation of infants is difficult. It is most effective to invite normal infants and parents to class to practice these techniques.
2. Direct music activities. Cue parents to stimulate infants and approve responses.
3. Place special emphasis on noticing subtle responses.
4. Evaluate infant responses in auditory, visual, and physical areas.

Music Specifications:
1. Music to stimulate auditory (cooing, laughing), visual (eye tracking), and physical responses (moving, kicking, head turning).

Recommended Time Limit: 15 minutes

Criteria For Objective:

Checklist 3: Minimum scores in each category
Overall minimum score = 75

Techniques Included: *Cuing*
Approving
Infant Stimulation
Evaluating/Data

Discussion for Transfer:
1. Why would parents need training in the stimulation of handicapped infants? How could parents' attention be directed to subtle changes in the infant's responses?

OBJECTIVE 3.14

Use music to increase social interaction.

Group: Mainstreamed hearing impaired and normally hearing adolescents

Procedure:

PREPARATION:
1. Select songs and signs. Practice according to procedures in Objective 1.10.
2. Plan ways to increase social interaction opportunities between groups, i.e., breaking into small groups and letting students practice together and tutor each other; giving decisions to groups and letting them work out a solution, etc.
3. Develop form to assess interaction between the two groups.

IMPLEMENTATION:
1. Teach songs and signs.
2. Insure opportunities for social interaction between hearing impaired and normally hearing persons.
3. Approve *all* spontaneous positive, social interaction between hearing and non-hearing persons.
4. Evaluate results of activity.

Music Specifications:
1. Song with signs that would be of interest to adolescents.

Recommended Time Limit: 20 minutes

Criteria For Objective:
Checklist 3: Minimum scores in each category
Overall minimum score = 75

Techniques Included: *Approving*
Evaluating
Signing to Music
Teaching Social Interaction

Discussion for Transfer:
1. What would be the probability of increasing social interaction between hearing and nonhearing adolescents using this activity? What kind of music or decisions would increase this probability?
2. How could adolescents be motivated to continue such social interaction outside the music class?

OBJECTIVE 3.15

Use music to help retarded adults learn to make decisions by planning a group leisure activity.

Group: Retarded adults who are residents of independent group living setting

Procedure:

PREPARATION:
1. Select music and activity to teach decision making: identifying options, identifying pros and cons of each option, arriving at consensus on one option, implementing decision.
2. Develop form to assess decision making.
3. Gather information about leisure opportunities, transportation in the community, e.g., newspaper ads with dates, times, cost, bus routes, etc.

IMPLEMENTATION:
1. Direct music activity and teach decision making skills.
2. Introduce topic of deciding on a group leisure activity.
3. Cue group to use decision making skills.
4. Approve all spontaneous use of these skills,
5. Review formulated plan and cue issues group might have omitted.
6. Assess decision making skills.

Music Specifications:
1. Student's choice

Recommended Time Limit: 20 minutes

Criteria For Objective:

Checklist 3: Minimum scores in each category
Overall minimum score = 75

Techniques Included: *Cuing*
Approving
Teaching Decision Making
Evaluating/Data

Discussion for Transfer:

1. Why might planning a leisure activity be highly motivating to these clients? What type of music activity might be attractive to these clients as an affordable leisure endeavor?
2. What issues would need to be considered besides date, time, cost, transportation? Are there activities that the community would view as inappropriate for retarded persons? Should a group leader help plan such activities?

OBJECTIVE 3.16

Use music to help parents have a positive interaction with their children.

Group: Children and parents with tendency to abuse their children

Procedure:

PREPARATION:
1. Select task with high frustration potential for parents (high probability of children's failure, very messy, high probability for children to engage in inappropriate behavior, etc.).
2. Select music activity to teach positive, controlled parenting techniques: positive touching and verbalization, correction without punishment, being proactive through structure rather than reactive to inappropriate behavior.
3. Develop means of evaluating activity.

IMPLEMENTATION:
1. Divide group into parents and children.
2. Conduct music activity and teach positive, effective parenting techniques: controlled, positive verbalizations; controlled, positive touching; correcting without punishing, etc.
3. Direct task with high frustration potential and cue parents to use positive, controlled techniques. Stop any interactions in which frustration begins to develop and have parents leave the room. Teach these parents it is good to leave *before* becoming frustrated.
4. Approve parents who are using techniques and remaining calm.
5. Evaluate effectiveness of activity.

Music Specifications:
1. Student's choice

Recommended Time Limit: 20 minutes

Criteria For Objective:

Checklist 3: Minimum scores in each category
Overall minimum score = 75

Techniques Included: *Cuing*
Approving
Evaluating
Parenting Techniques

Discussion for Transfer:
1. Why would parents need to practice new parenting techniques in the presence of the leader prior to trying them alone?
2. How can parents be motivated to walk away from correcting their child rather than to lose their temper?
3. If the parents knew how to *prevent* problems from developing, there would be no need for coping techniques. How could the activity be structured so that the children are less likely to engage in inappropriate behavior?

OBJECTIVE 3.17

Use a rhythm instrument activity to teach creativity, social interaction, and rhythmic skills.

Group: Geriatric clients

Procedure:

PREPARATION:
1. Select rhythm or percussion instruments with excellent musical sound that are age appropriate.
2. Plan rhythms to accompany a selected favorite song of this group.
3. Develop form to assess creativity, social interaction, and rhythmic skill.

IMPLEMENTATION:
1. Pass out instruments and teach how each is played.
2. Sing song and let each person play along.
3. Divide group into sections and teach each a different rhythm.
4. Teach group to play softly and let individuals take turns doing a solo, dancing, singing, etc.
5. Approve creativity, rhythmic accuracy, and all spontaneous interactions.
6. Assess these three areas.

Music Specifications:

1. Favored song of geriatric clients.
2. Quality of instruments.

Recommended Time Limit: 15 minutes

Criteria For Objective:

Checklist 3: Minimum scores in each category
Overall minimum score = 75

Techniques Included: *Approving*
Evaluating
Stimulating Creativity

Discussion for Transfer:

1. Might geriatric clients feel demeaned by toylike rhythm instruments?
2. Would geriatric clients need "permission" or prompting to express their creativity or to perform a solo?

OBJECTIVE 3.18

Use music to teach group to extinguish inappropriate, stereotyped mannerisms, to wait for a turn and to identify their written name.

Group: Emotionally disturbed children

Procedure:

PREPARATION:
1. Select music activity that requires taking turns.
2. Review *approving* and *ignoring* techniques (Objective 2.30 and 2.31).
3. Develop form to assess specified behaviors.
4. Select *incompatible responses* for stereotyped behaviors.
5. Prepare cards with each person's name.

IMPLEMENTATION:
1. Assign stereotyped behaviors to each person.
2. Direct music activity and teach name recognition.
3. Approve *incompatible responses*, correct name recognition, and waiting for a turn.
4. *Ignore* inappropriate behavior.
5. Assess effect of activity.

Music Specifications:
1. Student's choice

Recommended Time Limit: 15 minutes

Criteria For Objective:

Checklist 3: Minimum scores in each category
Overall minimum score = 75

Techniques Included: *Approving*
Ignoring
Teaching Incompatible Responses
Evaluating

Discussion for Transfer:
1. How did teaching an incompatible response effect the stereotyped behaviors?
2. Could music interruption be incorporated into this activity?

OBJECTIVE 3.19

Use music to teach clients to reduce stress.

Group: General hospital patients with stress related diagnoses

Procedure:

PREPARATION:
1. Select relaxation/imagery routine (Objective 2.09).
2. Select music.
3. Determine physiological and cognitive assessment of relaxation.

IMPLEMENTATION:
1. Conduct relaxation/imagery routine with music.
2. Teach clients to assess their own relaxation.
3. Have each person write a list of stimuli that generate stress.
4. Help each one make a plan to schedule daily relaxation routine and use of supplementary routines under conditions of stress.

Music Specifications:

1. Student's choice

Recommended Time Limit: 15 minutes

Criteria For Objective:

Checklist 3: Minimum scores in each category
Overall minimum score = 75

Techniques Included: *Relaxation*
Imagery
Evaluating

Discussion for Transfer:

1. How could persons with uncontrolled reactions to stress monitor themselves cognitively and physically?
2. How often would relaxation routines need to be practiced? Daily, several times a day?

OBJECTIVE 3.20

Use music to teach a group of adults with a fear of leaving the house (agoraphobiacs) one action step leading to the reduction of this fear.

Group: Adults with agoraphobia

Procedure:

PREPARATION:
1. Learn a relaxation routine (Objective 2.09) and plan desensitization imagery for leaving house on a short trip (grocery store, mall).
2. Select music.
3. Plan role-playing situations.
4. Develop feedback forms.

IMPLEMENTATION:
1. Direct relaxation routine followed by imagery. Use music.
2. Have group role-play going on selected trip in imagery routine.
3. Motivate group to attempt this trip during the week.
4. Hand out feedback forms so clients can fill them out after the trip and bring back to therapy next week.

Music Specifications:
1. Student's choice

Recommended Time Limit: 20 minutes

Criteria For Objective:

Checklist 3: Minimum scores in each category
Overall minimum score = 75

Techniques Included: *Relaxation*
Imagery
Role-Playing
Client Self-Evaluating/Data

Discussion for Transfer:

1. Self-evaluation is often an effective way to get explicit information about how a client feels about an experience. What are the problems with relying solely on self-report data? What other types of data collection would be desirable?
2. How could persons with agoraphobia be helped to generalize relaxation techniques to a variety of situations?

LEVEL 4 COMPETENCIES

Tasks at this level are designed to teach:

a)   the ability to plan music activities to achieve *multiple group objectives* for a variety of client populations;

b)   the development of an extensive music *repertoire* for a variety of therapy activities;

c)   *adapting* a planned activity in response to specific problems of individuals within the group;

d)   the ability to *evaluate* success in achieving group objectives.

See Index by Techniques (page 173) for assistance with specific activities.

> Note: Individual roles within the group should be assigned by the instructor prior to the class. Time limits may be extended for more realistic pacing of techniques.

OBJECTIVE 4.01

Teach hemodialysis patients to use music and relaxation techniques to reduce the discomforts of dialysis, e.g., boredom, pain, nausea, blood pressure fluctuations, etc.

Group: Kidney dialysis patients; at least one will be critically ill, another will be severely depressed.

Procedure:

PREPARATION:
1. Plan relaxation routine to music.
2. Plan adaptation for critically ill person.
3. Plan intervention for depressed person.
4. Plan evaluation for group and individual objectives.

IMPLEMENTATION: As planned

Music Specifications:

1. Provide a list of fifty music selections (ten in each of five categories of different types of music) from which patients can select preferred music for use during the four hours of each dialysis session.
2. Relaxation routine to music.

Recommended Time Limit: 20 minutes

Criteria For Objective:

Checklist 3: Overall Score = 75 or above
Evaluation of group objective and two individual objectives

Techniques Included: *Relaxation*
Others By Student's Choice
Evaluating

Discussion for Transfer:

1. In hemodialysis situations, what would be the role of the therapist vs. the music? Could the music be available and independently selected by each patient with no therapist present?
2. What techniques would be necessary in this situation to deal with people as individuals?

OBJECTIVE 4.02

Teach group members to empathize with the role of a client in group therapy.

Group: Peers; one will be verbally domineering, one will be withdrawn, one will be hostile to situation.

Procedure:

PREPARATION:
1. Plan to have each student describe a personal situation which was very embarrassing.
2. Plan to deal with the group members who were assigned to be problematical through approving *incompatible responses.*
3. Plan to lead a focused group discussion to have students describe how they felt discussing intimate events in public. Make transfers to clients in group therapy.
4. Plan use of music.
5. Plan evaluation of your leadership skills.

IMPLEMENTATION: As planned

Music Specifications:
1. Student's choice

Recommended Time Limit: 20 minutes

Criterion For Objective:

Checklist 3:   Overall Score = 75 or above

Techniques Included: *Use of Incompatible Responses*
Leading Focused Group Discussion
Others By Student's Choice
Evaluating

Discussion for Transfer:

1. Did the group reveal the most embarrassing, intimate details about themselves or were these censored? What degree of trust would it take for each to reveal censored details? How did the group deal with embarrassment–laughter/lack of eye contact/blushing/ hostility?
2. How was this situation like one that a client in group therapy might experience? What skills would a group leader need to establish trust within the group?
3. Under what circumstances should a leader *not* encourage a client to make *public confessions* in the group?

OBJECTIVE 4.03

Use music and art to help patients deal with their feelings.

Group: Terminally ill persons; one will be uncommunicative, one will be angry.

Procedure:

PREPARATION:
1. Plan for patients to draw to music.
2. Plan to lead a focused group discussion of a positive objective using content of pictures. Decide before discussion starts what the objective of the discussion will be. Make plans to deal with persons with problems.
3. Plan to evaluate your skills as leader and whether objectives were achieved.

IMPLEMENTATION: As planned

Music Specifications:

1. Student's choice

Recommended Time Limit: 20 minutes

Criterion For Objective:

Checklist 3: Overall Score = 75 or above

Techniques Included: *Drawing To Music*
Leading Focused Group Discussion
Others By Student's Choice
Evaluating

Discussion for Transfer:

1. What effect did the music selection have on the drawing? How would other types of music have functioned in this situation?
2. Was the group discussion resolved in a beneficial way indicating some acceptance of the illness? What were the indicators of this?
3. How was leader effectiveness evaluated?

OBJECTIVE 4.04

Teach a music task using signs and demonstrate differential feedback to 5-year-old hearing impaired children.

Group: Hearing impaired children aged 5 years

Procedure:

PREPARATION:
1. Plan to approve the following:
    Child 1 – approve for following directions
    Child 2 – approve for speaking in two-word phrases
    Child 3 – approve for reduced hyperactivity
    Child 4 – approve for eye contact
    Others in group – approve for correct musical responses.
2. Learn signs necessary for teaching the musical task.
3. Practice teaching the task with signs.
4. Prepare evaluation form for assessing your feedback.

IMPLEMENTATION: As planned

Music Specifications:
1. Student's choice

Recommended Time Limit: 20 minutes

Criterion For Objective:

Checklist 3:   Overall Score = 75 or above

Techniques Included: *Signing*
                          Approving
                          Evaluating

Discussion for Transfer:
1. How does a leader's skill in differential feedback affect the ability to individualize instruction within a group?
2. Why would hearing impaired preschoolers require as much individualized instruction as possible?

OBJECTIVE 4.05

Teach a music task to the group and, additionally, teach an incompatible response to each of the persons with the problems listed below.

Group: Retarded adults; one will be withdrawn, one will be socially inappropriate, one will give incorrect answers to questions.

Procedure:

PREPARATION:
1. Plan music task and teach procedure for retarded persons.
2. Review procedures for teaching an incompatible response (Objective 2.02).

IMPLEMENTATION: As planned

Music Specifications:
1. Student's choice

Recommended Time Limit: 15 minutes

Criterion For Objective:

Checklist 3: Overall Score = 75 or above

Techniques Included: *Teaching Incompatible Responses*

Discussion for Transfer:

1. An incompatible response is an appropriate *valued* response that is mutually exclusive of the specific *in*appropriate behavior in which the person has been engaging. Were the selected, taught responses in this situation incompatible? Were expectations readily apparent to the individual? How did the leader prompt or cue the *desired* responses?

OBJECTIVE 4.06

Use music to teach an aspect of accepting responsibility for one's actions to clients in a juvenile detention center.

Group: Juvenile delinquents; one will be hostile, one will constantly interrupt.

Procedure:

PREPARATION:
1. Develop a few role-playing situations where accepting responsibility for one's actions results in positive consequences (awards, approval) and a few where it results in negative consequences (detention, suspension, disapproval).
2. Plan to deal with group members with behavior problems.
3. Plan the use of music for this objective.
4. Plan to lead a focused group discussion on accepting responsibility for one's actions and how this is evidenced (no excuses), i.e., no one makes excuses for the things they do that result in positive consequences.
5. Plan to evaluate effect of the session by having each person write "What I did to be here" without excuses.

IMPLEMENTATION: As planned

Music Specifications:
1. Student's choice

Recommended Time Limit: 20 minutes

Criterion For Objective:

Checklist 3:   Overall Score = 75 or above

Techniques Included: *Role-Playing*
                         Leading a Focused Group Discussion
                         Evaluating

Discussion for Transfer:
1. Why would you be cautious about having the group tell each other what they did to be in detention?
2. How could you evaluate the ability to accept responsibility from what each person wrote?
3. What other ways could acceptance of responsibility be taught?

OBJECTIVE 4.07

Use music to teach acute psychotic patients who have been in facility one month to select and implement a self-shaping project.

Group: Acute psychotic persons; one will begin hallucinating.

Procedure:

PREPARATION:
1. Plan a psychiatric diagnosis for each member of the group. Plan techniques to deal with the potential problems of each diagnosis and the hallucinatory person, i.e., say name loudly to startle, then approve for being on-task to the group.
2. Plan to have each member select one behavior they would like to self-shape.
3. Plan to teach group how to implement a self-shaping program for their objective: specify objective, measure it, consequate it and evaluate results.
4. Plan to get group to take first action step in implementation of their individual program.
5. Plan use of music.
6. Develop evaluation procedures.

IMPLEMENTATION: As planned

Music Specifications:
1. Student's choice

Recommended Time Limit: 20 minutes

Criterion For Objective:

Checklist 3: Overall Score = 75 or above

Techniques Included: *Teaching An Action Step*
Evaluating

Discussion for Transfer:
1. What kind of follow-up would be necessary to assist psychiatric clients in actually implementing their plan?
2. How could a self-shaping project provide transition between facility and home after discharge?
3. What skills would a leader need to motivate each person to select an objective with significant impact upon his/her overall problem?

OBJECTIVE 4.08

Use music in a desensitization program for animal phobia.

Group: Persons with animal phobia; one will hyperventilate at beginning of approach to animal, one will refuse to participate.

Procedure:

PREPARATION:
1. Select music, relaxation routine and specific animal to which group will be desensitized.
2. Plan how to deal with person who refuses to participate.
3. Plan desensitization hierarchy for physical proximity to animal following relaxation training and adaptation for person who will hyperventilate.
4. Plan imagery to maximize pleasure following approach to animal.
5. Develop evaluation procedures.

IMPLEMENTATION: As planned

Music Specifications:
1. Student's choice

Recommended Time Limit: 20 minutes

Criterion For Objective:

Checklist 3:   Overall Score = 75 or above

Techniques Included: *Relaxation*
Desensitization
Imagery
Evaluating

Discussion for Transfer:
1. How would this technique vary for other specific phobias or for generalized phobias such as agoraphobia or "panic attacks"?
2. What is the function of a) music in this situation, b) the relaxation routine, c) the desensitization hierarchy, d) the imagery?
3. How would a leader help the group move from cognitive rehearsal to action?

OBJECTIVE 4.09

Conduct a music activity to stimulate socialization, then help group plan a group leisure activity with emphasis on feasibility. Insure that the group is independent from you in making decisions.

Group: Geriatric persons in senior center or nursing home; one will be hard of hearing, one will refuse to participate.

Procedure:

PREPARATION:
1. Plan music socialization activity and adaptation for persons with problems.
2. Decide how to guide group in planning the leisure activity.
3. Plan approvals for instances of *independent*, yet realistic, ideas.
4. Plan how to maintain high level of socialization during decision-making.
5. Develop evaluation procedures.

IMPLEMENTATION: As planned

Music Specifications:
1. Student's choice

Recommended Time Limit: 20 minutes

Criterion For Objective:

Checklist 3:   Overall Score = 75 or above

Techniques Included: *Leading Focused Group Discussion*
Approving
Socialization
Evaluating

Discussion for Transfer:
1. Why would independence in planning leisure activities be an important goal for persons in a senior center or nursing home?
2. What skills would a leader use to facilitate decision-making without allowing the group to become *dependent* upon the leader?

OBJECTIVE 4.10

Use music to teach decision-making skills.

Group: Retarded adults in group living home; one will engage in stereotyped rocking, one will interrupt verbally.

Procedure:

PREPARATION:
1. Select activity requiring several decisions.
2. Select music.
3. Review procedures for decision making: define the problem, identify options, identify pros and cons of each option, select preferred option, act upon selection and deal with consequences.
4. Prepare form for homework assignment.
5. Plan to teach incompatible responses for the problem.
6. Develop evaluation procedures.

IMPLEMENTATION: As planned

Music Specifications:
1. Student's choice

Recommended Time Limit: 20 minutes

Criterion For Objective:

Checklist 3:   Overall Score = 75 or above

Techniques Included: *Decision Making*
                              Approving
                              Role Playing
                              Homework Assignments
                              Use of Incompatible Responses
                              Evaluating

Discussion for Transfer:
1. When retarded persons are taught decision-making skills, what discrimination would also be important to teach?
2. How might decision making cause a retarded person to be viewed as inappropriate?
3. Are there decisions retarded people should never be allowed to make? What are the civil rights of retarded persons?

OBJECTIVE 4.11

Use music to stimulate positive verbal and physical responses between spouses.

Group: Persons in marital counseling; one will be nonparticipatory, one will be verbally negative.

Procedure:

PREPARATION:
1. Select music activity that stimulates feedback to group members.
2. Select role-playing activity.
3. Plan to deal with uncooperative group members.

IMPLEMENTATION:
1. Conduct music activity.
2. Approve all positive responses in a hierarchy from music, to leader, to other group members, to spouse. Approve verbal and physical proximity responses.
3. Focus discussion on commitment to positive interactions.
4. Role-play problematical home situation with emphasis on positive responses.
5. Develop evaluation procedure.

Music Specifications:
1. Student's choice

Recommended Time Limit: 20 minutes

Criterion For Objective:

Checklist 3: Overall Score = 75 or above

Techniques Included: *Approving*
Role-Playing
Leading Focused Group Discussion
Evaluating

Discussion for Transfer:

1. Do all couples in marital counseling have the goal of trying to respond positively to each other?
2. Could persons planning a divorce benefit from learning to respond positively to each other?
3. Could a positive response to an alienated spouse be learned in one session?

OBJECTIVE 4.12

Use music activities to structure positive parent visits and maintain child's developmental level.

Group: Children in general hospital (one will cry easily, one will be totally dependent, one will regress to baby talk) and their parents.

Procedure:

PREPARATION:
1. Plan variety of music activities appropriate to various age levels to motivate self-feeding, self-toileting, self-dressing, etc.
2. Plan a variety of activities that can be left with child to self-structure time: coloring music instruments, music crossword puzzles, music quizzes for interviewing families, medical staff, etc.

IMPLEMENTATION:
1. Conduct various music activities.
2. Approve all independent, self-help skills. Ignore all whining, "sick" responses.
3. Teach parents to positively interact with their child and to use music and approving to help their child remain at developmental level with self-help skills. Utilize evaluation procedures.
4. Leave variety of music activities for children to complete during the week.

Music Specifications:
1. Student's choice.

Recommended Time Limit: 20 minutes

Criterion For Objective:

Checklist 3:   Overall Score = 75 or above

Techniques Included: *Approving*
Ignoring
Self-Help Skills
Positive Interaction
Evaluating

Discussion for Transfer:

1. Parents may be reluctant to ignore "crying," "sick," or "feeling bad" responses of their child. How could doing the music activities *first* help them get perspective on this issue?
2. What is the problem if a child regresses and loses developmental milestones due to hospitalization?

OBJECTIVE 4.13

Use music to teach role function and help each family member select a satisfactory role.

Group: Families in therapy; one father will be a whiner, one mother will be autocratic, one mother will be a victim.

Procedure:

PREPARATION:
1. Plan activity to assess current roles in family interactions. (Possibilities would be autocrat, nurturer, irritant, whiner, nagger, victim, initiator, attention seeker, etc.).
2. Select music.
3. Plan activity to role-play positive roles.
4. Plan to deal with problems of individuals.

IMPLEMENTATION:
1. Assess roles.
2. Role-play positive roles. Approve use of positive roles.
3. Help each family as a group to select satisfactory roles for each member through discussion.
4. Conduct music activity. Cue each person to use their pre-selected role. Cue family members to give feedback to the new role.

Music Specifications:
1. Student's choice

Recommended Time Limit: 20 minutes

Criterion For Objective:

Checklist 3:   Overall Score = 75 or above

Techniques Included: *Role-Playing*
Group Decision Making
Cuing
Role Assessment

Discussion for Transfer:

1. How can role clarification or selection help achieve harmony in a family grouping?
2. What type of feedback would family members need to learn in response to another's role?

OBJECTIVE 4.14

Use music and breathing routines to teach labor management to pregnant women.

Group: Pregnant women and their partners in Lamaze class; one couple will continuously seek attention.

Procedure:

PREPARATION:
1.   Plan breathing routines with music for labor stages I, II, and III.
2.   Plan attention focusing and muscle relaxation cues.
3.   Teach assistance role to partners.
4.   Approve *incompatible responses* for couple with attention-seeking problem.

IMPLEMENTATION:
1.   Teach breathing routine, attention focusing, and muscle relaxation.
2.   Approve partners for assisting correctly.
3.   Approve *incompatible responses* for couple with problem.

Music Specifications:
1.   Student's choice

Recommended Time Limit: 20 minutes

Criterion For Objective:

Checklist 3:   Overall Score = 75 or above

Techniques Included: *Lamaze Breathing Techniques*
Focusing Attention
Relaxing Muscles
Approving
Using Incompatible Responses

Discussion for Transfer:
1.   What are the cues that a woman is moving to the next stage of labor? How can the music be coordinated with changes to the next stage of labor?
2.   How can breathing routines to music, focused attention, and muscle relaxation be compatible? How can the partner monitor these without interrupting?

OBJECTIVE 4.15

Use music to teach "speaking in sentences" and asking questions.

Group: Language delayed children; one child will interrupt, one will be passively off-task.

Procedure:

PREPARATION:
1. Plan music activity and cues for sentences and questions.
2. Develop evaluation procedures.

IMPLEMENTATION:
1. Teach music activity. Cue verbal responses. Approve complete sentences and questions.
2. Approve all appropriate classroom behaviors, i.e., waiting turn, following directions, paying attention, etc.
3. Approve *incompatible responses* for interrupting and off-task.
4. Evaluate.

Music Specifications:
1. Student's choice

Recommended Time Limit: 20 minutes

Criterion For Objective:
Checklist 3: Overall Score = 75 or above

Techniques Included: *Cuing*
Approving
Using Incompatible Responses
Evaluating

Discussion for Transfer:
1. What would indicate the child has the skills to learn to speak in sentences or ask questions?
2. What would be the next developmental language skill to teach after this?
3. What other persons in the child's environment would need to be cued to help the child maintain a language skill?

OBJECTIVE 4.16

Use music to teach appropriate, positive interactions between normal and special education children in mainstreamed music class.

Group: Special education and "normal" children in mainstreamed music class; one special education child will have a behavior problem, one normal child will be verbally negative.

Procedure:

PREPARATION:
1. Plan to deal with ED, HI, and CP children in regular music class and plan to deal with behavior problems.
2. Plan variety of activities, music, teaching techniques, use of peer tutors, etc.
3. Develop evaluation procedures.

IMPLEMENTATION:
1. Cue and approve *positive interactions between normal and special education children.*
2. Approve all appropriate classroom behavior. Ignore all inappropriate behavior.
3. Evaluate.

Music Specifications:
1. Student's choice

Recommended Time Limit: 20 minutes

Criterion For Objective:

Checklist 3:   Overall Score = 75 or above

Techniques Included: *Approving*
Ignoring
Peer Tutoring
Evaluating

Discussion for Transfer:

1. Research shows that music can facilitate positive interactions in mainstreamed classes. What structure should the teacher add to the music to insure this?
2. What would be the indicators of positive interactions between normal and handicapped children?

OBJECTIVE 4.17

Use music to teach adolescents to deal with peer pressure.

Group: Adolescents; all will be somewhat reluctant to participate initially.

Procedure:

PREPARATION:
1. Select music activity to overcome reluctance to participate.
2. Select music and activity to introduce the topic of peer pressure.
3. Plan role-playing to deal with peer pressure for leaving school, shoplifting, getting pregnant, etc.
4. Develop evaluation procedures.

IMPLEMENTATION:
1. Conduct music activity. Approve participation.
2. Teach values clarification and *a priori* decision making with regard to the above issues.
3. Have students role-play above situations with peer pressure to deviate from *a priori* decision making.
4. Approve students who remain in control under peer pressure.
5. Evaluate.

Music Specifications:
1. Student's choice

Recommended Time Limit: 20 minutes

Criterion For Objective:

Checklist 3: Overall Score = 75 or above

Techniques Included: *Role-Playing*
Decision Making
Approving
Evaluating

Discussion for Transfer:

1. To what extent can adolescents deal with peer pressure through values clarification and *a priori* decision making?
2. Should adolescents be taught techniques to sway peer pressure toward their own values? How could this become a problem for them?

OBJECTIVE 4.18

Use music to help parents set realistic goals for their children.

Group: Parents of handicapped children; all will have unrealistic goals (too negative, too protective, too lofty, etc.).

Procedure:

PREPARATION:
1. Plan activities to help parents clarify the expectations of self vs. others, realistic goals and appropriate parenting techniques.
2. Develop evaluation procedures.

IMPLEMENTATION:
1. Conduct music activity.
2. Lead focused group discussion on above topics. Help parents individually to achieve closure on each issue.
3. Conduct role-playing activity to help parents practice their desired techniques and goal setting skills.
4. Evaluate.

Music Specifications:
1. Student's choice

Recommended Time Limit: 20 minutes

Criterion For Objective:

Checklist 3:   Overall Score = 75 or above

Techniques Included: *Leading Focused Group Discussion*
Role-Playing
Evaluating

Discussion for Transfer:
1. How might parents' expectations for their children differ from those of others in the family? Might parents sometimes feel stress due to pressure from others without realizing it?
2. At what point should future goals for the child be determined by the child?

OBJECTIVE 4.19

Use music to reduce awareness of pain.

Group: Chronic pain patients; one will complain continuously, one will refuse to participate due to pain.

Procedure:

PREPARATION:
1. Prepare exercise routine to music.
2. Plan indicators for improved endurance, participation.
3. Plan evaluation procedures.

IMPLEMENTATION:
1. Cue and approve participation, endurance/duration, and positive verbalizations during exercises. Ignore complaining and lack of participation.
2. Let group members be leaders of exercise routine and cue and approve others.
3. Evaluate.

Music Specifications:

1. Student's choice

Recommended Time Limit: 20 minutes

Criterion For Objective:

Checklist 3:   Overall Score = 75 or above

Techniques Included: *Cuing*
Approving
Ignoring
Evaluating

Discussion for Transfer:

1. Research shows music can reduce awareness of pain. Why would cuing and approving be important to the use of music with exercise?

OBJECTIVE 4.20

Use music to improve math skills.

Group: Learning disabled middle school students; one will have frequent frustration responses, one will be negative about his/her abilities.

Procedure:

PREPARATION:
1. Select math problems at middle school level.
2. Select music activities.
3. Plan evaluation procedures.

IMPLEMENTATION:
1. Conduct math/music activities.
2. Approve correct answers and appropriate social behaviors: attending, positive verbalizations, etc. Ignore negative verbalizations and frustration responses.
3. Evaluate.

Music Specifications:
1. Student's choice

Recommended Time Limit: 20 minutes

Criterion For Objective:

Checklist 3:   Overall Score = 75 or above

Techniques Included: *Approving*
Ignoring
Evaluating

Discussion for Transfer:
1. Music can be an effective reinforcer for academic subject matter. Would it appeal to middle school students? What music would be most preferred? How could this be determined?
2. Females often reject math skills as being unattractive. How can this value be changed?
3. Assuming that frustration is a learned response, identify some incompatible behaviors that can be taught to offset it.

LEVEL 5 COMPETENCIES

Spontaneous Demonstration

Level 5 is designed to allow the student to demonstrate competencies across a variety of tasks without relying on extensive prior planning.

Its purpose is to give the student experience in:

      a) planning quickly,
      b) building and utilizing repertoire that is memorized with materials that are readily available, and
      c) spontaneously handling unexpected client responses.

Tasks at this level are derived from the following form which has an array of choices for the instructor in the categories of leadership techniques, client objectives, use of music, client age, client disability, type of service site, and client characteristics.

The instructor selects a different set of specifications for each student by checking the appropriate blanks and distributes the forms at the beginning of class. The class is given five minutes of planning time and then each student conducts a short (5 minutes) activity to meet the individual set of specifications. Students may utilize any instruments or materials available in the classroom.

SPONTANEOUS SKILL DEMONSTRATION FORM

Name	Date Due	Order	Time Limit

Objective:
- _____ accepting responsibility for actions
- _____ verbal interaction
- _____ social interaction
- _____ reduction of hyperactivity
- _____ reduction of aggression
- _____ attending
- _____ decision-making
- _____ memory
- _____ academic information
- _____ motor response
- _____ self-help skill
- _____ reality orientation
- _____ rule following
- _____ parenting techniques
- _____ relationship development
- _____ stress reduction

Group:

A. Age

- _____ infant
- _____ child
- _____ adolescent
- _____ adult
- _____ geriatric

B. Disability

- _____ retarded
- _____ mentally ill
- _____ delinquent
- _____ visually impaired
- _____ hearing impaired
- _____ physically handi-capped
- _____ emotionally disturbed
- _____ health problem
- _____ persons in crisis
- _____ distressed family
- _____ terminally ill
- _____ mentally ill

Procedure:

PREPARATION:
1. Take 5 minutes to plan a music activity to achieve the desired objective for identified group. Use memorized repertoire and materials readily available in room.
2. Plan to deal with the following client behavior problems:
   - _____ withdrawn
   - _____ hyperactive
   - _____ negative
   - _____ suicidal
   - _____ depressed
   - _____ disoriented
   - _____ aggressive
   - _____ off-task
   - _____ nonparticipatory
   - _____ hostile

IMPLEMENTATION
As planned

Music Specifications:
- _____ accompanying instrument
- _____ recorded music
- _____ singing
- _____ moving to music
- _____ rhythmic activity

Recommended Time Limit: 5 minutes

Criterion for Objective:

Checklist 3: Overall score 80 or above

Techniques to be Included:

_____ Approving	_____ Role-Playing
_____ Modeling	_____ Teaching Action Steps
_____ Cuing	_____ Signing to Music
_____ Ignoring	_____ Leading Focused Group Discussion
_____ Chaining	_____ Use of Relaxation Procedures
_____ Scanning	_____ Use of Rules
_____ Approving an Incompatible Response	_____ Use of Range of Motion Exercises

Therapy Orientation:

_____ Rogersian	_____ Rational-Emotive
_____ Reality	_____ Action Counseling
_____ TA	_____ Behavioral

PART III:
REFERENCE

DISCOGRAPHY BY COUNSELING TOPIC

ACTIVE CHANGE

Title	Artist
Beautiful	Carole King
Changes	Olivia Newton-John
Changes in Attitude, Changes in Latitude	Jimmy Buffet
Cool Change	Little River Band
Do What You Think You Should	Exile
Do What You Want, Be What You Are	Darryl Hall and John Oates
Everything Is Kinda All Right	The Charlie Daniels Band
Follow That Dream	Elvis Presley
Games People Play	Joe South
I Can See Clearly Now	Johnny Nash
I Gotta Try	Michael McDonald
I'm Easy	Keith Carradine
I've Gotta Be Me	Sammy Davis, Jr.
It's Up to You	Teddie Pendergrass
Let the Sunshine in	The 5th Dimension
Long Promised Road	The Beach Boys
Lookin' Out for Number One	Bachman-Turner Overdrive
Man in the Mirror	Michael Jackson
My Life	Billy Joel
My Way	Frank Sinatra
Only Heaven Can Wait	Roberta Flack
People Gotta Be Free	Martha Reeves
Present	Cupid
Rehumanize Yourself	Police
That's Why	Michael McDonald
The Need to Be	Jim Weatherly
This Gift of Life	Teddie Pendergrass
Time After Time	Ivory
Wait a Little While	Kenny Loggins
We've Only Just Begun	The Carpenters
What Do I Need to Be Me	The 5th Dimension
Where Will I Be	Crosby & Nash
You Haven't Done Nothin'	Stevie Wonder

ADDICTIONS/SUBSTANCE ABUSE

Title	Artist
Addicted to Love	Robert Palmer
Be Smart, Don't Start	The Jets
Bottoming Out	Lou Rawls
Cloud Nine	Diana Ross & the Supremes with the Temptations
Control	Janet Jackson
Don't Try Suicide	Queen
Drinking Again	Tasha Thomas
Fat Man	Jethro Tull
I Got Stoned and I Missed It	Jim Stafford
I Want a New Drug	Huey Lewis and the News
Kicks	Paul Revere & the Raiders
Rappin'	Snack Attack

ADDICTIONS/SUBSTANCE ABUSE (cont)

Title	Artist
Reasons to Quit	Merle Haggard and Willie Nelson
Sign of the Times	Prince
Shot to Hell	Henry Paul Band
10538 Overture	E.L.O.
That Smell	Lynyrd Skynyrd
That Needle and the Damage Done	Neil Young
The Raid	Parker
Tragic Surf	The Motels
We All Had a Real Good Time	Edgar Winter
Whiskey Man	Milly Hatchet
Whiskey River	Willie Nelson
Whiskey Talkin'	Henry Paul Band
Wino	Lynyrd Skynyrd

ADOLESCENCE

Title	Artist
At Seventeen	Janis Ian
Bus Rider	The Guess Who
Father & Son	Cat Stevens
How Will I Know	Whitney Houston
Kicks	Paul Revere & The Raiders
Papa Don't Preach	Madonna
Problem Child	Parker
Spotlight	Madonna
Summer – The First Time	Bobby Goldsboro
What Do I Need to Be Me	The 5th Dimension
Younger Generation	The Lovin' Spoonful

AGING

Title	Artist
Are the Good Times Really Over	Merle Haggard
Cat's in the Cradle	Harry Chapin
Circle Game	Joni Mitchell
Forever Young	Laura Branigan
I Wish I Was 18 Again	George Burns
It Was a Very Good Year	Frank Sinatra
Memories	The Beatles
Old Folks	Kenny Rogers
Old Man in Our Town	Kenny Rogers
Rings of Life	Michael Murphey
September Song	Willie Nelson
Time in a Bottle	Jim Croce
Up on the Shelf	Harry Chapin
Where Did the Spring Go	The Kinks
With a Child's Heart	Stevie Wonder
Younger Generation	The Lovin' Spoonful

ANGER

Title	Artist
Brain Damage	Pink Floyd
I Am a Rock	Simon & Garfunkel
Insane Again	The J. Geils Band
Love I Never Had	Tavares
Nobody Knows	John Simons
No Tears	Furs
Rain Song	John Simons
Rage in a Cage	The J. Geils Band
The Sounds of Silence	Simon & Garfunkel
Take This Job and Shove It	Johnny Paycheck

CHILD ABUSE

Title	Artist
Dear Mr. Jesus	Shannon Bass

CRISIS INTERVENTION

Title	Artist
Anywhere's a Better Place to Be	Harry Chapin
At Seventeen	Janis Ian
Desperado	Eagles
Don't Cry Out Loud	Melissa Manchester
Dreams of the Everyday Housewife	Glen Campbell
Honey	Bobby Goldsboro
Love I Never Had	Tavares
Lyin' Eyes	Eagles
Nowhere Man	The Beatles

DECISION MAKING

Title	Artist
Believe in You	Twisted Sister
Come Home America	Billy Joel
Everybody Has a Dream	Johnny Rivers
Goodbye Yellow Brick Road	Elton John
High Time	Heart
I Am, I Said	Neil Diamond
I Believe in Myself Again	Janis Ian
I Can See Clearly Now	Ray Charles
Low Budget	The Kinks
Road to Freedom	Robin Trower
Secret of Life	Jethro Tull
So Many Paths	Little River Band
Take a Look at Yourself	Miracle Lick
The Circle Game	Joni Mitchell
The Going Ups and Coming Downs	Gladys Knight & The Pips
Things That Dreams Are	The Human League
Tomorrow	Barbra Streisand
Was I Right or Was I Wrong?	Lynyrd Skynyrd
We May Never Pass This Way Again	Seals & Croft
Wheel of Fortune	The Doobie Brothers

DECISION MAKING (cont.)

Title	Artist
Where Do You Go?	Cher
Wind in Our Sails	Black Oak Arkansas
You Can't Always Get What You Want	The Rolling Stones
You're the One that I Want	Olivia Newton-John

DEPRESSION/LONELINESS

Title	Artist
Ain't No Good Life	Lynyrd Skynyrd
Alfie	Cher
All By Myself	Eric Carmen
All the Time	Barry Manilow
Anywhere's a Better Place to Be	Harry Chapin
Are You Lonesome Tonight	Elvis Presley
Beautiful	Carole King
Comin' Home	Johnny Mathis
Deep River Blues	Darryl Hall & John Oates
Desperado	Eagles
Don't Cry Out Loud	Melissa Manchester
Don't Forget Me When I'm Gone	Glass Tiger
Does Anybody Know I'm Here?	The Dells
Everyday I Have the Blues	B. B. King
Fool on the Hill	The Beatles
Helpless	Crosby, Stills, Nash & Young
I Am a Rock	Simon & Garfunkel
I Don't Live Today	Jimi Hendrix
I'm Sad and I'm Lonely	Carl Sandburg
I'm So Lonesome I Could Cry	Hank Williams
Loneliness	Paul Williams
Lonely Children	Foreigner
Lonely People	America
Loner	Neil Young
Nowhere Man	The Beatles
Only the Lonely	Roy Orbison
Rainy Days and Mondays	The Carpenters
Sad Lisa	Cat Stevens
Send in the Clowns	Stephen Sondheim
Traces	Classic IV
Whoever Finds This, I Love You	Mac Davis
Words Get in the Way	Miami Sound Machine

DISAPPOINTMENT

Title	Artist
Comin' Home	Johnny Mathis
Don't Cry Out Loud	Melissa Manchester
Hey Jude	The Beatles
Lyin' Eyes	Eagles
Yesterday's Wine	Merle Haggard & George Jones

EMOTIONAL INVOLVEMENT

Title	Artist
All the Time	Barry Manilow
Believe It or Not	Joey Scarbury
Desperado	Eagles
Don't Cry Out Loud	Melissa Manchester
Dust in the Wind	Kansas
I'd Like to Get to Know You	Spanky & Our Gang
I Don't Know How to Love Him	Yvonne Elliman
I Honestly Love You	Olivia Newton-John
I Love How You Love Me	The 5th Dimension
If I Could Feel	Richard Pryor
In Your Eyes	Peter Gabriel
Let's Wait Awhile	Janet Jackson
Love Songs	James Taylor
Poor Pitiful Me	Linda Rondstadt
The First Time Ever I Saw Your Face	Roberta Flack
You Light Up My Life	Debby Boone
You'll Never Find Another Love Like Mine	Lou Rawls

MARITAL ISSUES

Title	Artist
Another Grey Morning	James Taylor
B. S. U. R.	James Taylor
Changes	Olivia Newton-John
Daddy's Little Man	Mac Davis
Doesn't Anybody Stay Together Anymore?	Phil Collins
Don't Think Twice, It's All Right	Peter, Paul & Mary
I Never Meant to Hurt You	Barbra Streisand
It Ain't No Use	Stevie Wonder
Legal Boys	Elton John
Love I Never Had	Tavares
Never Was a Day	The 5th Dimension
On My Own	Patti LaBelle
Pen in Hand	Bobby Goldsboro
Second Avenue	Art Garfunkel
Separate Ways	Elvis Presley
She's Not the Same	Gordon Lightfoot
Tell Her About It	Billy Joel
Traces	Classic IV
The Way We Were	Barbra Streisand
We Can Work It Out	The Beatles
With You All the Way	New Edition
You'd Better Sit Down Kids	Cher

PROBLEM SOLVING

Title	Artist
Hey Jude	The Beatles
If You Want It	Niteflyte
Life's What You Make It	Talk Talk
Lizzy and the Rainman	Tanya Tucker
Spring	Tanya Tucker

RELATIONSHIPS

Title	Artist
Always on My Mind	Willie Nelson
Angels, Roses and Rain	Dickey Lee
Back Stage	The Temptations
Battle Stations	Wham!
Believe It or Not	Joey Scarbury
Blind Man in the Bleachers	David Geddes
Bridge Over Troubled Waters	Simon & Garfunkel
Cat's in the Cradle	Harry Chapin
Cry to Me	Heart
Daddy's Little Man	Mac Davis
Ebony and Ivory	Paul McCartney & Stevie Wonder
Father and Son	Cat Stevens
Games People Play	Joe South
He Ain't Heavy, He's My Brother	Neil Diamond
Here to Love You	The Doobie Brothers
Honesty	Billy Joel
I Am a Rock	Simon & Garfunkel
I'd Like to Get to Know You	Spanky & Our Gang
I Don't Know How to Love Him	Yvonne Elliman
If You Could Read My Mind	Gordon Lightfoot
I Love How You Love Me	The 5th Dimension
It's Too Late	Carole King
Just the Way You Are	Billy Joel
Lean on Me	Bill Withers
Livin' on a Prayer	Bon Jovi
My Friends	Simon & Garfunkel
Old Man	Neil Young
People	Barbra Streisand
Put a Little Love in Your Heart	Martha Reeves
Solitary Sing Song	Kenny Young
Solitude Solitaire	Peter Cetera
Standing on the Top	The Temptations
Superstar	The Temptations
That's What Friends Are For	Dionne Warwick
The Long and Winding Road	The Beatles
United We Stand	Brotherhood of Man
We Are Family	Sister Sledge
We Are the World	USA for Africa
We Never Really Say Goodbye	Captain & Tenille
Where Peaceful Waters Flow	Gladys Knight & The Pips
Willie Jones	The Charlie Daniels Band
You and Me Against the World	Helen Reddy
You Are the Sunshine of My Life	Stevie Wonder
You Give Love a Bad Name	Bon Jovi
You're the Inspiration	Peter Cetera
You've Got a Friend	Carole King

SUICIDE

Title	Artist
Don't Try Suicide	Queen
Lyin' Eyes	Eagles
I Think I'm Going to Kill Myself	Elton John
Sign of the Times	Prince

TERMINAL ILLNESS/CATASTROPHE

Title	Artist
And When I Die	Blood, Sweat & Tears
Autumn of My Life	Bobby Goldsboro
Daniel	Elton John
Everybody's Gotta Go	Atlanta Rhythm Section
Flight	John Denver
I Can See Clearly Now	Gladys Knight & The Pips
I Don't Live Today	Jimi Hendrix
My Life	Billy Joel
My Way	Frank Sinatra
Old Shep	Elvis Presley
Sometimes It Snows in April	Prince
Spring	Tanya Tucker
'Til I Die	The Beach Boys
Tonight's the Night	Neil Young
The Bookend	Simon & Garfunkel
Waterfall	Chris Williamson
We Never Really Say Goodbye	Captain & Tenille

INDEXES TO COMPETENCY TASKS

INDEX BY POPULATION

POPULATION	TASK	STUDENT OBJECTIVE	TECHNIQUES
Adolescents	2.17	Teach circle dance to EMR	Chaining Cuing Task Analysis
	2.18	Teach choral performance skills to EMR	Modeling Cuing Fading Approving Incompatible Response
	2.30	Teach on-task behavior	Approving/Disapproving Ratio
	2.39	Teach acceptance of responsibility for actions	Leading Group Discussion Role-Playing
	2.40	Teach rhythmic activity/rules	Use of Rules Approving Evaluating
	2.41	Teach anger control	Controlling Anger Leading Group Discussion Overcompensation
	2.42	Teach nonsexual relationships with opposite sex	Establishing Relationships Role-Playing
	2.43	Teach resistance to peer pressure	Role-Playing
	3.03	Reduce inappropriate behavior in lunchroom	Music Interruption Focused Group Discussion Approving Self-Evaluating
	3.14	Increase social interaction between mainstreamed hearing impaired & normally hearing	Approving Evaluating Signing Social Interaction
	4.06	Teach accepting responsibility for one's actions	Role-Playing Leading Focused Group Discussion
	4.17	Teach appropriate response to peer pressure	Role-Playing Decision Making Approving

Agoraphobia	3.20	Reduce fear of leaving house	Relaxation Imagery Role-Playing
Cerebral Palsy Adults	2.36	Teach group interaction	Group Interaction
Children	2.35	Teach range of motion exercises	Range of Motion Exercises
	3.07	Teach academic skills/social behavior	Cuing Approving Ignoring Evaluating
Child Abusers	2.51	Teach anger control	Anger Control Role-Playing
	3.16	Reduce tendency to abuse	Cuing Approving Evaluating
Educable Mentally Retarded	2.17	Teach circle dance to adolescents	Chaining Cuing Task Analysis
	2.18	Teach choral performance skills	Modeling Cuing Fading Approving Incompatible Responses
Emotionally Disturbed	2.29	Reduce hyperactivity in 8 year olds & increase incompatible response	Reducing Hyperactivity Modeling Cuing Approving Incompatible Response
	2.30	Teach on-task; 4:1 Approval Ratio	Approving/Disapproving in 4:1 Ratio
	2.31	Teach rule following to 10-year-olds	Rule Following Ignoring
	3.18	Teach children to extinguish stereotyped mannerisms, wait for turn & identify written name	Approving Ignoring Teaching Incompatible Response
Epileptics	2.14	Teach monitoring of fatigue/tension to reduce seizure activity	Relaxation Techniques
Families (of/in) Distress	2.56	Identify roles of family members in group interaction	Leading Group Discussion Role Analysis
	2.57	Help family have positive interaction	Rapping/Composing Family Counseling Evaluating

Families (of/in) Distress (cont)	3.04	Teach how to improve family relationships	Teaching Interpersonal Skills Role-Playing Evaluating
Organ Donor	2.55	Teach how to be comfortable with decision for organ donation	Leading Group Discussion Empathy Role-Playing
Terminally Ill	2.54	Enhance relationships between family members	Establishing Relationship Role-Playing
Therapy	4.13	Teach role function and selection	Role Assessment Cuing Role-Playing Group Decision Making
Geriatric Clients	2.44	Teach three Reality Orientation Objectives	Composing Cuing
	2.45	Teach exercises synchronized to music	Group Leadership Exercises Cuing Scanning
	2.46	Increase social interaction	Stimulating Group Interaction
	2.47	Plan musical performance	Leading Group Discussion
	2.48	Increase interaction between clients and staff	Approving Leading Group Discussion
	3.17	Teach creativity, social inter-action & rhythmic skill	Approving Evaluating Stimulating Creativity
	4.09	Stimulate socialization & plan group leisure activity	Leading Focused Group Discussion Approving Socializing
Group Therapy Clients	4.02	Teach empathy with role of client in group therapy	Incompatible Response Leading Focused Group Discussion
Hearing Impaired	2.32	Teach signs to well-known song	Songleading Chaining Modeling Cuing Signing to Music
	2.33	Teach 16 measure rhythm	Group Leadership–Rhythm Cuing Chaining Modeling

Hearing Impaired (cont.)	2.34	Teach an auditory discrimination task	Signing Auditory Discrimination
	3.14	Increase social interaction between mainstreamed hearing impaired and normally hearing adolescents	Approving Evaluating Signing Social Interaction
	4.04	Teach music task using signs & demonstrate differential feedback	Signing Approving
Juvenile Delinquents	4.06	Teach acceptance of responsibility for actions	Role-Playing Leading Focused Group Discussion
Kidney Dialysis	4.01	Reduce discomforts of dialysis	Leading Relaxation
Language Delayed	4.15	Teach speaking in sentences & asking questions	Cuing Approving Incompatible Responses
Learning Disabled	2.15	Teach spelling concept	Composing Songleading Chaining Cuing Evaluating
	2.16	Improve reading	Composing Songleading Approving Cuing Evaluating
	4.20	Improve math skills	Approving Ignoring Evaluating
Pain	4.01	Reduce discomforts of dialysis	Relaxation
	4.19	Reduce awareness of pain	Cuing Approving Ignoring
Parents	2.37	Teach reinforcement	Approving Ignoring
	2.38	Parenting techniques	Lead Group Discussion Role-Playing
	3.02	Teach response to child's drug problems	Focusing Group Discussion Role-Playing Evaluating
	4.12	Structure visits with hospitalized child	Approving Ignoring Self-Help Skills Positive Interaction

Parents (cont.)	4.18	Teach parents to set realistic goals for children	Leading Group Discussion Role-Playing

Passive-
Aggressive
Persons
	3.01	Teach assertiveness/anger control & discrimination	Action Techniques/
			  Anger Control
			Action Techniques/
			  Assertiveness
			Discrimination
			Role-Playing
			Evaluating

Patients Chronic Pain	4.19	Reduce awareness of pain	Cuing Approving Ignoring
General Hospital	2.50	Teach stress reduction	Relaxation Techniques
	3.19	Teach stress reduction	Relaxation Imagery Evaluation
	4.12	Structure parent visits to maintain child's developmental level	Approving Ignoring Self-Help Skills Positive Interaction
Hemodialysis	4.01	Reduce discomforts of dialysis	Relaxation
Presurgical	2.49	Teach how to use music to relieve postoperative pain	Focusing Attention Music Listening
Terminally Ill	2.52	Demonstrate "realistic life goals"	Leading Group Discussion Empathetic Listening
	2.53	Teach action step to deal with diagnosis	Teaching Action Steps
	2.54	Enhance relationships with family	Role-Playing Evaluating
	4.03	Teach emotional adjustment	Drawing to Music Leading Focused Group Discussion
Psychiatric Acute	2.60	Facilitate reality-based verbalizations	Leading Group Discussion Ignoring Approving
	2.61	Teach action steps to resolve a problem	Role-Playing Teaching Action Steps
	2.62	Plan dance with entry criteria	Leading Focused Group Discussion Teaching Social Skills Role-Playing
	4.07	Teach to select & implement self-shaping project	Teaching Action Steps

Psychiatric			
Chronic	2.58	Teach square dance to improve social skills	Chaining Cuing Task Analysis Peer Tutoring Approving
	2.59	Teach social interaction in a chorus rehearsal	Stimulating Group Interaction
	2.62	Plan facility-wide dance to increase social skills	Leading Focused Group Teaching Social Skills
	3.05	Teach reality-based, appropriate social behavior using dance	Music to Reinforce Cuing Approving Evaluating
Depressed	3.06	Teach action behavior to reduce depression	Teaching Action Steps Role-Playing Evaluating

Passive-Aggressive Persons	3.01	Teach assertiveness/anger control & discrimination	Action Techniques/
			  Anger Control
			Action Techniques/
			  Assertiveness
			Discrimination
			Role-Playing
			Evaluating

Peers	1.01	Lead well-known, unaccompanied song	Songleading Scanning
	1.02	Accompany with most advanced technique & lead well-known song	Songleading Accompanying Scanning
	1.03	Accompany with most advanced technique & teach new song	Songleading Accompanying Scanning Chaining Modeling
	1.04	Accompany with second best instrument & teach new song	Songleading Accompanying Scanning Chaining Modeling
	1.05	Teach group to play autoharp	Songleading Teaching from Task Analysis Cuing Modeling

Peers (cont.)	1.05		Approving Correcting
	1.06	Compose "hello" song: teach to group and accompany it	Composing Songleading Accompanying Chaining Modeling Scanning
	1.07	Compose "good-bye" song: teach to group and accompany it	Composing Songleading Accompanying Chaining Modeling Scanning
	1.08	Teach new round	Chaining Cuing Fading
	1.09	Teach 16 measure rhythm task	Group Leadership–Rhythm Cuing Chaining Modeling
	1.10	Teach signs to simple song	Songleading Chaining Modeling Cuing Signing
	1.11	Teach synchronized exercises: ten sequential steps	Group Leadership– Exercises Cuing Chaining Evaluating
	1.12	Teach simple dance of at least ten sequential steps	Group Leadership–Dance Cuing Chaining Evaluating
	1.13	Conduct group sing-along	Songleading Accompanying Using Repertoire
	2.01	Use music to maintain group contact with you	Songleading Maintaining Eye Contact Scanning

Peers (cont.)	2.02	Eliminate talking in group	Songleading Scanning Approving Incompatible Response

	2.03	Teach appropriate peer touching	Structuring Music to
			    Elicit Specific
			    Response
			Approving
			Scanning
			Evaluating

	2.04	Create 100% on-task	Approving Incompatible Response Evaluating
	2.05	Teach academic task	Composing Songleading Chaining Cuing Evaluating
	2.06	Teach paired nonsense syllables	Composing Chaining Cuing Fading Evaluating
	2.07	Teach vocabulary pronunciation	Composing Chaining Cuing Fading Evaluating
	2.08	Teach foreign language vocabulary	Composing Chaining Cuing Fading Evaluating

	2.09	Use music to teach relaxation	Synchronizing Activity
			    to Background Music
			Directing Relaxation
			    Routine
			Evaluating

	2.10	Teach group two action steps to deal with disappointment	Role-Playing Teaching Action Steps
	2.11	Shape unanimous group decision	Shaping Group Discussion Accompanying

	2.12	Introduce topic of drugs/alcohol
		    & lead group discussion to
		    formulate guidelines
			Leading Group Discussion
			Shaping Group Discussion

Peers (cont.)	2.13	Teach how to assist grand mal seizures	Handling Seizures
	4.02	Teach empathy with role of client in group therapy	Teaching Incompatible Response Leading Focused Group Discussion
Phobia	3.20	Teach agoraphobics to leave house	Relaxation Imagery Role-Playing Self-Evaluating
	4.08	Desensitize animal phobia	Relaxation Desensitization Imagery
Pregnant Women	4.14	Teach labor management	Lamaze Focused Attention Relaxing Muscles Approving Incompatible Responses
Retarded Adults	3.15	Teach decision making	Cuing Approving Decision Making Evaluating
	4.05	Teach music task & three differentiated incompatible responses	Incompatible Responses
	4.10	Teach decision-making skills	Decision Making Approving Role-Playing Homework Assignment Incompatible Responses
Educable	2.17	Teach circle dance to adolescents	Chaining Cuing Task Analysis
	2.18	Teach choral performance skills to adolescents	Modeling Cuing Fading Approving Incompatible Responses
	2.20	Teach two chords on guitar (color coded)	Task Analysis Cuing Modeling Approving Correcting
	2.36	Teach group interaction	Stimulating Interaction

Retarded (cont.) Trainable	2.19	Teach manners appropriate for adult social occasion	Modeling Cuing Evaluating Teaching Social Skills
	2.21	Teach children to follow two-part directions	Composing Chaining Cuing Guided Assistance
	2.22	Teach honesty to children	Composing Modeling Approving
Severe/Profound	2.23	Teach language development task	Cuing Approving
	2.24	Teach one color	Cuing Approving
	2.25	Teach responses to three types of stimulation	Infant Stimulation Evaluating Cuing Approving
	3.13	Teach infant stimulation	Infant Stimulation Evaluating Cuing Approving
Special Education	4.16	Teach appropriate positive inter-actions between children in mainstreamed music class	Approving Ignoring Peer Tutoring
Spouses	2.51	Teach anger control with spouses & children	Anger Control Role-Playing
	3.10	Teach improved communication	Teaching Interpersonal Skills Evaluating
	4.11	Stimulate positive verbal & physical responses between spouses	Approving
Stroke Victims	3.11	Improve gait and ambulation	Gait Training Approving Intermittent Interruption of Music Evaluating
	3.12	Conduct range of motion exercises while teaching sign language for basic daily needs	Range of Motion Exercises Sign Language Evaluating

Substance Abusers	3.09	Discuss negative consequences of drug abuse	Leading Focused Group Discussion Nonverbal Approving Evaluating
Suicidal Clients	3.08	Teach skills to establish relationship with others	Teaching Interpersonal Skills Leading Focused Group Discussion Teaching Action Steps Evaluating
Teachers	3.02	Teach response to students' drug problems	Focused Group Discussion Role-Playing Evaluating
Trainable Mentally Retarded	2.19	Teach manners appropriate for adult social occasion	Modeling Cuing Evaluating Teaching Social Skills
	2.21	Teach children to follow two-part directions	Composing Chaining Cuing Guided Assistance
	2.22	Teach honesty to children	Composing Modeling Approving
Visually Impaired	2.26	Teach body parts to children	Cuing Approving
		children; reduce stereotyped behaviors	Task Analysis Approving Incompatible Response
	2.28	Extinguish inappropriate verbal behavior while teaching mobility task to adults	Mobility Training Cuing Successive Approximation

INDEX BY TECHNIQUE

TECHNIQUE	TASK #	POPULATION	STUDENT OBJECTIVE
Accompanying	1.02	Peers	Lead well-known song
	1.03	Peers	Teach new song
	1.04	Peers	Teach new song
	1.06	Peers	Compose "hello" song; teach
	1.07	Peers	Compose "good-bye" song; teach
	1.13	Peers	Lead group sing-along; ten song repertoire
	2.11	Peers	Shape group decision on song
Action Steps	2.10	Peers	Teach to deal with disappointment
	2.53	Terminally ill	Teach adjustment to diagnosis
	2.61	Acute psychiatric	Teach resolution of a problem
	3.06	Depressed	Teach reduction of depression
	3.08	Suicidal clients	Teach to establish relationship with others
	4.07	Acute psychiatric	Teach to implement self-shaping project
Anger Control	2.41	Adolescents	Teach anger control
	2.51	Child abusers	Teach anger control
	3.01	Passive-aggressive	Teach assertiveness/anger control
Approving	1.05	Peers	Teach group to play autoharp
	1.08	Peers	Teach new round
	2.03	Peers	Teach appropriate touching
	2.16	Learning disabled	Teach reading fluidity, comprehension & pleasure
	2.20	EMR	Teach two guitar chords
	2.22	TMR	Teach honesty concept
	2.23	Severe/profound MR	Teach language development
	2.24	Severe/profound MR	Teach one color
	2.26	Visually impaired	Teach body parts
	2.29	Emotionally disturbed	Reduce hyperactivity; increase incompatible response
	2.37	Parents of MR	Teach reinforcement & feedback
	2.40	Adolescents	Teach rhythmic activity & roles
	2.43	Adolescents	Resist peer pressure
	2.48	Geriatric	Increase positive interactions
	2.57	Family	Teach positive interactions
	2.58	Chronic psychiatric	Teach square dance and improve social skills
	2.60	Acute psychiatric	Teach reality-based verbalizations
	3.03	Adolescents	Reduce inappropriate lunchroom behavior
	3.05	Chronic psychiatric	Teach reality-based, social behavior
	3.07	Cerebral palsied	Teach academic skills and social behavior
	3.11	Stroke victims	Improve gait & ambulation
	3.13	Multihandicapped infants & parents	Teach infant stimulation techniques

Approving (cont.)	3.14	Hearing impaired & normal hearing adolescents	Increase social interaction
	3.15	Retarded adults	Teach decision making
	3.16	Child abusers	Teach position interactions
	3.17	Geriatric clients	Teach creativity, interaction & rhythmic skills
	3.18	Emotionally disturbed	Extinguish stereotyped mannerisms; wait turn; identify name
	4.04	Hearing impaired	Teach signs & music
	4.09	Geriatric	Teach socialization & group decision making
	4.10	Retarded adults	Teach decision-making skills
	4.11	Marital counselees	Teach positive verbal and physical responses
	4.12	Hospitalized child	Structure parent visit; maintain developmental level
	4.14	Pregnant women	Teach labor management
	4.15	Language delayed	Teach speaking in sentences; asking questions
	4.16	Special ed. and normal	Teach positive interactions
	4.17	Adolescents	Teach response to peer pressure
	4.19	Chronic pain	Reduce awareness of pain
	4.20	Learning disabled	Improve math skills
Approving/ Disapproving Ratio	2.30	Emotionally disturbed	Teach on-task behavior
Approving Incompatible Response	2.02	Peers	Extinguish talking
	2.04	Peers	Teach on-task behavior
	2.18	EMR	Teach choral performance skills
	2.27	Visually impaired	Teach two grooming skills & reduction of stereotyped behaviors
Approving-Nonverbal	3.09	Substance abusers	Teach to formulate/use guidelines
Assertiveness	3.01	Passive-aggressive	Teach assertiveness/anger control
Auditory Discrimination	2.34	Hearing impaired	Teach auditory discrimination task
Autoharp	1.05	Peers	Teach use of autoharp
Chaining	1.03	Peers	Teach new song
	1.04	Peers	Teach new song
	1.06	Peers	Teach composed "hello" song
	1.07	Peers	Teach composed "good-bye" song
	1.08	Peers	Teach new round
	1.09	Peers	Teach 16 measure rhythm
	1.10	Peers	Teach signing to simple song
	1.12	Peers	Teach simple dance
	2.05	Peers	Compose & teach vocabulary song
	2.06	Peers	Teach memory of paired nonsense syllable; compose song
	2.07	Peers	Teach vocabulary pronunciation; compose song

Chaining (cont.)	2.08	Peers	Teach foreign vocabulary; compose song
	2.15	Learning disabled	Teach spelling concept; compose song
	2.17	EMR	Teach circle dance
	2.21	TMR	Teach following two-part directions
	2.32	Hearing impaired	Sign recorded song
	2.33	Hearing impaired	Teach 16 measure rhythm
	2.58	Chronic psychiatric	Teach square dance & social skills
Composing	1.06	Peers	Teach composed "hello" song
	1.07	Peers	Teach composed "good-bye" song
	2.05	Peers	Compose & teach vocabulary song
	2.06	Peers	Teach paired nonsense syllables; compose song
	2.07	Peers	Teach vocabulary pronunciation; compose song
	2.08	Peers	Teach foreign language vocabulary; compose song
	2.15	Learning disabled	Teach spelling concept; compose song
	2.16	Learning disabled	Increase reading fluidity, comprehension & pleasure
	2.21	TMR	Teach following two-part directions
	2.22	TMR	Teach honesty concept
	2.44	Geriatric	Teach Reality Orientation objectives
	2.57	Family	Teach positive interaction
Correcting	1.05	Peers	Teach group to play autoharp
	1.08	Peers	Teach new round
	2.20	EMR	Teach two guitar chords
Cuing	1.05	Peers	Teach group to play autoharp
	1.08	Peers	Teach new round
	1.09	Peers	Teach 16 measure rhythm
	1.10	Peers	Teach signing to simple song
	1.11	Peers	Teach exercises to music
	1.12	Peers	Teach simple dance
	2.05	Peers	Compose & teach vocabulary song
	2.06	Peers	Teach paired nonsense syllables; compose song
	2.07	Peers	Teach vocabulary pronunciation; compose song
	2.08	Peers	Teach foreign language vocabulary; compose song
	2.15	Learning disabled	Teach spelling concept; compose song
	2.16	Learning disabled	Increase reading fluidity, comprehension & pleasure
	2.17	EMR	Teach circle dance
	2.18	EMR	Teach choral performance skills
	2.19	TMR	Teach manners for social occasion
	2.20	EMR	Teach two guitar chords
	2.21	TMR	Teach following two-part directions
	2.22	TMR	Teach honesty concept
	2.23	Severe/profound MR	Teach language development

Cuing	2.24	Severe/profound MR	Teach one color
(cont.)	2.25	Severe/profound MR	Teach response to stimulation
	2.26	Visually impaired	Teach body parts
	2.27	Visually impaired	Teach two grooming skills; reduce stereotyped behaviors
	2.28	Visually impaired	Teach mobility
	2.29	Emotionally disturbed	Reduce hyperactivity; increase incompatible response
	2.32	Hearing impaired	Teach signing to recorded song
	2.33	Hearing impaired	Teach 16 measure rhythm
	2.44	Geriatric	Teach Reality Orientation Objectives
	2.45	Geriatric	Teach exercises to music
	2.58	Chronic psychiatric	Teach square dance; social skills
	3.05	Chronic psychiatric	Teach reality-based, appropriate social behavior
	3.07	Cerebral palsied	Teach academic skills, social behavior
	3.13	Multihandicapped infants	Teach infant stimulation techniques
	3.15	Retarded adults	Teach decision making
	3.16	Child abusers	Teach positive interactions
	4.15	Language delayed	Teach speaking in sentences; asking questions
	4.19	Chronic pain	Reduce awareness of pain
Data Collection	1.12	Peers	Teach simple dance
	2.01	Peers	Maintain group eye contact
	2.02	Peers	Extinguish talking
	2.03	Peers	Teach appropriate touching
	2.04	Peers	Teach on-task behavior
	2.05	Peers	Compose & teach vocabulary song
	2.06	Peers	Teach paired nonsense syllables; compose song
	2.09	Peers	Use music to teach relaxation
	2.15	Learning disabled	Teach spelling concept; compose song
	2.17	EMR	Teach circle dance
	2.19	TMR	Teach manners for social occasion
	2.28	Visually impaired	Teach mobility
	2.29	Emotionally disturbed	Reduce hyperactivity; increase incompatible response
	2.30	Emotionally disturbed	Teach on-task behavior
	2.57	Family	Teach positive interactions
	3.01	Passive-aggressive	Teach assertiveness/anger control
	3.03	Adolescents	Reduce inappropriate lunchroom behavior
	3.06	Depressed	Teach reduction of depression
	3.11	Stroke victims	Improve gait & ambulation
	3.13	Multihandicapped infants & parents	Teach infant stimulation techniques
	3.15	Retarded adults	Teach decision making
	3.20	Agoraphobics	Reduce fear of leaving house

Decision	3.15	Retarded adults	Teach decision-making skills
Making	4.10	Retarded adults	Teach decision-making skills
	4.13	Families	Teach role function
	4.17	Adolescents	Teach response to peer pressure
Desensitization	4.08	Phobics	Desensitize animal phobia
Drawing to Music	4.03	Terminally ill	Teach emotional expression
Discrimination	3.01	Passive-aggressive	Teach assertiveness/anger control
Empathy	2.52	Terminally ill	Teach identification of "realistic life goals"
	2.55	Families of organ donors	Teach empathy & positive decision making
	4.02	Peers	Teach empathy with role of clients in group therapy
Evaluating	1.10	Peers	Teach signs to simple song
	1.12	Peers	Teach simple dance
	2.01	Peers	Maintain group eye contact
	2.02	Peers	Extinguish talking
	2.03	Peers	Teach appropriate touching
	2.04	Peers	Teach on-task behavior
	2.05	Peers	Compose & teach vocabulary song
	2.06	Peers	Teach paired nonsense syllables; compose song
	2.07	Peers	Teach vocabulary pronunciation; compose song
	2.08	Peers	Teach foreign vocabulary; compose song
	2.09	Peers	Use music to teach relaxation
	2.15	Learning disabled	Teach spelling concept; compose song
	2.16	Learning disabled	Teach reading fluidity, comprehension & pleasure
	2.19	TMR	Teach manners for social occasion
	2.25	Severe/profound MR	Teach response to stimulation
	2.57	Family	Teach positive interactions
Eye Contact	2.01	Peers	Maintain group eye contact
Fading	1.08	Peers	Teach new round
	2.06	Peers	Teach paired nonsense syllables; compose song
	2.07	Peers	Teach vocabulary pronunciation; compose song
	2.08	Peers	Teach foreign vocabulary; compose
	2.18	EMR	Teach choral performance skills
Family	2.56	Families	Teach to identify family roles
Counseling	2.57	Families	Teach positive interactions
Focused Attention	2.49	Presurgical patients	Teach to relieve postoperative pain
	4.14	Pregnant women	Teach labor management
Gait Training	3.11	Stroke victims	Improve gait & ambulation
Group	2.11	Peers	Shape group decision on song
Discussion	2.12	Peers	Teach to formulate guidelines
Skills	2.38	Parents of handicapped	Teach parenting techniques

Group **Discussion** **Skills** (cont.)	2.39	Adolescents	Teach to accept responsibility
	2.41	Adolescents	Teach to control anger
	2.47	Geriatric	Plan musical performance
	2.48	Geriatric	Increase positive interactions
	2.52	Terminally ill	Teach to demonstrate "realistic life goals"
	2.55	Families of organ donors	Teach empathy & positive decision making
	2.56	Families	Teach to identify family roles
	2.60	Acute psychiatric	Teach reality-based verbalizations
	2.62	Chronic psychiatric	Teach social skills
	3.02	Parents/teachers of adolescents	Teach to identify drugs & symptoms of abuse; develop guidelines
	3.03	Adolescents	Reduce inappropriate lunchroom behavior
	3.08	Suicidal clients	Teach to establish relationship with others
	3.09	Substance abusers	Teach to formulate/use guidelines
	4.02	Peers	Teach empathy with role of clients in group therapy
	4.03	Terminally ill	Teach emotional adjustment
	4.06	Juvenile delinquent	Teach accepting responsibility
	4.09	Geriatric	Teach socialization & independent decision making
	4.18	Parents of handicapped	Teach realistic goal setting
Group **Leadership** **Skills**	1.09	Peers	Teach 16 measure rhythm
	1.11	Peers	Teach exercises to music
	1.12	Peers	Teach simple dance
	2.33	Hearing impaired	Teach 16 measure rhythm
	2.45	Geriatric	Teach exercises to music
Guided **Assistance**	2.21	TMR	Teach following two-part directions
Homework **Assignments**	4.10	Retarded adults	Teach decision-making skills
Hyperactivity **Reduction**	2.29	Emotionally disturbed	Reduce hyperactivity; increase incompatible response
Ignoring	2.31	Emotionally disturbed	Teach role following
	2.37	Parents of MR child	Teach reinforcement & feedback techniques
	2.60	Acute psychiatric	Teach reality-based verbalizations
	3.07	Cerebral palsied	Teach academic skills; social behavior
	3.18	Emotionally disturbed	Extinguish stereotyped mannerisms; wait turn; identify name
	4.12	Hospitalized child	Structure parent visit; maintain developmental level
	4.16	Special ed. and normal	Teach positive interactions
	4.19	Chronic pain	Reduce awareness of pain
	4.20	Learning disabled	Improve math skills
Imagery	3.19	General hospital patients	Teach stress reduction
	3.20	Agoraphobics	Reduce fear of leaving house
	4.08	Phobics	Desensitize animal phobia

Incompatible Responses	2.29	Emotionally disturbed	Reduce hyperactivity; increase incompatible response
	3.18	Emotionally disturbed	Extinguish stereotyped mannerisms; wait turn; identify name
	4.02	Peers	Teach empathy with role of client in group therapy
	4.05	Retarded adults	Teach music task & incompatible response
	4.10	Retarded adults	Teach decision-making skills
	4.14	Pregnant women	Teach labor management
	4.15	Language delayed	Teach speaking in sentences & asking questions
Infant Stimulation	2.25	Severe/profound MR infants	Teach responses to stimulation
	3.13	Multihandicapped infants	Teach infant stimulation techniques
Interpersonal Skills	3.04	Families	Teach to improve family relationships
	3.08	Suicidal	Teach to establish relationship with others
	3.10	Marital counselees	Teach communication techniques
Lamaze Techniques	4.14	Pregnant women	Teach labor management
Mobility Training	2.28	Visually impaired	Extinguish inappropriate verbal behavior
Modeling	1.03	Peers	Teach new song
	1.04	Peers	Teach new song
	1.05	Peers	Teach group to play autoharp
	1.06	Peers	Compose "hello" song; teach
	1.07	Peers	Compose "good-bye" song; teach
	1.09	Peers	Teach 16 measure rhythm
	1.10	Peers	Teach signs to simple song
	2.18	EMR	Teach choral performance skills
	2.19	TMR	Teach manners for social occasion
	2.20	EMR	Teach two guitar chords
	2.22	TMR	Teach honesty concept
	2.29	Emotionally disturbed	Reduce hyperactivity; increase incompatible response
	2.32	Hearing impaired	Teach signing to recorded song
	2.33	Hearing impaired	Teach 16 measure rhythm
	3.01	Passive-aggressive	Teach assertiveness/anger control
Music Interruption	3.03	Adolescents	Reduce inappropriate lunchroom behavior
	3.11	Stroke victims	Improve gait & ambulation
Music Listening	2.49	Presurgical patients	Teach how to relieve postoperative pain
	4.01	Kidney dialysis	Reduce discomforts of dialysis
Over-compensation	2.41	Adolescents	Teach to control anger
Parenting Techniques	2.37	Parents of MR	Teach reinforcement & feedback
	2.38	Parents of handicapped	Teach parenting techniques
	2.51	Child abusers	Teach anger control

Parenting Techniques (cont.)	3.13	Multihandicapped infants	Teach infant stimulation techniques
	3.16	Child abusers	Teach positive parenting techniques
	4.12	Hospitalized children	Structure parent visit; maintain developmental level
	4.18	Parents of handicapped	Teach realistic goal setting
Peer Tutoring	2.58	Chronic psychiatric	Teach square dance; social skills
	4.16	Special ed. & normal	Teach positive interactions
Positive Interactions	2.48	Geriatric	Increase positive interactions
	4.12	Hospitalized children	Structure parent visit; maintain developmental level
	4.16	Special ed. & normal	Teach positive interactions
Range of Motion Exercises	2.35	Cerebral palsied	Teach range of motion exercises
	3.12	Stroke victims	Conduct range of motion exercises; teach signs for basic daily needs
Rap	2.57	Families	Teach positive interaction
	2.60	Acute psychiatric	Teach reality based verbalizations
Relationships	2.42	Adolescents	Teach nonsexual relationships with opposite sex
	2.54	Terminally ill	Enhance relationship among family members
	3.04	Families	Teach improved family relationships
	3.08	Suicidal	Teach to establish relationships
	4.13	Families	Teach role function
Relaxation Techniques	2.09	Peers	Use music to teach relaxation
	2.14	Epileptic	Teach how to monitor fatigue/tension
	2.50	General hospital patients	Teach stress reduction
	3.19	General hospital patients	Teach stress reduction
	3.20	Agoraphobics	Reduce fear of leaving house
	4.01	Kidney dialysis	Reduce discomforts of dialysis
	4.08	Phobics	Desensitize animal phobia
	4.14	Pregnant women	Teach labor management
Repertoire	1.13	Peers	Lead group sing-along; ten song repertoire
Role-Playing	2.10	Peers	Teach dealing with disappointment
	2.38	Parents of handicapped	Teach parenting techniques
	2.39	Adolescents	Teach to accept responsibility
	2.42	Adolescents	Teach nonsexual relationships with opposite sex
	2.43	Adolescents	Teach resistance to peer pressure
	2.51	Child abusers	Teach anger control
	2.54	Terminally ill	Enhance relationships among family members
	2.56	Families	Teach to identify family roles
	2.61	Acute psychiatric	Teach to resolve a problem
	3.01	Passive-aggressive	Teach assertiveness/anger control
	3.02	Parents/teachers of adolescents	Teach to identify drugs & symptoms of abuse; develop guidelines
	3.04	Families	Teach positive family relationships

Role-Playing (cont.)	3.06	Depressed	Reduce depression
	3.20	Agoraphobics	Reduce fear of leaving house
	4.06	Juvenile Delinquents	Teach to accept responsibility
	4.10	Retarded adults	Teach decision-making skills
	4.13	Families	Teach role function
	4.17	Adolescents	Teach response to peer pressure
	4.18	Parents of handicapped	Teach realistic goal setting
Rules	2.31	Emotionally disturbed	Teach rule following
	2.40	Adolescents	Teach rhythmic activity; reinforce rules
Scanning	1.01	Peers	Lead well-known song
	1.02	Peers	Lead well-known song & accompany
	1.03	Peers	Teach new song
	1.04	Peers	Teach new song
	1.06	Peers	Compose "hello" song; teach
	1.07	Peers	Compose "good-bye" song; teach
	1.11	Peers	Teach exercises to music
	2.01	Peers	Maintain group eye contact
	2.02	Peers	Extinguish talking
	2.03	Peers	Teach appropriate touching
	2.45	Geriatric	Teach exercises to music
Seizure Assistance	2.13	Peers	Teach to assist grand mal seizure
Self-Help Skills	4.12	Hospitalized children	Structure parent visits; maintain developmental level
Signing	1.10	Peers	Teach signs to simple song
	2.32	Hearing impaired	Teach signs to recorded song
	2.34	Hearing impaired	Teach auditory discrimination task
	3.12	Stroke victims	Conduct range of motion exercises; teach signs for basic daily needs
	3.14	Hearing impaired & normal hearing	Increase social interaction
	4.04	Hearing impaired	Teach music task using signs; demonstrate differential feedback
Socialization	2.36	Cerebral palsied MR	Teach group interaction
	2.46	Geriatric	Teach social interaction
	2.59	Chronic psychiatric	Teach social interaction
	3.14	Hearing impaired & normal hearing	Increase social interaction
	4.09	Geriatric	Stimulate socialization; plan group leisure activity
Social Skills	2.19	TMR	Teach manners for social occasion
	2.62	Chronic psychiatric	Increase social skills
Songleading	1.01	Peers	Lead well-known song
	1.02	Peers	Lead well-known song & accompany
	1.03	Peers	Teach new song
	1.04	Peers	Teach new song
	1.05	Peers	Teach group to play autoharp
	1.06	Peers	Compose "hello" song; teach
	1.07	Peers	Compose "good-bye" song; teach
	1.10	Peers	Teach signs to simple song

Songleading (cont.)	1.13	Peers	Lead group sing-along
	2.01	Peers	Maintain group eye contact
	2.02	Peers	Extinguish talking
	2.05	Peers	Compose & teach vocabulary song
	2.15	Learning disabled	Teach spelling concept; compose song
	2.16	Learning disabled	Teach signs to recorded song
	2.48	Geriatric	Increase positive interactions
Successive Approximation	2.28	Visually impaired	Teach mobility
Task Analysis	1.05	Peers	Teach group to play autoharp
	2.17	EMR	Teach circle dance
	2.20	EMR	Teach two guitar chords
	2.27	Visually impaired	Teach two grooming skills & reduction of stereotyped behaviors
	2.58	Chronic psychiatric	Teach square dance; social skills

INDEX BY STUDENT OBJECTIVE

STUDENT OBJECTIVE	TASK #	POPULATION	TECHNIQUES
Academic Tasks			
Teach vocabulary	2.05	Peers	Composing Songleading Chaining Cuing Evaluating
Teach paired nonsense syllables	2.06	Peers	Composing Chaining Cuing Fading Evaluating
Teach vocabulary pronunciation	2.07	Peers	Composing Chaining Cuing Evaluating
Teach foreign language vocabulary	2.08	Peers	Composing Chaining Cuing Fading Evaluating
Teach spelling concept	2.15	Learning disabled	Composing Songleading Chaining Cuing Evaluating
Increase reading fluidity, comprehension & pleasure	2.16	Learning disabled	Composing Songleading Cuing Approving Evaluating
Teach circle dance	2.17	EMR – 15 yrs	Chaining Cuing Task Analysis
Teach a color	2.24	Severe/Profound MR - 6 yrs	Cuing Approving
Teach body parts	2.26	Visually impaired – 4 yrs	Cuing Approving

Academic Tasks (cont.) Teach academic and individual- ized social behavior	3.07	Cerebral palsied preschoolers	Cuing Approving Ignoring Evaluating
Improve gait and ambulation	3.11	Stroke victims	Gait training Approving Music interruption Evaluating
Improve math skills	4.20	Learning disabled	Approving Ignoring Evaluating
Action Steps Teach action steps	2.10	Peers	Role-Playing Teaching Action Steps Evaluating
Teach anger control	2.41	Adolescents with problems	Teaching Anger Control Leading Group Discussion Overcompensating Evaluating
	2.51	Parents/abused child	Teaching Anger Control Role-Playing Evaluating
Teach responsibility acceptance	2.39	Adolescents with problems	Leading Group Discussion Role-Playing Evaluating
	4.06	Juvenile delinquents	Role-Playing Leading Focused Group Discussion Evaluating
Facilitate nonsexual relation- ships	2.42	Adolescents with problems	Establishing Relationships Teaching Actions Steps Role-Playing Evaluating
Teach emotional adjustment	2.53	Terminally ill	Teaching Action Steps Evaluating
Teach decision acceptance	2.55	Families of organ donors	Leading Group Discussion Role-Playing Teaching Action Steps Evaluating
Teach problem solving	2.61	Acute psychiatric patients	Role-Playing Teaching Action Steps Evaluating

Action Steps (cont.)			
Teach anger control/ assertive behavior	3.01	Passive/aggressive	Teaching Anger Control Teach Assertiveness Role-Playing Discriminating Evaluating
Reduce depression	3.06	Depressed patients	Teaching Action Steps Role-Playing Evaluating
Establish relationships	3.08	Suicidal clients	Teaching Action Steps Leading Group Discussion Evaluating
Teach reduction of agora-phobia	3.20	Agoraphobic adults	Relaxation Imagery Role-Playing Self-Evaluating
Teach implementation of self-shaping project	4.07	Acute psychiatric patients	Teaching Action Steps Evaluating
Decision Making			
Shape unanimous group decision	2.11	Peers	Shaping Group Discussion Singing Accompanying
Lead group discussion: alcohol/drugs	2.12	Peers	Leading/Shaping Group Discussion Nonverbal Approving Evaluating
	3.09	Substance Abuse	Leading Focused Group Discussion Nonverbal Approving Evaluating
Teach decision making	3.15	MR adults	Cuing Approving Decision Making Evaluating
Teach peer pressure resistance	2.43	Adolescents with problems	Role-Playing Approving Independent Decision Making
Teach decision making	4.10	MR adults - group home	Decision Making Approving Role-Playing Homework Assignment Incompatible Response Evaluating

Decision Making (cont.)			
Teach role function	4.13	Family in therapy	Role-Playing Group Decision Making Role Assessment Cuing
Teach dealing with peer pressure	4.17	Adolescents	Role-Playing Decision Making Approving Evaluating
Feedback			
Demonstrate differential feedback	4.04	Hearing impaired children – 5 yrs	Signing Approving Evaluating
Teach reinforcement and positive feedback	2.37	Parents of MR child	Approving Ignoring Evaluating
Group Discussion			
Teach parenting techniques	2.38	Parents of handicapped children	Leading Group Discussion Parenting Techniques Role-Playing Evaluating
Lead discussion on life goals	2.52	Terminally ill patients	Leading Group Discussion Empathetic listening Evaluating
Lead discussion on organ donation	2.55	Families of organ donors	Leading Group Discussion Role-Playing Evaluating Teaching Action Steps
Teach drug identification	3.02	Parents/teachers of adolescents	Focusing Group Discussion Role-Playing Evaluating
Teach focus on negative consequences	3.09	Drug abusers	Focusing Group Discussion Nonverbal Approving Evaluating
Reduce inappropriate behavior	3.03	Adolescents	Music Interruption Focusing Group Discussion Approving Self-Evaluation
Teach empathy with client	4.02	Peers	Incompatible Responses Leading Focused Group Discussion Evaluating

Group Discussion (cont.)			
Teach to establish relationships	3.08	Suicidal clients	Leading Focused Group Discussion Teaching Action Steps Evaluating
Language			
Teach signs	1.10	Peers	Songleading Chaining Modeling Cuing Signing Evaluating
Teach signs	2.32	Hearing impaired – 5 yrs	Songleading Chaining Modeling Cuing Signing Evaluating
	3.12	Stroke victims	Songleading Chaining Modeling Cuing Signing Range of Motion Exercises
Teach language development task	2.23	Severe/Profound MR – 8 yrs	Cuing Approving
Teach auditory discrimination task	2.34	Hearing impaired – 5 yrs	Signing Auditory Discrimination Evaluating
Teach speaking in sentences and asking questions	4.15	Language delayed child	Cuing Approving Incompatible Responses Evaluating
Movement			
Teach simple dance	1.12	Peers	Group Leading Designing Dance Cuing Chaining Evaluating
Teach exercises	1.11	Peers	Group Leading Designing Exercise Cuing Scanning Evaluating

Movement (cont.) Teach exercises	2.45	Geriatric clients	Group Leading Designing Exercise Cuing Scanning Evaluating
Teach mobility	2.28	Visually impaired	Mobility Training Cuing Successive Approximation Evaluating
Teach range of motion exercises	2.35	Cerebral palsied – 10 yrs	Range of Motion Exercises Evaluating
Teach square dance and social skills	2.58	Chronic psychiatric patients	Chaining Cuing Task Analysis Peer Tutoring Approving Evaluating
Improve gait	3.11	Stroke victims	Gait Training Approving Music Interruption Evaluating
Teach range of motion exercises and signs	3.12	Stroke victims	Songleading Chaining Modeling Cuing Signing Range of Motion Exercises Evaluating
Reduce awareness of pain	4.19	Chronic pain patients	Cuing Approving Ignoring Evaluating
Music Lead unaccompanied, known song	1.01	Peers	Songleading Scanning
Accompany/lead well-known song	1.02	Peers	Songleading Accompanying Scanning
Accompany/teach new song	1.03	Peers	Songleading Accompanying Scanning Chaining Modeling

Music (cont.)			
Accompany on second best instrument; teach new song	1.04	Peers	Songleading Accompanying Scanning Chaining Modeling
Teach autoharp accompaniment	1.05	Peers	Songleading Task Analysis Cuing Modeling Approving Correcting
Compose song/teach/ accompany	1.06	Peers	Composing Songleading Accompanying Chaining Modeling Scanning
	1.07	Peers	Composing Songleading Accompanying Chaining Modeling Scanning
Teach new round	1.08	Peers	Chaining Cuing Fading
Lead sing-along/ten song repertoire	1.13	Peers	Songleading Accompanying Developing Repertoire
Teach rhythm reading task	1.09	Peers	Group Leading Cuing Chaining Modeling
	2.33	Hearing impaired 12–15 yrs	Group Leading Cuing Chaining Modeling
Teach choral performance skills	2.18	EMR adolescents	Modeling Cuing Fading Approving Incompatible Response
Teach two guitar chords	2.20	EMR children	Task Analysis Cuing Modeling Approving

Music (cont)			
Plan musical performance	2.47	Geriatric clients	Lead Group Discussion Conducting Musical Warm-Up
Reality Orientation/ Awareness			
Teach Reality Orientation objectives	2.44	Geriatric clients	Composing Cuing Teaching Reality Orientation Objectives Evaluating
Facilitate reality-based verbalizations	2.60	Acute psychiatric patients	Leading Group Discussion Ignoring Approving Rapping Evaluating
Teach realistic goal setting	4.18	Parents of handicapped children	Leading Focused Group Discussion Role-Playing Evaluating
Reinforcement			
Teach positive feedback	2.37	Parents of MR children	Approving Ignoring
Relationships/Interaction			
Teach group interaction	2.36	Cerebral palsied/ retarded adults	Stimulating Group Interaction Evaluating
	2.46	Geriatric clients	Stimulating Group Interaction Cuing Evaluating
	2.59	Chronic psychiatric patients	Stimulating Group Interaction Cuing Evaluating
Facilitate nonsexual relationships	2.42	Adolescents with problems	Establishing Relationships Teaching Action Steps Role-Playing Evaluating
Increase positive interactions	2.48	Geriatric clients	Approving Leading Group Discussion Songleading
Facilitate positive family interaction	2.54	Families of terminally ill	Establishing Relationships Role-Playing Evaluating
	2.56	Distressed family	Role Analysis Leading Group Discussion Evaluating

Relationships/Interaction (cont.)			
Facilitate positive family interaction	2.57	Distressed family	Rapping Approving Comparing Leading Group Discussion
	3.04	Distressed family	Teaching Interpersonal Skills Role-Playing Evaluating
	3.16	Child abusers	Cuing Approving Parenting Techniques Evaluating
Teach relationships with others	3.08	Suicidal clients	Teaching Interpersonal Skills Leading Focused Group Discussion Teaching Action Steps Evaluating
Improve communications	3.10	Couples in marital counseling	Teaching Interpersonal Skills Evaluating
Increase social interaction	3.14	Mainstream hearing impaired and normal hearing adolescents	Approving Evaluating Signing Teaching Social Interaction
Teach creativity, social interaction, rhythmic skill	3.17	Geriatric clients	Approving Evaluating Stimulating Creativity
Facilitate emotional expression	4.03	Terminally ill	Drawing to Music Leading Focused Group Discussion Evaluating
Facilitate positive verbal and physical responses	4.11	Couples in marital counseling	Approving Role-Playing Leading Focused Group Discussion Evaluating
Facilitate socialization	4.09	Geriatric clients	Leading Focused Group Discussion Approving Socialization Evaluating

Relationships/Interaction (cont.)			
Structure positive parent visits; maintain developmental level	4.12	Hospitalized children	Approving Ignoring Self-Help Skills Teaching Interaction Evaluating
Teach positive interactions	4.16	Special Education and normal children	Approving Ignoring Peer Tutoring Evaluating
Relaxation			

Teach relaxation	2.09	Peers	Synchronizing Activity/
			  Background Music
			Leading Relaxation
			  Routine
			Evaluating

Teach fatigue/tension reduction	2.14	Epileptics	Using Relaxation Techniques
Relieve postoperative pain	2.49	Presurgical patients	Focusing Attention Evaluating
Teach stress reduction	2.50	General hospital patients	Teaching Relaxation Techniques Evaluating
	3.19	General hospital Patients	Teaching Relaxation Techniques Imagery Evaluating
Teach reduction of agoraphobia	3.20	Agoraphobic adults	Teaching Relaxation Techniques Imagery Role-Playing Self-Evaluating
Reduce hemodialysis discomfort	4.01	Kidney dialysis patients	Relaxation Evaluating
Desensitize animal phobia	4.08	Animal phobics	Teaching Relaxation Techniques Desensitizing Imagery Evaluating

Relaxation (cont.)			
Teach labor management	4.14	Pregnant women/ partners	Breath Exercises Focusing Attention Teaching Relaxation Techniques Approving Incompatible Responses
Social Skills			
Maintain group eye contact	2.01	Peers	Songleading Maintaining Eye Contact Scanning Evaluating
Extinguish talking in group	2.02	Peers	Songleading Scanning Approving Incompatible Responses Evaluating
Teach appropriate peer touching	2.03	Peers	Structure Music/Elicit Responses Approving Scanning Evaluating
Teach 100% on-task	2.04	Peers	Approving Incompatible Responses
Teach how to handle *grand mal* seizure	2.13	Peers	Handling Seizures
Teach manners for social occasion	2.19	TMR adults	Modeling Cuing Evaluating Social Skills
Teach following two-part directions	2.21	TMR – 5 yrs	Composing Chaining Cuing Assisting
Teach honesty	2.22	TMR – 12 yrs	Composing Modeling Approving
Teach responses to stimulation	2.25	Severe/Profound MR infants	Infant Stimulation Evaluating
Teach infant stimulation	3.13	Multi-handicapped infants/parents	Cuing Approving Infant stimulation Evaluating

Social Skills (cont.)			
Teach grooming skills	2.27	Visually impaired – 8 yrs	Cuing Task Analysis Incompatible Responses
Teach on-task behavior	2.30	Emotionally disturbed adolescents	Approving/Disapproving 4:1 Ratio
Extinguish pity seeking behavior	2.28	Visually impaired adults	Mobility Training Cuing Evaluating
Reduce hyperactivity	2.29	Emotionally disturbed children - 8 yrs	Reduce hyperactivity, Modeling Cuing Approving Incompatible Response
Teach rule following	2.31	Emotionally disturbed children – 10 yrs	Rule Following Ignoring
Teach role enforcement	2.40	Adolescents with problems	Rule Following Approving Evaluating
Increase social skills	2.62	Chronic psychiatric patients	Leading Focused Group Discussion Social Skills Role-Playing
Teach appropriate social behavior	3.05	Chronic psychiatric patients	Music Reinforcement Cuing Approving Evaluating
Extinguish stereotyped behavior	3.18	Emotionally disturbed	Approving Ignoring Incompatible Responses Evaluating
Teach individualized incompatible responses	4.05	Retarded adults	Incompatible Responses

MUSIC THERAPY BIBLIOGRAPHIES
GENERAL

Alvin, J.A.: *Music Therapy*. London: John Clare Books, 1978.

Bernstein, P.L.: *Theory and Methods in Dance-Movement Therapy: A Manual for Therapists, Students and Educators*. Dubuque, IA: Kendall-Hunt, 1985.

Birkenshaw, L.: *Music for Fun, Music for Learning*. (3rd ed.) St. Louis, MO: MMB Music, Inc., 1982.

Bitcon, C.H.: *Alike and Different: The Clinical and Educational Use of Orff-Schulwerk*. (rev. ed.) St. Louis, MO: MMB Music, Inc., 1991.

Bonny, H.L. & Savary, L.M.: *Music and Your Mind: Listening with a New Consciousness*. New York: Harper and Row, 1973.

Boxhill, E.H.: *Music Therapy for the Developmentally Disabled*. Rockville, MD: Aspen Systems Corporation, 1985.

Bright, R.: *Practical Planning in Music Therapy for the Aged*. Van Nuys, CA: Alfred, 1984.

Brown, F.: *Come Join the Geritones – Starter Kit*. Lake Forest, IL: Geritones, 1977.

Burton, K. & Hughes, W.: *Music Play – Learning Activities for Young Children*. Menlo Park, CA: Addison-Wesley Publishing Co., 1980.

Caplow-Lidner, E., Harpay, L., & Samberg, S.: *Therapeutic Dance/Movement: Expressive Activities for Older Adults*. New York: Human Sciences Press, 1979.

Clark, C. & Chadwick, D.: *Clinically Adapted Instruments for the Multiply Handicapped: A Sourcebook*. (rev. ed.): St. Louis, MO: MMB Music, Inc., 1980.

Cole, F.: *Music For Children with Special Needs*. CA: Bowman Records, 1965.

Coleman, J., Schoepfle, I.L., & Templeton, V.: *Music for Exceptional Children*. Evanston, IL: Summy-Birchard Co., 1964.

Costonis, M. (Ed.): *Therapy in Motion*. New York: Harper & Row, 1978.

DePeters, A., Gordon, L., & Wertman, J.: *The Magic of Music*. Buffalo, NY: Potentials Development for Health & Aging Services, 1981.

Dickinson, P.I.: *Music with Exceptional (ESN) Children*. Atlantic Highland, NJ: Humanities Press, 1985.

Dobbs, J.P.: *The Slow Learner and Music*. London: Oxford University Press, 1985.

Douglass, D.: *Accent on Rhythm: Music Activities for the Aged*. (3rd ed.) St. Louis, MO: MMB Music, Inc., 1985.

Eagle, C.T., Jr.: *Music Therapy Index, Vol. 1*. Lawrence, KS: NAMT, Inc., 1976.

Eagle, C.T., Jr.: *Music Psychology Index, Vol. 2*. Denton, TX: Institute for Therapeutic Research, 1976.

Eagle, C.T., Jr. & Minter, J.J. (Eds.): *Music Psychology Index, Vol 3*. Phoenix, AZ: Onyx Press, 1984.

Edwards, E.M.: *Music Education for the Deaf*. South Waterford, MA: Merriam-Eddy.

Furman, C. (Ed.): *Effectiveness of Music Therapy Procedures: Documentation of Research and Clinical Practice*. Washington, DC: NAMT, 1988.

Gallina, M. & Gallina, J.: *Sing a Song of Sounds*. Long Branch, NJ: Kimbo Educational.

Gallina, M. & Gallina, J.: *Alphabet in Action*. Long Branch, NJ: Kimbo Educational.

Gaston, E.T.: *Music in Therapy*. New York, NY: Macmillan Press, 1968.

Gfeller, K. (Ed.): *Fiscal, Regulatory-Legislative Issues for the Music Therapist*. Washington, DC: NAMT, Inc, 1985.

Ginglend, D.R. & Stiles, W.E.: *Music Activities for Retarded Children*. New York: Abingdon Press, 1985.

Graham, R.M. (Ed.): *Music for the Exceptional Child*. Reston, VA: Music Educators National Conference, 1975.

Graham, R.M. & Beer, A. S.: *Teaching Music to the Exceptional Child*. Englewood Cliffs, NJ: Prentice-Hall, Inc., 1980.

Hanser, S.B.: *Music Therapy Practicum: A Manual for Behavior Change Through Music Therapy*. Stockton, CA: University of the Pacific Press, 1980.

Hanser, S.B.: *Music Therapist's Handbook*. St. Louis, MO: Warren N. Green, Inc., 1988.

Hap Palmer Record Library. Freeport, NY: Educational Activities, Inc.
   Learning Basic Skills Through Music – Vol 1. Album AR 514
   Learning Basic Skills Through Music – Building Vocabulary. Album AR 521
   Learning Basic Skills Through Music – Health and Safety. Album AR 526

Simplified Folk Songs - Special Edition, Grades K-3. Album AR 518
Folk Song Carnival. Album AR 524
Holiday Songs and Rhythms - Primary-Intermediate. Album AR 538
Singing Multiplication Tables (from the 2's through the 12's) Album AR 45
Creative Movement and Rhythmic Exploration. Album AR 533
Modern Tunes for Rhythms and Instruments. Album AR 523
Patriotic and Morning Time Songs – Grades 1-4. Album AR 519
Mod Marches. Album AR 527
Hardesty, K.W.: *Music for Special Education.* Morristown, NJ: Silver-Burdett, 1985.
Henry, D.G., Knoll, C. & Reuer, B.: *Music Works: A Handbook of Job Skills for Music Therapists.* Stephenville, TX: MusicWorks, 1986.
Hoshizaki, M.K.: *Teaching Mentally Retarded Children Through Music.* Springfield IL: Charles C. Thomas, 1983.
Janiak, W.: *Songs for Music Therapy.* Long Branch, NJ: Kimbo Educational, 1978.
Laker, M.: *Nursing Home Activities for the Handicapped.* Springfield, IL: Charles C. Thomas, 1980.
Lathom, W.B. & Eagle C.T. (Eds.): *Music Therapy for Handicapped Children.* Denton, TX: Institute for Therapeutic Research, 1982.
    Cormeir, Sr. L.: *Deaf Blind.*
    Paul, D.W.: *Emotionally Disturbed.*
    Beuchler, J.: *Hearing Impaired.*
    Carter, S.A.: *Mentally Retarded.*
    Pfeifer, St. M.: *Multi-Handicapped.*
    Schwankowsky, L.M. & Guthrie, P.T.: *Other Health Impaired.*
    Miller, S.G.: *Speech Impaired.*
    Codding, P.: *Visually Impaired.*
    Eagle, C.T., Jr.: *An Annotated and Indexed Bibliography.*
Licht, S.: *Music in Medicine.* Boston, MA: New England Conservatory of Music, 1946.
Lingerman, H.A.: *The Healing Energies of Music.* Wheaton, IL: Theosophical Publishing House, 1983.
Madsen, C.H., Jr. & Madsen, C.K.: *Teaching/Discipline: A Positive Approach for Educational Development.* (3rd ed.) Raleigh, NC: Contemporary Publishing Co., 1983.
Madsen, C.K.: *Music Therapy: A Behavioral Guide for the Mentally Retarded.* Lawrence, KS: NAMT, Inc., 1981.
Madsen, C.K. & Madsen, C.H. Jr.: *Parents and Children: Love and Discipline: A Positive Guide to Behavior Modification.* Arlington Heights, IL: Harlan Davidson, 1975.
Madsen, C.K. & Prickett, C.A., (Eds.): *Applications of Research in Music Behavior.* Tuscaloosa, AL: The University of Alabama Press, 1987.
Maranto, C.D. & Bruscia, K. (Eds.): *Perspectives on Music Therapy Education and Training.* Philadelphia: Temple University, 1987.
Maranto, C.D. & Bruscia, K.: *Methods of Teaching and Training the Music Therapist.* Philadelphia: Temple University, 1988.
Merrill, T.: *Activities with the Aged and Infirmed: A Handbook for the Untrained Worker.* Springfield, IL: Charles C. Thomas, 1967.
Michel, D.E.: *Music Therapy: An Introduction to Therapy and Special Education Through Music.* Springfield, Il: Charles C. Thomas, 1976.
Munro, S.: *Music Therapy in Palliative/Hospice Care.* St. Louis, MO: MMB Music, Inc., 1984.
Nocera, S.D.: *Reaching the Special Learner Through Music.* Morristown, NJ: Silver-Burdett, 1979.
Nordoff, P. & Robbins, C.: *Creative Music Therapy: Individualized Treatment for the Handicapped Child.* New York: John Day & Co., 1977.
Nordoff, P. & Robbins, C.: *Therapy in Music for Handicapped Children.* North Pomfret, UT: Trafalgar Square, 1971.
Nordoff, P. & Robbins, C.: *Music for Handicapped Children.* London: Gollancz, 1973.
Orff, G.: *The Orff Music Therapy: Active Furthering of the Development of the Child.* London, UK: Schott, 1980.
Plach, T.: *The Creative Use of Music in Group Therapy.* Springfield, IL: Charles C. Thomas, 1980.
Priestley, M.: *Music Therapy in Action.* St. Louis, MO: MMB Music, Inc., 1975.
Purvis, J. & Samet, S. (Eds.): *Music in Developmental Therapy.* Baltimore: University Park Press, 1976.
Robbins, C. & Robbins, C.: *Music for the Hearing Impaired.* St. Louis, MO: MMB Music, Inc., 1985.

Ruud, E.: *Music Therapy and Its Relationship to Current Treatment Theories.* St. Louis, MO: MMB Music, Inc., 1985.

Schulberg, C.: *The Music Therapy Sourcebook: A Collection of Activities Categoried and Analyzed.* St. Louis, MO: MMB Music, Inc., 1985.

Schullian, E. & Schoen, M. (Eds.): *Music and Medicine.* New York: Abelard-Schuman, Ltd., 1971.

Slyoff, M.R.: *Music for Special Education.* Fort Worth, TX: Harris Music, 1979.

Smith, R.B. & Flohr, J.W.: *Music Dramas for Children with Special Needs.* Denton, TX: Troostwyk Press, 1984.

Soibelman, D. *Therapeutic and Industrial Uses of Music.* New York: Columbia University Press, 1948.

Steele, A.E. (Ed.): *The Music Therapy Levels System: A Manual of Principles and Applications.* Cleveland, OH: The Cleveland Music School Settlement, 1985.

Thurman, L. & Langness, A.P.: *Heartsongs: A Guide to Active Pre-Birth and Infant Parenting Through Language and Singing.* Englewood, CO: Music Study Services, 1986.

Tomat, J.H. & Krutzky, C.D.: *Learning Through Music for Special Children and Their Teachers.* South Waterford, MA: Merriam-Eddy, 1975.

Van de Wall, W.: *Music in Hospitals.* New York: Russell Sage Foundation, 1946.

Van de Wall, W.: *Music In Institutions.* New York: Russell Sage Foundation, 1936.

Ward, D.: *Sing A Rainbow: Musical Activities with Mentally Handicapped Children.* London: Oxford University Press, 1979.

Ward, D.: *Hearts and Hands and Voices: Music in the Education of Slow Learners.* London: Oxford University Press, 1976.

ADDICTIONS/SUBSTANCE ABUSE

Brooks, H.B.: The role of music in a community drug abuse prevention program. *JMT*, 1973, **10**(1), pp. 3-6.

Browne, H.E.: Psychiatric treatment with drug LSD and music therapy for alcoholics. *Proceedings of the NAMT*, 1961, **10**, pp. 154-162.

Daughtery, K.: Music therapy in the treatment of the alcoholic client. *Music Therapy*, 1984, **1**, pp. 47-54.

Eagle, C.T.: Music and LSD: An empirical study. *JMT*, 1972, **9**, pp. 23-36.

Freed, B.S.: Songwriting with the chemically dependent. *Music Therapy Perspectives*, 1987, **4**, pp. 13-18.

Gaston, E.T. & Eagle, C.: Function of music in LSD therapy for alcoholic patients. *JMT*, 1970, **7**(1), p.3

Miller, A.S.: Music therapy for alcoholics at a Salvation Army Center. *JMT*, 1970, **7**, p. 136.

Murphy, M.: Music therapy: A self-help group experience for substance abuse patients. *Music Therapy*, 1983, **1**, pp. 52-62.

Smith, S.M.: Using music therapy with short term alcoholic and psychiatric patients. *Hospital and Community Psychiatry*, 1975, **26**(7), p. 420.

Wheeler, B.: The relationship between musical and activity elements of music therapy sessions and client responses: An exploratory study. *Music Therapy*, 1985, **1**, pp. 52-60.

Winich, C. & Nyswander, M.: Psychotherapy of successful musicians who are drug addicts. *American Journal of Orthopsychiatry*, 1961, **31**, pp. 622-636.

ADOLESCENT

Bean, L.J.: Music at Indiana State Prison. *Music Journal*, 1969, **27**, p. 31.

Gardstrom, S.C.: Positive peer culture: A working definition for the music therapist. *Music Therapy Perspectives*, 1987, **4**, pp. 19-23.

Johnson, E.R.: The role of objective and concrete feedback in self-concept treatment of juvenile delinquents in music therapy. *JMT*, 1981, **18**, pp. 137-147.

Kivland, M.J.: The use of music to increase self-esteem in a conduct disordered adolescent. *JMT*, 1986, **23**, pp. 25-29.

Larson, B.A.: Auditory and visual rhythmic recognition by emotionally disturbed and normal adolescents. *JMT*, 1981, **18**, pp. 128-136.

Lindecker, J.M.: Music therapy in a juvenile detention home. *Music Therapy*, 1953, pp. 108-114.

Madsen, C.K. & Madsen, C.H.: Music as a behavior modification technique with a juvenile delinquent. *JMT*, 1968, **5**(3), p. 72.

Patterson, W.: Our own thing. *JMT*, 1972, **9**, pp. 119.

Ragland, Z.: Community music therapy with adolescents. *JMT*, 1974, **11**, p. 147.

Steele, L.: Three year study of a music therapy program in a residential treatment center. *JMT*, 1975, **12**, p. 67.

GERONTOLOGY AND GERIATRIC

Allen, D.M.: Music therapy with geriatric patients. *British Journal of Music Therapy*, 1977, **8**, pp. 2-6.

Altman, K.P.: The effect of a music participation program on self concept and extraversion of senior citizens in a day treatment facility (doctoral dissertation, California School of Professional Psychology, 1977). *Dissertation Abstracts International*, 1977, **38**, pp. 3863A.

Altshuler, I.M.: The value of music in geriatrics. In: E.H. Schneider, (Ed.), *Music Therapy 1959*. Lawrence, KS: Allen Press, 1960, pp. 109-115.

Anderson, M.: Music therapy. *Professional Nursing Home*, 1965, **7**, pp. 14, 16 & 18.

Armstrong, M.: *Music Therapy and Physical Excersises for Frail Elderly Residents of a Therapeutic Community*. Ann Arbor: University of Michigan-Wayne State University, 1974.

Bartlett, J.C. & Snelus, P.: Lifespan memory for popular songs. *American Journal of Psychology*, 1980, **93**, pp. 551-560.

Boxberger, R.: Music for the geriatric wards. *Bulletin for NAMT*, 1960, **9**, P. 7, 10.

Boxberger, R. & Cotter, V.W.: Music therapy for geriatric patients. In: E. Thayer Gaston (Ed.), *Music in Therapy*. New York: The Macmillan Company, 1968, pp. 271-281.

Bright, R.: Music and the management of grief reactions. In: I.M. Burnside, (Ed.), *Nursing and the Aged*. New York: McGraw-Hill, Inc., 1981, pp. 137-142.

Bright, R.: *Practical Planning in Music Therapy for the Aged*. Van Nuys, CA: Alfred, 1984.

Bright, R.: *Music in Geriatric Care*. Sydney: Angus and Robertson, Ltd., 1972. Lynbrook, NY: Musicgraphics, 1980.

Brown, T.D.: Elderhostel. *MEJ*, February 1981, p. 57.

Browne, H.E. & Winkelmayer, R.A.: Structured music therapy program in geriatrics. In: E. Thayer Gaston (Ed.), *Music in Therapy*. New York: The Macmillan Company, 1968, pp. 285-290.

Burnside, I.M. (Ed.): *Nursing and the Aged*. New York: McGraw-Hill, Inc., 1976.

Carle, I.L.: Music therapy in a different key. *Music Therapy*, 1982, 2(1), pp. 63-71.

Caplow-Linder, E., Harpaz, L. & Samberg, S.: *Therapeutic Dance/Movement, Expressive Activities for Older Adults*. New York: Human Sciences, Press, 1979, pp. 156-160.

Catron, B.S.: Class piano for senior citizens. *Clavier*, 1977, **16**, p. 23.

Coates, P.: Sixty and still growing. *MEJ*, 1984, **70**, pp. 34-35.

Cotter, V.W.: *Effects of the Use of Music on the Behavior of Geriatric Patients*. Unpublished master's thesis, University of Kansas, Lawrence, KS, 1959.

Curran, J.M.: A design for the development of a beginning group piano curriculum for leisure age adults (doctoral dissertation, the University of Oklahoma, 1982). *Dissertation Abstracts International*, 1982, **43**, p. 319A.

Davidson, J.B.: Music for the young at heart. *MEJ*, 1982, **68**, pp. 33-35.

Davidson, J.B.: Music and gerontology: A young endeavor. *MEJ*, 1980, **66**, pp. 26-31.

Davidson, J.B.: The status of music programs for residents of sheltered housing, nursing and domiciliary care in Maryland (doctoral dissertation, the University of Maryland, 1978). *Dissertation Abstracts International*, 1978, **40**, p. 145A.

Donahue, W.: The challenge of growing older. In: M. Bing (Ed.), *Music Therapy 1953*. Lawrence, KS: Allen Press, 1954.

Douglass, D.: *Accent on Rhythm: Music Activities for the Aged*. (3rd Ed.) St. Louis, MO: MMB Music, Inc., 1985.

Eberly, J.W.: The aptitude of elderly people for learning to play the piano. In: M. Bing (Ed.), *Music Therapy 1953*. Lawrence, KS: Allen Press, 1954.

Eberly, J.W.: *The Aptitude of Elderly People for Learning the Piano*. Unpublished doctoral dissertation, University of Nebraska, Lincoln, NB, 1952.

Ebersole, P. & Hess, P.: *Toward Healthy Aging, Human Needs and Nursing Responses*. St. Louis, MO: C.V. Mosby Co., 1985.

Eckerle, M.J.: Expanding our pedagogy programs. *American Music Teacher*, 1982, **31**, pp. 33-34.

Fisher, R.G.: Beginning keyboard instruction as a nonverbal intervention for elderly persons to stimulate reminiscence, to structure life review, and to improve psychological well-being and adjustment (doctoral dissertation, University of Georgia, 1984). *Dissertation Abstracts International*, 1984, **44**, pp. 2399A.

Flynn, P.T. & Rich, A.J.: Photographic enlargement of printed music: Technique, application and implications. *The Gerontologist*, 1982, **22**, pp. 540-543.

Gaston, E.T. (Ed.): *Music in Therapy*. New York: The Macmillan Co., 1968.

Gibbons, A.C.: Stop babying the elderly. *MEJ*, 1985, **71**(7), pp. 48-51.

Gibbons, A.C.: Primary measures of music audiation scores in an institutionalized elderly population. *JMT*, 1983, **20**, pp. 21-29.

Gibbons, A.C.: Musical skill level self-evaluation in non-institutionalized elderly. *Activities, Adaptation and Aging*, 1982, **3**, pp. 61-67.

Gibbons, A.C.: Music aptitude profile scores in a non-institutionalized, elderly population. *Journal of Research in Music Education*, 1982, **30**, pp. 23-29.

Gibbons, A.C.: Music aptitude profile scores in the elderly and their relationships to morale and selected other variables (doctoral dissertation, University of Kansas, 1979). *Dissertation Abstracts International*, 1979, **41**, p. 150A.

Gibbons, A.: Popular music preferences of older people. *JMT*, 1977, **14**, pp. 180-189.

Gilbert, J. & Beal, M.: Preferences of elderly individuals for selected music activities. *Journal of Research in Music Education*, 1982, **30**, pp. 247-253.

Gilbert, J.P.: Music therapy perspectives on death and dying. *JMT*, 1977, **14**, pp. 165-171.

Gilliland, E.G.: Music in geriatrics. In: M. Bing (Ed.), *Music Therapy 1953*. Lawrence, KS: Allen Press, 1954.

Glassman, L.R.: The talent show: Meeting the needs of the healthy elderly. *Music Therapy*, 1983, **3**, pp. 82-93.

Glassman, L.R.: *The Use of Music with a Geriatric Population: Its Effects on Self-Esteem*. Unpublished master's thesis, Hahnemann Medical College, 1966.

Glynn, N.J.: The therapy of music. *Journal of Gerontological Nursing*, 1985, **12**, pp. 7-10.

Grant, R.E.: *Sing Along Senior Citizens*. Springfield, IL: Charles C. Thomas, 1977.

Greenwald, M.A. & Salzberg, R.S.: Vocal range assessment of geriatric clients. *JMT*, 1979, **16**, pp. 172-179.

Griffin, J.E.: *The Effects of a Planned Music Program on Habits of Incontinency and Interest in Music Activities of Geriatric Patients*. Unpublished master's thesis, University of Kansas, Lawrence, KS. 1959.

Griffin, J., Kurz, C. & Cotter, C.: The influence of music in geriatric patients. In: E. Thayer Gaston (Ed.), *Music in Therapy, 1957*. Lawrence, KS: NAMT, Inc., The Allen Press, 1957, p. 159, 168, 174.

Guerin, M.E.: Come sing along with me. *Geriatric Nursing*, 1982, **3**, pp. 70-71.

Hall, D.: Music activity for the older patient. In: E.T. Gaston, (Ed.), *Music Therapy 1956*, Lawrence, KS: Allen Press, 1957, pp. 115-118.

Hart, A.: The development of a music therapy program in a convalescent home. In: E.H. Schneider (Ed.), *Music Therapy, 1959*. Lawrence, KS: Allen Press, 1960.

Hauck, L.P. & Martin, P.L.: Music as a reinforcement in patient controlled duration of time out. *JMT*, 1970, **7**(2), pp. 43-53.

Hennessey, M.J.: Music and music therapy group work with the aged. In: I.M. Burnside, (Ed.), *Nursing and the Aged*. New York: McGraw-Hill, Inc., 1976, pp. 255-269.

Hennessey, M.J.: Music and music therapy groups. In: I.M. Burnside (Ed.), *Working with the Elderly: Group Processes and Techniques*. North Scituate, MA: Duxbury Press, 1978, pp. 255-274.

Hoffman, D.H.: *Pursuit of Arts Activities with Older Adults: An Administration and Programmatic Handbook*. Washington, DC: National Center on Arts and the Aging/National Council on the Aging, Inc., and the Center for Professional Development, University of Kentucky, 1980.

Holt, J.: *Never Too Late: My Musical Life Story*. New York: Delacorte Press/Seymour Lawrence, 1978.

James, M.R.: Implications of selected social psychological theories on life-long skill generalization: Considerations for the music therapist. *Music Therapy Perspectives*, 1987, **4**, pp. 29-33.

Jason, B. & Arrau, C.: New horizons in class piano. *Clavier*, 1983, **22**, pp. 46-47.

Jeanette, Sr. M.J.: Music for the aging. *Professional Nursing Home*, 1966, **8**, p. 12.

Kaplan, M.: Retirement is more than parties and gold watches. *MEJ*, 1980, **67**, p. 31 & 64.

Kartman, L.: The use of music as a program tool with regressed patients. *Journal of Gerontological Nursing*, 1977, **3**, pp. 38-42.

Kartman, L.L.: The power of music with patients in a nursing home. *Activities, Adaptations, and Aging*, 1980, **1**(1), pp. 9-17.

Kartman, L.L.: Music hath charms. *Journal of Gerontological Nursing*, 1984, **10**(6), pp. 20-24.

Kellman, R.H.: The development of a music education program for older adults suitable for use in senior citizens centers, retirement homes, or other sites. *Dissertation Abstracts International*, 1984, **46**, p. 95A. (University Microfilms No. 85-05-458).

Kurz, C.E.: The effects of a planned music program on the day hall sound level and personal appearance of geriatric patients. In: *Music Therapy*. Lawrence, KS: Allen Press, 1957.

Lancaster, E.L.: The beginner, the retread, the retiree. *Clavier*, 1979, **18**, p. 27.

Landon, E.A.: Piano workshop for senior citizens. *Clavier*, 1981, **20**, p. 40.

Larson, P.S.: An exploratory study of lifelong musical interest and activity: Case studies of twelve retired adults (doctoral dissertation, Temple University, 1983). *Dissertation Abstracts International*, 1983, **44**, p. 100A.

Lathom, W.B., Peterson, M. & Havlicek, L.: Music preferences of older people attending nutrition sites. *Educational Gerontology: An International Bimonthly Journal*, 1982, **8**, pp. 155-165.

Leonhard, C.: Expand your classroom. *MEJ*, 1981, **68**(54), pp. 61-62.

Liederman, P.C.: Music and rhythm group therapy for geriatric patients. *JMT*, 1967, **4**, pp. 11-27.

Leitner, M.J.: The effects of intergenerational music activities on senior day care participants and elementary school children (doctoral dissertation, University of Maryland, 1981). *Dissertation Abstracts International*, 1981, **42**, p. 3752A.

Linoff, M. & West, C.: Relaxation training systematically combined with music: Treatment of tension headaches in a geriatric patient. *International Journal of Behavioral Geriatrics*, 1982, **1**, pp. 11-16.

Mason, C.: Musical activities with elderly patients. *Physiotherapy*, 1978, **64**(3), pp. 80-82.

McCullough, E.C.: An assessment of the musical needs and preferences of individuals 65 and over (doctoral dissertation, University of Arizona, 1981). *Dissertation Abstracts International*, 1982, **42**, p. 909A.

Miller, T.C. & Crosby T.W.: Musical hallucinations in a deaf elderly patient. *Annals of Neurology*, 1979, **5**, pp. 301-302.

Moore, E.C.: Using music with the elderly: Group processes and techniques. In: I.M. Burnside (Ed.), *Working with the Elderly: Group Processes and Techniques*. North Scituate, MA: Duxbury Press, 1978.

Munro, S. & Mount, B.: Music therapy in palliative care. *Canadian Medical Association Journal*, 1978, **119**, pp. 1029-1034.

Needler, W. & Baer, M.: Movement, music and remotivation with the regressed elderly. *Journal of Gerontological Nursing*, 1982, **8**, pp. 497-503.

Norman, J.S.: Arts programming for senior citizens (doctoral dissertation, University of Northern Colorado, 1978). *Dissertation Abstracts International*, 1978, **39**, p. 2611A.

Olson, B.K.: Player piano music as therapy for the elderly. *JMT*, 1984, **21**, pp. 35-45.

Palmer, M.O.: Music therapy in a comprehensive program of treatment and rehabilitation for the geriatric resident. *JMT*, 1977, **14**, pp. 190-197.

Palmer, M.D.: Music therapy and gerontology. *Activities, Adaptations and Aging*, 1980, **1**(1), pp. 37-40.

Palmer, M.: Music therapy in a comprehensive program of treatment and rehabilitation for the geriatric patient. *Activities, Adaptations, and Aging*, 1983, **3**(3), pp. 53-59.

Palmore, E.B.: The effects of aging on activities and attitudes. *The Gerontologist*, 1968, **8**, pp. 259-263.

Paulman, L.: Reaching the confused and withdrawn through music. *Aging*, 1982, **333-334**, pp. 7-11.

Phillips, J.R.: Music in the nursing of elderly persons in nursing homes. *Journal of Gerontological Nursing*, 1980, **6**, pp. 209-220.

Prickett, C.: Music therapy for the aged. In: C.E. Furman (Ed.), *Effectiveness of Music Therapy Procedures: Documentation of Research and Clinical Practice*. Washington, DC: NAMT, 1988, pp. 107-134.

Ramsay, D.: *Music Therapy and Depression in the Elderly*. Unpublished master's thesis, University of Kansas, Lawrence, KS, 1982.

Riegler, J.: Comparison of a reality orientation program for geriatric patients with and without music. *JMT*, 1980, **17**, pp. 26-33.

Riegler, J.: Most comfortable loudness level of geriatric patients as a function of seashore loudness discrimination scores, detection threshold, age, sex, setting and musical background. *JMT*, 1980, **17**, pp. 214-222.

Shapiro, A.: A pilot program in music therapy with residents of a home for the aged. *Gerontologist*, 1969, **9**, pp. 128-133.

Smith, D.S.: Preferences for differentiated frequency loudness levels in older adult music listening. Unpublished doctoral dissertation, Florida State University, 1987.

Smith, J.J.: A survey of avocational music activities for adults (doctoral dissertation, University of Michigan, 1973). *Dissertation Abstracts International*, 1973, **33**, p. 1910A.

Steele, A.L.: New audiences for young musicians (children perform for retirement and nursing homes). *American Music Teacher*, 1982, **31**, pp. 34-35.

Stern, J.: A plan for developing an adult music education program in Charlotte, North Carolina (doctoral dissertation, Columbia University, 1968). *Dissertation Abstracts International*, 1968, **29**, p. 460A.

Sterrett, D.E.: Music in the recreation program for the senior citizens in the state of Florida (doctoral dissertation, George Peabody College for Teachers, 1957). *Dissertation Abstracts International*, 1957.

Strang, C.D.: Music at night: An experiment in a geriatric ward. *Royal College of General Practitioners Journal*, 1970, **20**, pp. 246-247.

Tanaka, T.: Music therapy for psychiatric rehabilitation of the aged. *Kangogaku Zasshi*, 1980, **44**, pp. 500-502.

Tanner, D.R. & O'Briant, R.M.: Music can color a graying America. *MEJ*, 1980, **67**, pp. 28-30.

Toombs, M.R.: Musical activities for geriatric patients, music as a means toward revitalization. In: E.T. Gaston (Ed.), *Music Therapy, 1958*, NAMT, Inc. Lawrence KS: The Allen Press, 1958.

Vanderark, S., Newman, I. & Bell, S.: The effects of music participation on quality of life of the elderly. *Music Therapy*, 1983, **3**, pp. 71-81.

Walker, D.L.: A study of music education in community development continuing education, and correctional programming as reported by state arts agency directors in the United States (doctoral dissertation, George Peabody College for Teachers of Vanderbilt University, 1980). *Dissertation Abstracts International*, 1980, **40**, p. 3293A.

Watts, T.D.: Theories of aging: The difference in orientations. *JMT*, 1980, **17**, pp. 84-89.

Weissman, J.A.: Meeting selected needs and treatment goals of aged individuals in long-term care facilities through the therapeutic use of music activities (doctoral dissertation, New York University, 1981). *Dissertation Abstracts International*, 1981, **42**, p. 12B.

Weissman, J.A.: Planning music activities to meet the needs and treatment goals of aged individuals in long-term care facilities. *Music Therapy*, 1983, **3**, pp. 63-70.

Wells, A.: Rhythmic activities on wards of senile patients. In. M. Bing, (Ed.), *Music Therapy 1953*. Lawrence, KS: Allen Press, 1954, pp. 127-132.

Wilson, A.V.: Recharging retirement life. *MEJ*, 1983, **69**, pp. 27-28.

Wolfe, J.R.: The use of music in a group sensory training program for regressed geriatric patients. *Activities, Adaptations, and Aging*, 1983, **4**, pp. 49-62.

MEDICAL/DENTAL

Ainlay, G.W.: The place of music in military hospitals. In: D.M. Schullian & M. Schoen (Eds.), *Music in Medicine*. New York: Books for Libraries Press, 1948.

Anderson, W.: The effectiveness of audio-nitrous oxide-oxygen psychosedation on dental behavior of a child. *Journal of Pedodontics*, 1981, **5**(10), pp. 963-971.

Atterbury, R.A.: Auditory pre-sedation for oral surgery patients. *Audioanalgesia*, 1974, **38**(6), pp. 12-14.

Bailey, L.M.: The effects of live music versus tape-recorded music on hospitalized cancer patients. *Music Therapy*, 1983, **3**(1), pp. 17-28.

Bailey, L.M.: The use of songs in music therapy with cancer patients and their families. *Music Therapy*, 1984, **4**(1), pp. 5-17.

Bartlett, K.: Audio-analgesia evaluated as hypnosis. *The American Journal of Clinical Hypnosis*, 1967, **9**(4), pp. 275-284.

Bason, P.T.: Control of the heart rate by external stimuli. *Nature*, 1972, **4**, pp. 279-280.

Behrens, G.A.: *The Use of Music Activities to Improve the Capacity, Inhalation, and Exhalation Capabilities of Handicapped Children's Respiration*. Unpublished master's thesis, Kent State University, 1982.

Blass, B.: Sound analgesia. *Journal of the American Podiatry Association*, 1975, **65**(10), p. 963-971.

Bob, S.R.: Audioanalgesia in podiatric practice, a preliminary study. *Journal of the American Podiatry Association*, 1962, **52**, pp. 503-504.

Bonny, H.L. & Savary, L.M.: *Music and Your Mind: Listening with a New Consciousness*. New York: Harper and Row, 1973.

Bonny, H.L.: Music listening for intensive coronary care units: A pilot project. *Music Therapy*, 1983, **3**(1), pp. 4-16.

Borzecki, M. & Zakrzewski, K.: Music autohypnorelaxation in pain: Some objective correlates. *World Journal of Psychosynthesis*, 1978, **10**(4), pp. 22-25.

Boyle, M.E.: *Operant Procedures and the Comatose Patient*. Unpublished doctoral dissertation, Teachers College, Columbia University, 1981.

Burt, R.K. & Korn, G.W.: Audioanalgesia in obstetrics. White noise analgesia during labor. *American Journal of Obstetrics and Gynecology* , 1964, **88**, pp. 361-366.

Camp, W., Martin, R. & Chapman, L.F.: Pain threshold and discrimination of pain intensity during brief exposure to intense noise. *Science*, 1962, **135**, pp. 788-789.

Carlin, S., Ward, W.D., Gershon, A. & Ingraham, R.: Sound stimulation and its effect on dental sensation threshold. *Science*, 1962, **138**, pp. 1258-1259.

Chapman, J.S.: *The Relation Between Auditory Stimulation of Short Gestation Infants and Their Gross Motor Limb Activity*. Unpublished doctoral dissertation, New York University, 1975.

Cherry, H. & Pallin, I.: Music as a supplement in nitrous oxide oxygen anesthesia. *Anesthesiology*, 1948, **9**, pp. 391-399.

Chetta, H.D.: The effect of music and desensitization on preoperative anxiety in children. *JMT*, 1981, **18**, pp. 74-87.

Christenberry, E.: The use of music therapy with burn patients. *JMT*, 1979, **16**, pp. 138-148.

Clark, M.E.: Music therapy-assisted childbirth: A practical guide. *Music Therapy Perspectives*, 1986, **3**, pp. 34-41.

Clark, M.E., McCorkle, R.R. & Williams, S.B.: Music therapy-assisted labor and delivery. *JMT*, 1981, **18**, pp. 88-109.

Chetta, H.D.: The effect of music and desensitization on preoperative anxiety in children. *JMT*, 1981, **18**, pp. 74-87.

Cockrell, B.A.: Music therapy for T.B. patients. *Bulletin of the NAMT*, 1953, **2**, p. 9.

Codding, P.A.: *An Exploration of the Uses of Music in the Birthing Process*. Unpublished master's thesis, The Florida State University, 1982.

Corah, N.L., Gale, E., Pace, L. & Seyrek, S.: Relaxation and musical programming as means of reducing psychological stress during dental procedures. *Journal of the American Dental Association*, 1981, **103**(2), pp. 232-234.

Crago, B.R.: Reducing the stress of hospitalization for open heart surgery. *Dissertation Abstracts International*, 1981, **41**(7B), pp. 2752.

Crowe B.J.: Music therapy and physical medicine – expanding opportunities for employment. *Music Therapy*, 1985, **5**(1), pp. 44-51.

Curtis, S.L.: *The Effects of Music on the Perceived Degree of Pain Relief, Physical Comfort, Relaxation, and Contentment of Hospitalized Terminally Ill Patients.* Unpublished master's thesis, Florida State University, 1982.

Echternach, J.L.: Audioanalgesia as an adjunct to mobilization of the chronic frozen shoulder. *Journal of the American Physical Therapy Association,* 1966, **46**, pp. 839-846.

Ellis, D.S. & Brighthouse, G.: Effects of music on respiration and heart rate. *American Journal of Psychology,* 1952, **65**, pp. 39-47.

Epstein, L., Hersen, M. & Hemphill, D.: Music feedback in the treatment of tension headache: An experimental case study. *Journal of Behavior Therapy and Experimental Psychiatry,* 1974, **5**(9), pp. 59-63.

Fagen, T.S.: Music therapy in the treatment of anxiety and fear in terminal pediatric patients. *Music Therapy,* 1982, **2**(1), pp. 13-23.

Falb, M.: *The Use of Operant Procedures to Condition Vasoconstriction in Profoundly Mentally Retarded PMR Infants.* Unpublished master's thesis, Florida State University, 1982.

Field, T.M., Dempsey, J., Hatch, J., Ting, G. & Clifton, R.: Cardiac and behavioral responses to repeated tactile and auditory stimulation by pre-term and term neonates. *Developmental Psychology,* 1979, **15**(4), pp. 406-416.

Fisher, S. & Greenberg, R.: Selective effects upon women of exciting and calm music. *Perceptual and Motor Skills,* 1972, **34**, pp. 987-990.

Foutz, C.D.: Routine audio-nitrous oxide analgesia simplified. *Arizona Dental Journal,* 1970, **16**, pp. 15-16.

Froelich, M.A.R.: A comparison of the effect of music therapy and medical play therapy on the verbalization behavior of pediatric patients. *JMT,* 1984, **21**(1), pp. 2-15.

Gardner, W.J. & Licklider, J.C.: Auditory analgesia in dental operation. *Journal of the American Dental Association,* 1959, **59**, pp. 1144-1150.

Gardner, W.J., Licklider, J.C.R. & Weisz, A.Z.: Suppression of pain by sound. *Science,* 1960, **132**, pp. 32-33.

Gaston, E.T.: Dynamic music factors in mood change. *MEJ,* 1951, **20**, pp. 50-58.

Gatewood, E.L.: The psychology of music in relation to anesthesia. *American Journal of Surgery, Anesthesia Supplement,* 1921, **35**, pp. 47-50.

Gilbert, J.: Music therapy perspectives on death and dying. *JMT,* 1977, **14**(4), pp. 165-171.

Godley, C.A.S.: The use of music therapy in pain clinics. *Music Therapy Perspectives,* 1987, **4**, pp. 24-28.

Goloff, M.S.: The responses of hospitalized medical patients to music therapy. *Music Therapy,* 1981, **1**(1), pp. 51-56.

Gutheil, E. (Ed.): *Music and Your Emotions.* New York: Lineright Publishing Corp., 1952.

Hanser, S.B., Larson, S.C. & O'Connell, A.S.: The effect of music on relaxation of expectant mothers during labor. *JMT,* 1983, **20**(2), pp. 50-58.

Hanser, S.B.: Music therapy and stress reduction research. *JMT,* 1985, **22**(4), pp. 193-206.

Howitt, J.W.: An evaluation of audio-analgesia effects. *Journal of Dentistry for Children,* 1967, **34**, pp. 406-411.

Howitt, J.W. & Stricklerk, G.: Objective evaluation of audioanalgesia effects. *Journal of the ADA,* 1966, **73**, pp. 874-877.

Hyde, I.M.: Effects of music upon electrocardiograms and blood pressure. *Journal of Experimental Psychology,* 1924, **7**, pp. 213-224.

In this intensive care unit, the downbeat helps the heartbeats. *Modern Hospital,* 1972, **118**, p. 91.

Jacobs, I.H.: Use of stereo headphones for patient relaxation and surgical drape support during local anesthesia. *Opthalmic Surgery,* 1983, **14**(4), pp. 356-357.

Jacobson, E.: *Progressive Relaxation* (2nd Ed.). Chicago: University of Chicago Press, 1983.

Jacobson, H.L.: The effect of sedative music on the tensions, anxiety and pain experienced by mental patients during dental procedures. In: E.T. Gaston (Ed.), *Music Therapy 1956: Book of the proceedings of the NAMT, Inc.* Lawrence, KS: NAMT, Inc., 1957, pp. 231-234.

Jellison, J.A.: The effect of music on autonomic stress responses and verbal reports. In: C.K. Madsen, R.D.Greer, & C.H. Madsen, Jr., (Eds.), *Research in Music Behavior.* Teachers College Press, Columbia University, 1975, pp. 206-219.

Katz, V.: Auditory stimulation and developmental behavior of the premature infant. *Nursing Research,* 1971, **20**, pp. 196-201.

Kendall, P.C.: *Medical Psychology: Contributions to Medical Psychology.* New York: Academic Press, 1981.

Kendall, P.C.: Stressful medical procedures: Cognitive behavioral strategies for stress management prevention. In: Meichenbaum, D.H. & Jaremko, M.J. (Eds.), *Stress Management and Prevention: A Cognitive Behavioral Analysis.* New York: Plenum Press, 1983.

Kibler, V.E. & Rider, M.S.: The effect of progressive muscle relaxation and music on stress as measured by finger temperature response. *Journal of Clinical Psychology*, 1983, **39**(2), pp. 213-215.

Kozak, Y.A.: Music therapy for orthopedic patients in a rehabilitative setting. In: E.T.Gaston (Ed.), *Music in Therapy.* New York: The Macmillan Co., 1968, pp. 166-168.

Landreth, J. & Landreth, M.R.: Effects of music on physiological response. *Journal of Research in Music Education*, 1974, **22**(1), pp. 4-12.

Lavine, R., Buchsbaum, M. & Poncy, M.: Auditory analgesia: Somatosensory evoked response and subjective pain rating. *Psychophysiology*, 1976, **13**(2), pp. 140-148.

Levine-Gross, J. & Swartz, R.: The effects of music therapy on anxiety in chronically ill patients. *Music Therapy*, 1982, **2**(1), pp. 43-52.

Light, G.A., Love, D.M., Benson, D. & Morch, E.T.: Music in surgery. *Current Researches in Anesthesia and Analgesia*, 1954, **33**, pp. 258-264.

Linoff, M.G. & West, C.M.: Relaxation training systematically combined with music treatment of tension headaches in a geriatric patient. *Journal of Behavioral Geriatrics*, 1982, **1**(3), pp. 11-16.

Livingston, J.: Music for the childbearing family. *JOGN Nursing*, 1979, **8**, pp. 363-367.

Locsin, R.: The effect of music on the pain of selected post-operative patients. *Journal of Advanced Nursing*, 1981, **6**, pp. 19-25.

Logan, T.G. & Roberts, A.R.: The effects of different types of relaxation music on tension level. *JMT*, 1984, **21**, pp. 177-183.

Long, L. & Johnson, J.: Dental practice using music to aid relaxation and relieve pain. *Dental Survey*, 1978, **54**, pp. 35-38.

Lucia, C.M.: Toward developing a model of music therapy intervention in the rehabilitation of head trauma patients. *Music Therapy Perspectives*, 1987, **4**, pp. 34-39.

MacClelland, D.: Music in the operating room. *AORN Journal*, 1979, pp. 252-260.

Marley, L.S.: The use of music with hospitalized infants and toddlers: A descriptive study. *JMT*, 1984, **21**(3), pp. 126-132.

McDonnell, L.: Music therapy with trauma patients and their families on a pediatric service. *Music Therapy*, 1984, **4**(1), pp. 55-56.

McDowell, C.R.: Obstetrical applications of audioanalgesia. *Hospital Topics*, 1966, **44**, pp. 102-104.

Melzack, R., Weisz, A.Z. & Sprague, L.T.: Stratagems for controlling pain: Contributions of auditory stimulation and suggestion. *Experimental Neurology*, 1963, **8**(3), pp. 239-247.

Metera, A. & Metera, A.: Influence of music on the minute oxygen consumption and basal metabolism rate. *Anaesthesia, Resuscitation and Intensive Therapy*, July-September 1975, **3**, pp. 259-264, 265-269.

Metzger, L.K.: The selection of music for therapeutic use with adolescents and young adults in a psychiatric facility. *Music Therapy Perspectives*, 1986, **3**, pp. 20-24.

Miller, R.A. & Bornstein, P.H.: Thirty-minute relaxation: A comparison of some methods. *Journal of Behavior Therapy and Experimental Psychiatry*, 1977, **8**(3), pp. 291-294.

Monsey, H.L.: Preliminary report of the clinical efficacy of audioanalgesia. *Journal of California State Dental Association*, 1960, **36**, pp. 432-437.

Moore, W.M., McClure, J.C. & Hill, I.D.: Effect of white sound on pain threshold. *British Journal of Anaesthesia*, 1964, **36**, pp. 268-271.

Morosko, T.E. & Simmons, F.F.: The effect of audioanalgesia on pain threshold and pain tolerance. *Journal of Dental Research*, 1966, **45**, pp. 1608-1617.

Mowatt, K.S.: Background music during radiotherapy. *Medical Journal, Australia*, 1967, **1**, pp. 185-186.

Munro, S. & Mount, B.: Music therapy in palliative care. In: I. Ajemain and B. Mount (Eds.), *R.V.H. Manual on Palliative/Hospice Care.* New York: Arno Press, 1980.

Ohlsen, J.L.: Audioanalgesia in podiatry. *Journal of the American Podiatry Association*, 1987, **57**, pp. 153-156.

O'Moore, A.M.: Psychosomatic aspects in biopathic infertility: Effects of treatment with autogenic training. *Journal of Psychosomatic Research*, 1983, **27**, pp. 145-151.

Owens, L.D.: The effects of music on the weight loss, crying, and physical movement of newborns. *JMT*, 1979, **16**(2), pp. 83-90.

Oyama, T., Hatano, K., Sato, Y., Kudo, M., Spintge, R. & Droh, R.: Endocrine effect of anxiolytic music in dental patients. In: R. Droh & R. Spintge (Eds.), *Angst, Schmerz, Musik in der Anasthesie.* Basel: Editiones Roche, 1983, pp. 143-146.

Oyama, T., Sato, Y., Kudo, M., Spintge, R. & Droh, R.: Effect of anxiolytic music in endocrine function in surgical patients. In: R. Droh & R. Spintge (Eds.), *Angst, Schmerz, Musik in der Anasthesie.* Basel: Editiones Roche, 1983, pp. 147-152.

Padfield, A.: Letter: Music as sedation for local analgesia. *Anaesthesia,* 1976, **31**(2), pp. 300-301.

Peach, S.C.: Some implications for the clinical use of music facilitated imagery. *JMT,* 1984, **21**, pp. 27-34.

Peretti, P.O.: Changes in galvanic skin response as affected by musical selection, sex, and academic discipline. *Journal of Psychology,* 1975, **89**, pp. 183-187.

Peretti, P.O. & Swenson, K.: Effects of music on anxiety as determined by physiological skin responses. *Journal of Research in Music Education,* 1974, **22**, pp. 278-283.

Phillips, J.R.: Music in the nursing of elderly persons in nursing homes. *Journal of Gerontological Nursing,* 1980, **6**(1), pp. 37-39.

Pickerall, K.L., Metzger, J.T., Wilde, J.N., Broadbent, R.R. & Edwards, B.F.: The use and therapeutic value of music in the hospital and operating room. *Plastic and Reconstructive Surgery,* 1950, **6**, pp. 142-152.

Piekos, M. & Gaertner, H.: Own observations of the analgesia effects of music during dental treatment (English Summary). *Czas. Stomat.,* 1968, **21**, pp. 1181-1187.

Prokop, C.K. & Bradley, L.A. (Eds.): *Medical Psychology: Contributions to Behavioral Medicine.* New York: Academic Press, 1981.

Reynolds, S.B.: Biofeedback, relaxation training, and music: Homeostasis for coping with stress. *Biofeedback and Self-Regulation,* 1984, **9**(2), pp. 169-179.

Rider, M.S.: Entrainment mechanisms are involved in pain reduction, muscle relaxation, and music-mediated imagery. *JMT,* 1985, **22**(4), pp. 183-192.

Rider, M.S., Floyd, J. & Kirkpatrick, J.: The effect of music, imagery, and relaxation on adrenal corticosteroids and the re-entrainment of circadian rhythms. *JMT,* 1985, **22**, pp. 46-58.

Rider, M.S.: Music therapy: Therapy for debilitated musicians. *Music Therapy Perspectives,* 1987, **4**, pp. 40-43.

Robinson, D.: Music therapy in a general hospital. *Bulletin of the NAMT,* 1962, **11**(3), pp. 13-18.

Robson, J.G. & Davenport, H.T.: The effects of white sound and music upon the superficial pain threshold. *Canadian Anaesthetists' Society Journal,* 1962, **9**, pp. 105-108.

Sanderson, S.K.: *The Effect of Music on Reducing Preoperative Anxiety and Postoperative Anxiety and Pain in the Recovery Room.* Unpublished master's thesis, Florida State University, 1986.

Scartelli, J.P.: The effect of sedative music on electromyographic biofeedback assisted relaxation training of spastic cerebral palsied adults. *JMT,* 1982, **19**(4), pp. 210-218.

Scartelli, J.P.: The effect of EMG biofeedback and sedative music, EMG biofeedback only, and sedative music only on frontalis muscle relaxation ability. *JMT,* 1984, **21**(2), pp. 67-78.

Schermer, R.: Distraction analgesia using the stereogesic portable. *Military Medicine,* 1960, **125**, pp. 843-848.

Schneider, F.A.: Assessment and evaluation of audio-analgesic effects on the pain experience of acutely burned children during dressing changes. *Dissertation Abstracts International,* 1983, **43**(8-B), p. 2716.

Schultz, J. & Luthe, W.: *Autogenic Training: A Psychophysiologic Approach in Psychotherapy.* New York: Gruen & Stratton, 1959.

Schuster, B.L.: The effect of music listening on blood pressure fluctuations in adult hemodialysis patients. *JMT,* 1985, **22**(3), pp. 146-153.

Schwankovsky, L.M. & Guthrie, P.T.: *Music Therapy for Handicapped Children: Other Health Impaired.* In: W. Lathom & C. Eagle (Eds.), Project Music Monograph Series, Washington, DC: NAMT Inc,. 1982.

Sears, W.W.: The effect of music on muscle tonus. *Music Therapy,* 1958, **7**, pp. 250-261.

Segall, M.: *The Relationship Between Auditory Stimulation and Heart Rate Response of the Premature Infant.* Unpublished doctoral dissertation, New York University, 1970.

Seki, H.: Influence of music on memory and education, and the application of its underlying principles to acupuncture. *International Journal of Acupuncture and Electro-Therapeutic Research,* 1983, **8**, pp. 1-16.

Shapiro A.G. & Cohen, H.: Auxiliary pain relief during suction currettage. In: R. Droh & R. Spintge (Eds.), *Angst, Schmerz, Musik in der Anasthesie.* Basel: Editiones Roche, 1983, pp. 89-95.

Seigel, S.L.: *The Use of Music as Treatment In Pain Perception with Post Surgical Patients in a Pediatric Hospital.* Unpublished master's thesis, University of Miami, 1983.

Smith, C.A. & Morris, L.W.: Effects of stimulative and sedative music on cognitive and emotional components of anxiety. *Psychological Reports,* 1976, **38**, pp. 1187-1193.

Smith, C.A. & Morris, L.W.: Differential effects of stimulative and sedative music on anxiety, concentration and performance. *Psychological Reports,* 1977, **41**, pp. 1047-1053.
Snow, W. & Fields, B.: Music as an adjunct in the training of children with cerebral palsy. *Occupational Therapy,* 1950, **29**, pp. 147-156.
Standley, J.M.: Music research in medical/dental treatment: Meta-analysis and clinical applications. *JMT,* 1986, **23**(2), pp. 56-122.
Staum, M.J.: Music and rhythmic stimuli in the rehabilitation of gait disorders. *JMT,* 1983, **20**(2), pp. 69-87.
Staum, M.J.: Music for physical rehabilitation: An analysis of literature from 1950-1986 and applications for rehabilitation settings. In: C.E. Furman (Ed.), *Effectiveness of Music Therapy Procedures: Documentation of Research and Clinical Practice.* Washington, DC: NAMT, 1988, pp. 65-104
Stoudenmire, J.: A comparison of muscle relaxation training and music in the reduction of state and trait anxiety. *Journal of Clinical Psychology* 1975, **31**, pp. 490-492.
Stratton, V.N. & Zalanowski, A.H.: The relationship between music, degree of liking, and self-reported relaxation. *JMT,* 1984, **21**, pp. 184-191.
Sunderman, F.W.: Medicine, music, and academia. *Transactions of the College of Physicians of Philadelphia,* 1969, **37**, pp. 140-148.
Tanioka, F., Takazawa, T., Kamata, S., Kudo, M., Matsuki, A. & Oyama, T.: Hormonal effect of anxiolytic music in patients during surgical operations under epidural anesthesia. In: R. Droh & R. Spintge (Eds.), *Angst, Schmerz, Musik in der Anasthesie.* Basel: Editiones Roche, 1983, pp. 285-290.
Taylor, D.B.: Music in general hospital treatment from 1900 to 1950. *JMT,* 1981, **18**(2), pp. 62-73.
Turk, D.C. & Genest, M.: Regulation of pain: The application of cognitive and behavioral techniques for prevention and remediation. In: Kendall, P.C. & Hollon, S.D. (Eds.), *Cognitive Behavioral Interventions: Theory, Research, and Procedures.* New York: Academic Press, 1979, pp. 287-289.
Vincent, S. & Thompson, J.H.: The effects of music upon the human blood pressure. *The Lancet,* 1929, **1**, pp. 534-537.
Wagner, M.J.: Effect of music and biofeedback on alpha brain wave rhythms and attentiveness. *Journal of Research in Music Education,* 1975, **23**(1), pp. 3-13.
Wagner, M.J.: Brainwaves and biofeedback: A brief history. *JMT,* 1975, **12**, pp. 46-58.
Wallace, L.M.: Psychological preparation as a method of reducing the stress of surgery. *Journal of Human Stress: Research and Management,* 1984, **10**(2), pp. 62-76.
Webster, C.: Relaxation, music and cardiology: The physiological and psychological consequences of their interrelation. *Australian Occupational Therapy Journal,* 1973, **20**, pp. 9-20.
Weisbrod, R.L.: Audio-analgesia revisited. *Anesthesia Progress,* January, 1969 p. 8-15.
Wilson, C.U. & Aiken, L.S.: The effect of intensity levels upon physiological and subjective affective response to rock music. *JMT,* 1977, **14**, pp. 60-76.
Wilson, V.M.: Variations in gastric motility due to musical stimuli. *Music Therapy,* 1957, **6**, pp. 243-249.
Winokur, M.A.: *The Use of Music as an Audio-analgesia During Childbirth.* Unpublished master's thesis, Florida State University, 1984.
Winslow, G.A.: Music therapy in the treatment of anxiety in hospitalized high-risk mothers. *Music Therapy Perspectives,* 1986, **3**, pp. 29-33.
Wolfe, D.E.: Pain rehabilitation and music therapy. *JMT,* 1978, **15**(4), pp. 162-178.
Wolfe, D.E.: The effect of automated interrupted music on head posturing of cerebral palsied individuals. *JMT,* 1980, **17**(4), pp. 184-206.
Wolinsky, G.F. & Koehler, N.: A cooperative program in materials development for very young hospitalized children. *Rehabilitation Literature,* 1973, **34**(2), pp. 34-41.
Wylie, M.E. & Blom, R.C.: Guided imagery and music with hospice patients. *Music Therapy Perspectives,* 1986, **3**, pp. 25-28.
Zimny, G.H. & Weidenfeller, E.W.: Effects of music upon GSR and heart rate. *American Journal of Psychology,* 1963, **76**, pp. 311-314.

MENTAL HEALTH/PSYCHIATRIC

Adelman, E.J.: Multimodal therapy and music therapy: Assessing and treating the whole person. *Music Therapy*, 1985, **5**, pp. 12-21.

Ain, E.: *The Relationship of Musical Structure and Verbal Interaction Process During Adult Music Therapy*. Unpublished master's thesis. Hahnemann Medical College and Hospital, Philadelphia, 1978.

Allen, W.R. & White, W.F.: Psychodramatic effects of music as a psychotherapeutic agent. *JMT*, 1966, **3**, pp. 69-71.

Alvin, J.: Regressional techniques in music therapy. *Music Therapy*, 1981, **1**, pp. 3-8.

Applebaum, E., Egel, A., Koegel, R. & Imhoff, B.: Measuring musical abilities of autistic children. *Journal of Autism and Developmental Disorders*, 1979, **9**, pp. 279-287.

Arnold, M.: Music therapy in a transactional analysis setting. *JMT*, 1975, **12**, pp. 104-120.

Baumel, L.N.: Psychiatrist as music therapist. *JMT*, 1973, **2**, pp. 83-85.

Boenheim, C.: The importance of creativity in contemporary psychotherapy. *JMT*, 1967, **4**, pp. 3-6.

Boenheim, C.: The position of music and art therapy in contemporary psychotherapy. *JMT*, 1968, **5**, pp. 85-87.

Bolduc, T.E.: A psychologist looks at music therapy. *Proceedings of the NAMT*, 1962, **11**, pp. 40-42.

Bonny, H.L.: *Facilitating GIM sessions: GIM Monograph #1*. Baltimore: ICM Books, 1978.

Bonny, H.L.: Music and consciousness. *JMT*, 1975, **13**, pp. 121-135.

Bonny, H.L.: Preferred loudness of recorded music of hospitalized psychiatric patients and hospital employees. *JMT*, 1968, **2**, pp. 44-52.

Bonny, H.L. & Pahnke, W.: The use of music in psychedelic (LSD) psychotherapy. *JMT*, 1972, **9**, pp. 64-87.

Bonny, H.L. & Savary, L.M.: *Music and Your Mind*. New York: Harper and Row, 1973.

Braswell, C.: The future of psychiatric music therapy. *Proceedings of the NAMT*, 1962, **11**, pp. 65-76.

Braswell, C.: Psychiatric music therapy: A review of the profession. *Proceedings of the NAMT*, 1962, **11**, pp. 53-64.

Braswell, C., Brooks, D., Decuir, A., Humphrey, T., Jacobs, K. & Sutton, K.: Development and implementation of a music-activity therapy intake assessment for psychiatric patients. Part II: Standardization procedures on data from psychiatric patients. *JMT*, 1986, **23**(3), pp. 126-141.

Brooking, M.: Music therapy in British mental hospitals. *Music Therapy*, 1959, pp. 38-46.

Brown, M.E. & Selinger, M.: A nontherapeutic device for approaching therapy in an institutional setting. *International Journal of Group Psychotherapy*, 1969, **19**, pp. 88-95.

Brunner-Orne, M. & Flinn, S.S.: Music therapy at Westwood Lodge. *Music Therapy*, 1960, pp. 44-46.

Bryant, D.R.: A cognitive approach to therapy through music. *JMT*, 1987, **24**(1), pp. 27-34.

Cassity, M.D.: Influence of a music therapy activity upon peer acceptance, group cohesiveness, and interpersonal relationships of adult psychiatric patients. *JMT*, 1976, **13**(2), pp. 66-76.

Chace, M.: Report of a group project. St. Elizabeth Hospital. *Music Therapy*, 1954, pp. 187-190.

Clemetson, B.C. & Chen, R.: Music therapy in a day-treatment program. In: E. Thayer Gaston (Ed.), *Music in Therapy*. New York: The Macmillan Company, 1968, pp. 394-400.

Conrad, J.: A music therapy program for short-term psychiatric patients. *Bulletin of the NAMT*, 1962, **3**, pp. 7-12.

Cooke, R.M.: The use of music in play therapy. *JMT*, 1969, **6**, pp. 66-75.

Crocker, D.B.: Music as a projective technique. *Music Therapy*, 1955, pp. 86-97.

DeWolfe, A.S. & Konieczny, J.A.: Responsiveness in schizophrenia. *Journal of Personality Assessment*, 1973, **37**, pp. 568-573.

DeWolfe, A.S., Youkilis, H.D. & Konieczny, J.A.: Psychophysiological correlates of responsiveness in schizophrenia. *Journal of Consulting and Clinical Psychology*, 1975, **43**, pp. 192-197.

Dickens, G. & Sharpe, M.: Music therapy in the setting of a psychotherapeutic centre. *British Journal of Medical Psychology*, 1970, **43**, pp. 83-94.

Dickenson, M.: Music as a tool in psychotherapy for children. *Music Therapy*, 1957, pp. 97-104.

Diephouse, J.W.: Music therapy: A valuable adjunct to psychotherapy with children. *Psychiatric Quarterly Supplement*, 1986, **42**, pp. 75-85.

Douglass, D.R. & Wagner, M.K.: A program for the activity therapist in group psychotherapy. *JMT*, 1965, **2**, pp. 56-60.

Dreikurs, R.: The psychological and philosophical significance of rhythm. *Bulletin of the NAMT*, 1961, **10**, pp. 8-17.

Dreikurs, R. & Crocker, E.B.: Music therapy with psychotic children. *Music Therapy*, 1955, pp. 62-73.

Dvorkin, J.: Piano improvisation: A therapeutic tool in acceptance and resolution of emotions in a schizo-afffective personality. *Music Therapy*, 1982, **2**, pp. 53-62.

Egan, W.H.: Teaching medical student psychiatry through contemporary music. *Journal of Medical Education*, 1977, **52**, pp. 851-853.

Euper, J.A.: Contemporary trends in mental health work. *JMT*, 1970, **1**, pp. 20-27.

Farmer, R.: A musical activities program with young psychotic girls. *American Journal of Occupational Therapy*, 1963, **17**, pp. 116-119.

Farnan, L.A.: Composing music for use in therapy. *Music Therapy Perspectives*, 1987, **4**, pp. 8-12.

Ficken, T.: The use of song-writing in a psychiatric setting. *JMT*, 1976, **13**, pp. 163-172.

Forrest, C.: Music and the psychiatric nurse. *Nursing Times*, 1972, **68**, pp. 410-411.

Forrest, C.: Music in psychiatry. *Nursing Mirror*, 1968, **127**, pp. 22-23.

Friedman, E.R.: Psychological aspects of folk music. *American Psychological Proceedings of the Annual Convention*, 1968, **3**, pp. 449-450.

Friedrich, D., Beno, F. & Graham, H.: A second testing of paranoid schizophrenia on a dichotic listening task. *Journal of Abnormal Psychology*, 1976, **85**, pp. 622-644.

Froelich, M.: An annotated bibliography for the creative arts therapies. *JMT*, 1985, **22**(4), pp. 218-226.

Gibbons, A.: The development of square dancing activity in a music therapy program and Rockland State Hospital. *Music Therapy*, 1986, **6**, pp. 140-147.

Goldstein, C.: Music and creative arts therapy for an autistic child. *JMT*, 1964, **1**, pp. 235-238.

Goldstein, C., Lingas, C. & Sheafer, D.: Interpretive or creative movement as a sublimation tool in music therapy. *JMT*, 1965, **2**, pp. 11-15.

Glover, R.: New concepts in psychiatric treatment. *Proceedings of the NAMT*, 1962, **11**, pp. 48-49.

Greenburg, R.P. & Fisher, S.: Some differential effects of music on projective and structured psychological tests. *Psychological Reports*, 1971, **28**, pp. 817-818.

Greven, G.M.: Music as a tool in psychotherapy for children. *Music Therapy*, 1957, pp. 105-108.

Grossman, S.: An investigation of Crocker's music projective techniques for emotionally disturbed children. *JMT*, 1978, **15**(4), pp. 179-184.

Hadsell, N.: A sociological theory and approach to music therapy with adult psychiatric patients. *JMT*, 1974, **3**, pp. 113-124.

Hanser, S.: Music therapy and stress reduction research. *JMT*, 1986, **4**, pp. 193-207.

Hauck, L.P. & Martin, P.L.: Music as a reinforcer in patient-controlled duration of time out. *JMT*, 1970, **7**, pp. 43-53.

Hollander, F.M. & Juhrs, P.D.: Orff-Schulwerk, an effective tool with autistic children. *JMT*, 1974, **11**, pp. 1-12.

Howe, A.W.: Music therapy in the psychiatric treatment program. *Journal of the South Carolina Medical Association*, 1960, **56**, pp. 59-65.

Ishiyama, T.: Music as a psychotherapeutic tool in the treatment of a catatonic. *Psychiatric Quarterly*, 1963, **37**, pp. 437-461.

Kahans, D. & Calford, M.B.: The influence of music on psychiatric patients' immediate attitude change toward therapists. *JMT*, 1982, **19**(3), pp. 179-187.

Kantor, M. & Pinsker, H.: Musical repression of psychopathology. *Perspective in Biology and Medicine*, 1973, **16**, pp. 263-269.

King, H.E.: Incidental serial reaction time: Normal and schizophrenic response to the onset and cessation of auditory signals. *Journal of Psychology*, 1976, **93**, Part 2, pp. 299-311.

Koh, S.D. & Shears, G.: Psychophysical scaling by schizophrenics and normals: Line lengths and music preferences. *Archives of General Psychiatry*, 1970, **23**, pp. 249-259.

Korboot, P.J. & Damiani, N.: Auditory processing speed and signal detection in schizophrenia. *Journal of Abnormal Psychology*, 1976, **85**, pp. 287-295.

Lerner, J., Nachson, I. & Carmon, A.: Responses of paranoid and non-paranoid schizophrenics in a dichotic listening task. *Journal of Nervous and Mental Disease*, 1977, **164**, pp. 247-252.

Lewis, D.: Chamber music – proposed as a therapeutic medium. *JMT*, 1964, **4**, pp. 126-127.

Lord, W.: Communication of activity therapy rationale. *JMT*, 1971, **2**, pp. 68-71.

Matteson, C.A.: Finding the self in space. *MEJ*, April 1972, pp. 47-49.

Maultsby, M.C.: Combining music therapy and rational behavior therapy. *JMT*, 1977, **14**, pp. 89-97.

McClean, M.: One therapist; one patient: A success story. *Hospital and Community Psychiatry*, 1974, **25**, pp. 153-156.

Metzger, L.K.: The selection of music for therapeutic use with adolescents and young adults in a psychiatric facility. *Music Therapy Perspectives*, 1986, **3**, pp. 20-24.

Mitchell, G.C.: Bedtime music for psychotic children. *Nursing Mirror*, 1966, **122**, pp. 452.

Morgenstern, A.M.:   Group therapy: A timely strategy for music therapists.   *Music Therapy Perspectives*, 1982, **1**, pp. 16-20.

Moreno, J.J.:   Music psychodrama: A new direction in music therapy. *JMT*, 1980, **17**, pp. 34-42.

Myers, K.F.:   The relationship between degree of disability and vocal range, vocal range midpoint, and pitch-matching ability of mentally retarded and psychiatric clients, *JMT*, 1985, **22**(1), pp. 35-45.

Nass, M.L.:   Some considerations of a psychoanalytic interpretation of music. *Psychoanalytic Quarterly*, 1971, **40**, pp. 303-316.

Nelson, D.L., Anderson, V. & Gonzales, A.:   Music activities as therapy for children with autism and other pervasive developmental disorders. *JMT*, 1984, **21**(3), pp. 100-116.

Nolan, P.:   Insight therapy: Guided imagery and music in a forensic psychiatric setting. *Music Therapy*, 1983, **1**, pp. 43-51.

Nolan, P.:   *The Use of Guided Imagery and Music in the Clinical Assessment of Depression.* Unpublished master's thesis. Hahnemann University, 1981.

North, E.F.:   Music therapy as an important treatment modality with psychotic children. *JMT*, 1966, **3**, pp. 22-24.

Noy, P.:   The psychodynamic meaning of music, Parts I - V. *JMT*, 1966, **3**, pp. 126-134; 1967, **4**, pp. 45-51, 81-94.

Peach, S.C.:   Some implications for the clinical use of music facilitated imagery. *JMT*, 1984, **21**(1), pp. 27-34.

Pickler, A.G.:   Music as an aid in psychotherapy. *Proceedings of the NAMT*, 1962, **11**, pp. 23-29.

Pishkin, V. & Hershiser, D.:   White sound and schizophrenic's reaction to stress. *Journal of Oklahoma State Medical Association*, 1964, **57**, pp. 215-217.

Plach, T.:   *The Creative Use of Music in Group Therapy.* Springfield, IL: Charles C. Thomas, 1980.

Racker, H.:   Psychoanalytic considerations on music and the musician. *Psychoanalytic Review*, 1965, **52**, pp. 75-94.

Robbins, A.:   *Expressive Therapy.* New York: Human Sciences Press, 1980.

Robbins, L.:   Role of music therapy in a psychiatric treatment. *JMT*, 1966, **3**, p. 1.

Rollin, H.R.:   Music therapy in a mental hospital. *Nursing Times*, 1964, **60**, pp. 1219-1222.

Rollin, H.R.:   Therapeutic use of music in a mental hospital. *Transactions of the College of Physicians of Philadelphia*, 1962, **29**, pp. 130-136.

Rosenfeld, A.H.:   Music, the beautiful disturber. *Psychology Today*, December 1985, pp. 48-56.

Rubin, B.:   Music therapy in a community mental health program. *JMT*, 1975, **7**, p. 59.

Ruppenthal, W.:   "Scribbling" in music therapy. *JMT*, 1965, **2**, pp. 8-10.

Schmidt, J.A.:   Songwriting as a therapeutic procedure. *Music Therapy Perspectives*, 1983, **2**, pp. 4-7.

Schneider, S.J.:   Selective attention in schizophrenia. *Journal of Abnormal Psychology*, 1976, **85**, pp. 167-173.

Schneider, C.W.:   The effects of Dalcroze eurhythmics upon the motor processes of schizophrenia. *Proceedings of the NAMT*, 1961, **10**, pp. 132-140.

Sears, W.:   Processes in music therapy. In: E. Thayer Gaston (Ed.), *Music in Therapy*. New York: The Macmillan Company, 1968. pp. 30-40.

Seeley, M.C.:   Problems and techniques of a public radio broadcast from a mental hospital. *Bulletin of the NAMT*, 1960, **2**, pp. 7-8, 11.

Shashan, D.H.:   Group psychotherapy: Present trends in management of the more severe emotional problems. *Psychiatric Annals*, 1972, **2**, pp. 4-10.

Shatin, L., Kotter, W. & Douglas-Longmore, G.:   A psychological study of the music therapist in rehabilitation. *Journal of General Psychology*, 1964, **71**, pp. 193-205.

Shatin, L., Kotter, W. & Douglas-Longmore, G.:   Music therapy for schizophrenics. *Proceedings of the NAMT*, 1961, **11**, pp. 99-104.

Shatin, L., Kotter, W.L. & Douglas-Longmore, G.:   Music therapy for schizophrenia. *Journal of Rehabilitation*, 1961, **27**, pp. 30-31.

Shatin, L., Kotter, W. & Longmore, G.:   Psycho-social prescription for music therapy in hospital. *Diseases of the Nervous System*, 1967, **4**, pp. 231-233.

Shrodes, C.:   Bibliotherapy. An application of psychoanalytic therapy. *American Image*, 1960, **17**, pp. 311-317.

Slaughter, F.:   Approaches to the use of music therapy. In: E. Thayer Gaston (Ed.), *Music in Therapy*. New York: The Macmillan Company, 1968, pp. 238-244.

Slaughter, F.:   Some concepts concerning the therapeutic use of music in a psychiatric setting. *Bulletin of the NAMT*, 1960, **1**, p. 11.

Smith, S.M.:   Using music therapy with short-term alcoholic and psychiatric patients. *Hospital and Community Psychiatry*, 1975, **7**, pp. 420-421.

Sommers, D.T.: Music in the autobiographies of mental patients. *Mental Hygiene*, 1961, **45**, pp. 402-407.

Stanford, G.A.: Orchestration of the new mental hospital theme. *JMT*, 1964, **4**, pp. 124-128.

Staum, M.J.: An analysis of movement in therapy. *JMT*, 1981, **18**(1), pp. 7-24.

Steele, P.H.: Aspects of resistance in music therapy: Theory and technique. *Music Therapy*, 1984, **4**, pp. 64-72.

Stein, J. & Euper, J.A.: Advances in music therapy. In: J.H. Masserman, (Ed.), *Current Psychiatric Therapies* (Vol. 14). New York: Grune and Stratton, 1974, pp. 107-113.

Stein, J. & Thompson, S.V.: Crazy music: Theory. *Psychotherapy: Theory, Research, and Practice*, 1971, **8**, pp. 137-145.

Stephens, G.: Adele: A study in silence. *Music Therapy*, 1981, **1**, pp. 25-31.

Stephens, G.: Group supervision in music therapy. *Music Therapy*, 1984, **4**, pp. 29-38.

Stephens, G.: The use of improvisation for developing relatedness in the adult client. *Music Therapy*, 1983, **3**, pp. 29-42.

Sterba, R.F.: Psychoanalysis and music. *American Image*, 1965, **22**, pp. 96-111.

Sylwester, K., Barg, M., Frueh, B., Baker, K., Patrick, F. & Shaffer, S.: Music therapy in a decentralized hospital. *JMT*, 1971, **8**, p. 53.

Thomas, M.W.: Implications for music therapy as a treatment modality for the mentally ill deaf. *Voice of the Lakes*, 1976, **76**, pp. 19-22.

Toedter, A.D.: Music therapy for the criminally insane and the psychopath. *Music Therapy*, 1954, pp. 95-103.

Tunks, J.L.: The ward music therapy group and the integral involvement of nursing aides. *Music Therapy Perspectives*, 1983, **2**, pp. 23-24.

Tyson, F.: Child at the gate: Individual music therapy with a schizophrenic woman. *Art Psychotherapy*, 1979, **6**, pp. 77-83.

Tyson, F.: Individual singing instruction: An evolutionary framework for psychiatric music therapists. *Music Therapy Perspectives*, 1982, **1**, pp. 5-15.

Tyson, F.: Music therapy as a choice for psychotherapeutic intervention: A preliminary study of motivational factors among adult psychiatric patients. *Music Therapy Perspectives*, 1984, **1**, pp. 2-8.

Tyson, F.: Music therapy in private practices: Three case histories. *JMT*, 1966, **3**, p. 8.

Tyson, F.: *Psychiatric Music Therapy: Origin and Development*. New York: Creative Arts Rehabilitation Center, 1981.

Tyson, F.: Therapeutic elements in out-patient music therapy. *The Psychiatric Quarterly*, April 1965, pp. 315-327.

Tyson, F.: Analytically-oriented music therapy in a case of generalized anxiety disorder. *Music Therapy Perspectives*, 1987, **4**, pp. 51-55.

Wang, R.P.: Psychoanalytic theories and music therapy practice. *JMT*, 1968, **5**, pp. 114-116.

Warren, J.: Paired-associate learning in chronic institutionalized subjects using synthesized sounds, nonsense syllables, rhythmic sounds. *JMT*, 1980, **17**(1), pp. 16-25.

Wasserman, N.M.: Music therapy for the emotionally disturbed in a private hospital. *JMT*, 1972, **9**, pp. 99-104.

Wasserman, N., Plutchik, R., Deutsch, R. & Taketomo, Y.: The musical background of a group of mentally retarded psychotic patients: Implications for music therapy. *JMT*, 1973, **10**, pp. 78-82.

Weidenfeller, E.W. & Zimny, G.H.: Effects of music upon GSR of depressives and schizophrenics. *Journal of Abnormal Psychology*, 1962, **64**, pp. 307-312.

Weintraub, I.G.: Emotional responses of schizophrenics to selected musical compositions. *Delaware Medical Journal*, 1961, **33**, pp. 186-187.

Weisbrod, J.A.: Shaping a body image through movement therapy. *MEJ*, April 1971, pp. 50-53.

Wells, A.M.: Rhythm activities on wards of senile patients. *Music Therapy*, 1953, pp. 127-132.

Werbner, N.: The practice of music therapy with psychotic children. *JMT*, 1966, **3**, pp. 25-31.

West, B.: A music therapy technique for psychiatric patients. *Quodlibet*, January 1977, p. 16.

Wheeler, B.: The relationship between music therapy and theories of psychotherapy. *Music Therapy*, 1981, **1**, pp. 9-16.

Wheeler, B.L.: A psychotherapeutic classification of music therapy practices: A continuum of procedures. *Music Therapy Perspectives*, 1983, **2**, pp. 8-12.

Wilke, M.: Music therapy at work in the short-term psychiatric setting at Charity Hospital of New Orleans. *Bulletin of the NAMT*, 1960, **2**, pp. 5-6, 10.

Williams, G. & Dorow, L.G.: Changes in complaints and non-complaints of a chronically depressed psychiatric patient as a function of an interrupted music/verbal feedback package. *JMT*, 1983, **20**(3), pp. 143-155.

Wolfe, D.E.: Group music therapy in short-term psychiatric care. In: C.E. Furman (Ed.), *Effectiveness of Music Therapy Procedures: Documentation of Research and Clinical Practice*. Washington, DC: NAMT, 1988, pp. 175-205.

Wolfe, D.E., Burns, S., Stoll, M. & Wichmann, K.: *Analysis of Music Therapy Group Procedures*. Minneapolis, MN: Golden Valley Health Center, 1975.

Wolfgram, B.J.: Music therapy for retarded adults with psychotic overlay: A day treatment approach. *JMT*, 1978, **15**(4), pp. 199-207.

Wortis, R.P.: Music therapy for the mentally ill: The effect of music on emotional activity and the value of music as a resocializing agent. *Journal of General Psychology*, 1960, **62**, pp. 311-318.

Wright, B.: A study in the use of music therapy techniques for behavior modification at St. Thomas Psychiatric Hospital, Ontario. *Journal of the Canadian Association for Music Therapy*, 1976, **4**, pp. 2-4.

Zwerling, I.: The creative arts therapies as "real therapies." *Hospital and Community Psychiatry*, 1979, **30**, pp. 841-844.

SPECIAL EDUCATION

Music Educators Journal = MEJ
Journal of Music Therapy = JMT

Aebischer, D. & Sheridan, W.: For John, music makes a difference. *MEJ*, 1982, **68**(8), p. 29.

Albert, M., Sparks, R. & Helm, N.: Melodic intonation therapy for aphasia. *Archives of Neurology*, 1973, **29**(2), pp. 130-131.

Alford, R.L.: Music and the mentally retarded ethnic minority child. *The Pointer*, 1974, **19**(2), pp. 138-139.

Alley, J.M.: Education for the severely handicapped: The role of music therapy. *JMT*, 1977, **14**(2), pp. 50-59.

Alley, J.M.: Music in the IEP: Therapy/education. *JMT*, 1979, **16**(3), pp. 111-127.

Alley, J.M.: Music therapy. In: Reynolds, C.R. & Gutkin, T.B. (Eds.), *The Handbook of School Psychology*. New York: John Wiley & Sons, 1982, pp. 667-678.

Alvin, J.A.: *Music for the Handicapped Child*. London: Oxford University Press, 1965.

Alvin, J.A. Music therapy for severely subnormal boys. London: British Society for Music Therapy, 1969.

Alvin, J.A.: *Music Therapy for the Autistic Child*. London: Oxford University Press, 1978.

Alvin, J.A.: *Music Therapy*. London: John Clare Books, 1978.

Amir, D. & Schuchman, G.: Auditory training through music with hearing-impaired preschool children. *The Volta Review*, December 1985, pp. 333-343.

Anderson, V.G., Gonzales, A.D. & Nelson, D.L.: Music activities as therapy for children with autism and other pervasive developmental disorders. *JMT*, 1984, **21**(3), pp. 100-116.

Appell, M.J.: Arts for the handicapped: A researchable item. *JMT*, 1980, **17**(2), pp. 75-83.

Atterbury, B.W.: Musical differences in learning-disabled and normal-achieving readers, aged seven, eight, and nine. *Psychology of Music*, 1985, **13**(2), pp. 114-123.

Atterbury, B.W.: Music teachers need your help. *Journal of Learning Disabilities*, 1984,17(2), pp. 75-77.

Austen, M.P.: The effects of music on the learning of random shapes and syllables with institutionalized severely mentally retarded adolescents. *Contributions to Music Education*, 1977, **5**, pp. 54-69.

Bailey, J.Z.: *The Relationships Between the Colwell Music Achievement Tests I and II, the SRA Achievement Series, Intelligence Quotient, and Success in Instrumental Music in the Sixth Grade of the Public School of Prince William County, Virginia*. Unpublished doctoral dissertation, University of Illinois at Urbana-Champaign, 1976.

Banik, S.N. & Mendelson, M.A.: A comprehensive program for multiply handicapped, mentally retarded children. *Journal of Special Educators of the Mentally Retarded*, 1974, **11**(1), pp. 44-49.

Barber, E.: Music therapy with retarded children. *Australian Journal of Mental Retardation*, 1973, **2**(7), pp. 210-213.

Beal, M.R. & Gilbert, J.P.: Music curriculum for the handicapped. *MEJ*, 1982, **68**(8), pp. 52-55.

Beall, L.: The making of a special Oliver! *MEJ*, 1985, **71**(6), pp. 30-32.

Beer, A.S., Bellows, N.L. & Frederick, A.M.D.: Providing for different rates of music learning. *MEJ*, 1982, **68**(8), pp. 40-43.

Bellamy, T. & Sontag, E.: Use of group contingent music to increase assembly line production rates of retarded students in a simulated sheltered workshop. *JMT*, 1973, **10**(3), pp. 125-136.

Benigno, J.: Settlement music school advances music for the handicapped. *MEJ*, 1985, **71**(6), pp. 22-25.

Bennis, J.: The use of music as a therapy in the special education classroom. *JMT*, 1969, **6**, pp. 15-18.

Berel, M., Diller, L. & Orgel, M.: Music as a facilitator for visual motor sequencing tasks in children with cerebral palsy. *Developmental Medicine and Child Neurology*, 1971, **13**, pp. 335-342.

Bevans, J.: The exceptional child and Orff. *MEJ*, 1969, **55**(7), pp. 41-43.

Bibliography of mainstreaming materials. *MEJ*, 1982, **68**(8), pp. 56-57.

Birkenshaw, L.: Teaching music to deaf children. *The Volta Review*, 1965, **67**(5), pp. 352-358, 387.

Birkenshaw, L.: Consider the lowly kazoo. *The Volta Review*, 1975, **77**(7), pp. 440-444.

Birkenshaw, L.: *Music for Fun, Music for Learning*. (3rd Ed.) St. Louis, MO: MMB Music, Inc., 1982.

Bitcon, C.H.: *Alike and Different: The Clinical and Educational Use of Orff-Schulwerk*. (rev. ed.) St. Louis, MO: MMB Music, Inc., 1991.

Bitcon, C. & Ball, T.: Generalized imitation and Orff-Schulwerk. *Mental Retardation*, 1974, **12**(34), pp. 36-39.

Bixler, J.: Operetta production with physically handicapped children. In: *Music Therapy*. Lawrence, KS: Allen Press, 1960, p. 101.
Bixler, J.: Musical aptitude in the educable mentally retarded child. *JMT*, 1968, **5**(2), pp. 41-43.
Blos, J.: Traditional nursery rhymes and games: Language learning for preschool blind children. *New Outlook for the Blind*, 1974, **68**, pp. 268-274.
Bokor, C.R.: A comparison of musical and verbal responses of mentally retarded children. *JMT*, 1976, **13**(2), pp. 101-108.
Bove, C.F. & Flugrath, J.M.: Frequency components of noisemakers for use in pediatric audiological evaluations. *The Volta Review*, 1973, **75**(9), pp. 551-556.
Boxill, E.H.: *Music Therapy for the Developmentally Disabled*. Rockville, MD: Aspen Systems Corporation, 1985.
Breen, J. and Cratty, B.: *Educational Games for Physically Handicapped Children*. Denver, CO: Love Publishing, 1982.
Brick, R.M.: Eurythmics: One aspect of audition. *The Volta Review*, 1973, **75**, pp. 155-160.
Briller, S. & Morrison, B.: Teaching rock and roll dancing to totally blind teenagers. *The New Outlook for the Blind*, 1971, **65**(4), pp. 129-131.
Brooks, B.H., Huck, A.M. & Jellison, J.A.: Structuring small groups and music reinforcement to facilitate positive interactions and acceptance of severely handicapped students in the regular music classroom. *Journal of Research in Music Education*, 1984, **32**(4), pp. 243-264.
Bruner, O.: Music to aid the handicapped child. *Music Therapy*, 1951, pp. 1-46.
Cameron, R.: The uses of music to enhance the education of the mentally retarded. *Mental Retardation*, 1970, **8**, pp. 32-34.
Campbell, D.: *Introduction to the Musical Brain*. St. Louis, MO: MMB Music, Inc., 1986.
Campbell, D.: One out of twenty: The LD. *MEJ*, 1972, **58**(4), pp. 38-39.
Careers in Music Issue. *MEJ*, 1982, **69**(2), entire issue. (Gives overview and information about possible careers in music including music education and music therapy.)
Cartwright, J. & Huckaby, G.: Intensive preschool language program. *JMT*, 1972, **9**, p. 137.
Case, M.: *Recreation for Blind Adults*. Springfield, IL: Charles C. Thomas, 1966.
Cassity, M.D.: Nontraditional guitar techniques for the educable and trainable mentally retarded residents in music therapy activities. *JMT*, 1977, **14**(1), pp. 39-42.
Cassity, M.D.: Social development of TMR's involved in performing and nonperforming groups. *JMT*, 1978, **15**(2), pp. 100-105.
Cassity, M.D.: The influence of a socially valued skill on peer acceptance in a music therapy group. *JMT*, 1981, **18**(3), pp. 148-154.
Chadwick, D.R.: Speech disorders and music. *Instrumentalist*, 1976, **31**(1), pp. 28-30.
Chadwick, D.R. & Clark, C.A.: Adapting music instruments for the physically handicapped. *MEJ*, 1980, **67**(3), pp. 56-59.
Clark, C. & Chadwick, D.: *Clinically Adapted Instruments for the Multiply Handicapped: A Sourcebook*. (rev. ed.): St. Louis, MO: MMB Music, Inc., 1980.
Clegg, J.C.: *The Effect of Non-Contingent and Contingent Music on Work Production Rate of Mentally Retarded Adults in a Work Activity Center*. Unpublished master's thesis, Florida State University. 1982.
Cleland, C.C. & Swartz, J.D.: The blind retardate – three program suggestions. *Training School Bulletin*, 1970, **67**(3), pp. 172-177.
Coates, P.: "Is it functional?" A question for music therapists who work with the institutionalized mentally retarded. *JMT*, 1987, **24**(3), pp. 170-175.
Codding, P.: Music in the education/rehabilitation of visually disabled and multi-handicapped persons: A review of literature from 1946 - 1987. In: C.E. Furman (Ed.), *Effectiveness of Music Therapy Procedures: Documentation of Research and Clinical Practice*. Washington, DC: NAMT, 1988, pp. 107-134.
Cole, F.: *Music for Children with Special Needs*. North Hollywood, CA: Bowar Records, Inc., 1965
Cohen, G., Averbach, J. & Katz, E.: Music therapy assessment of the developmentally disabled client. *JMT*, 1978, **15**(2), pp. 88-99.
Cohen, G., & Gericke, L.: Music therapy assessment: Requisite for determining patient objectives. *JMT*, 1972, **9**, pp. 161-189.
Coleman, J.L., *et al.*: *Music for Exceptional Children*. Evanston, IL: Summy-Birchard Co., 1964.
Cook, M. & Freethy, M.: The use of music as a positive reinforcer to eliminate complaining behavior. *JMT*, 1973, **10**(4), pp. 213-216.
Cooke, R.M.: The use of music in play therapy. *JMT*, 1969, **6**(3), p. 66.
Cortazzi, D.: The bottom of the barrel. *Journal of Mental Subnormality*, 1969, **15**(1), p. 3.

Cotter, V.W.: Effects of music on performance of manual tasks with retarded adolescent females. *American Journal of Mental Deficiency*, 1971, **78**(2), pp. 242-248.

Cotter V.W. & Toombs, S.: A procedure for determining the music preferences of mental retardates. *JMT*, 1966, **3**(2), pp. 57-64.

Couch, K.: *The Effect of the Art + Reading, Writing, Arithmetic + Music + Science Project (AR³-MS) on the Acquisition of Reading Skills*. Unpublished master's thesis, Florida State University, 1984.

County School Board of Fairfax County. *Project Beacon: Perceptual Motor Activities Handbook Music Supplement*. Fairfax, VA: County School Board, 1978.

Cratty, B.: *Developmental Games for Physically Handicapped Children*. Palo Alto, CA: Peer Publications, 1969.

Cripe, F.F.: Rock music as therapy for children with attention deficit disorder: An exploratory study. *JMT*, 1986, **23**(1), pp. 30-37.

Crocker, D.B.: Music therapy for the blind. *Music Therapy*, 1956, pp. 175-196.

Danhauer, J.L., Johnson, C. & Asp, C.W.: Hearing-impaired children's performance on the Edgerton and Danhauer nonsense syllable test. *The Journal of Auditory Research*, 1984, **24**, pp. 231-238.

Darrow, A.A.: The beat reproduction responses of subjects with normal and impaired hearing: An empirical comparison. *JMT*, 1979, **16**, pp. 91-98.

Darrow, A.A.: A comparison of rhythmic responsiveness in normal and hearing impaired children and an investigation of the relationship of rhythmic responsiveness to the suprasegmental aspects of speech perception. *JMT*, 1984, **2**(2), pp. 48-66.

Darrow, A.A.: Music for the deaf. *MEJ*, February 1985, **71**(6), pp. 33-35.

Darrow, A.A.: An investigative study: The effect of hearing impairment on musical aptitude. *JMT*, 1987, **24**(2), pp. 88-96.

Darrow, A.A. & Gfeller, K.: Music therapy with hearing-impaired children. In: C.E. Furman (Ed.), *Effectiveness of Music Therapy Procedures: Documentation of Research and Clinical Practice*. Washington, DC: NAMT, 1988, pp. 137-172.

Decuir, A.A.: Vocal responses of mentally retarded subjects of four musical instruments. *JMT*, 1975, **12**(1), pp. 40-43.

Denenholz, B.: The use of music with mentally retarded children. In: M. Bing (Ed.), *Annual Book of Proceedings NAMT, Inc., 1953*. Lawrence, KS: Allen Press, p. 55.

DePeters, J., Gordon, L. & Wertman, A.: *The Magic of Music*. Buffalo, NY: Potentials Development, Inc., 1981.

Dervan, N.: Building Orff ensemble skills with mentally handicapped adolescents. *MEJ*, 1982, **68**(8), pp. 35-36.

Deutsch, M. & Parks, A.: The use of contingent music to increase appropriate conversational speech. *Mental Retardation*, 1978, **16**(1), pp. 33-36.

Diephouse, D.A.: Music therapy in a child psychiatry clinic school. *American Music Teacher*, 1968, **17**(3), pp. 27-28, pp. 39-40.

Dileo, C.L.: The use of a token economy program with mentally retarded persons in a music therapy setting. *JMT*, 1975, **12**(3), pp. 155-160.

Dileo, C.L.: The relationship of diagnostic and social factors to the singing ranges of institutionalized mentally retarded persons. *JMT*, 1976, **13**(1), pp. 16-28.

Dobbs, J.P.B.: *The Slow Learner and Music*. New York: Oxford University Press, 1966.

Dorow, L.G.: Conditioning music and approval as new reinforcers for imitative behavior with the severely retarded. *JMT*, 1975, **12**(1), pp. 30-39.

Dorow, L.G.: Televised music lessons as educational reinforcement for correct mathematical responses with the educable mentally retarded. *JMT*, 1976, **13**(2), pp. 77-86.

Dorow, L.G. & Horton, J.: Effect of the proximity of auditory stimuli and sung versus spoken stimuli on activity levels of severely/profoundly mentally retarded females. *JMT*, 1982, **19**(2), pp. 114-124

Douglass, D.: *Accent on Rhythm: Music Activities for the Aged*. (3rd Ed.) St. Louis, MO: MMB Music, Inc., 1985.

Dryer, J. & Dix, J.: Reaching the blind child through music therapy. *Journal of Emotional Education*, 1968, **8**(4), pp. 202-211.

Dunton, M.J.: Handicapped children respond to music therapy. *International Musician*, 1969, **8**(4), p. 2.

Dykman, R.A.: In step with PL 94-142. *MEJ*, 1979, **65**(5), pp. 58-63.

Eagle, C.T. & Lathom, W.: Music for the severely handicapped. *MEJ*, 1982, **68**(8), pp. 30-31.

Eddy, G.: No fingers to play a horn. *MEJ*, 1972, **58**(4), pp. 61-62.

Edwards, E.M.: *Music Education for the Deaf*. South Waterford, ME: Merriam-Eddy Co., 1974.

Eisenstein, S.R.: Effect of contingent guitar lessons on reading behavior. *JMT*, 1974, **11**, pp, 138-146.

Eisenstein, S.R.: A successive approximation procedure for learning music symbol names. *JMT*, 1976, **13**(4), pp. 173-179.

Epley, C.: In a soundless world of music enjoyment. *MEJ*, 1972, **58**(4), p. 55.

Fahey, J. & Birkenshaw, L.: Bypassing the ear: The perception of music by feeling and touch. *MEJ*, 1972, **58**(4), pp. 44-49, 127-128.

Falb, M.E.: *The Use of Operant Procedures to Condition Vasoconstriction in Profoundly Mentally Retarded (PMR) Infants.* Unpublished master's thesis, Florida State University, 1982.

Feil, N.: *Validation/Fantasy/Therapy.* Cleveland, OH: Edward Feil Productions, 1982.

Fellendorf, G.: The verbotonal method. *The Volta Review*, 1969, **71**, pp. 213-224.

Fisher, G.L.: *The Effect of Instrumental Music Instruction on Fine Motor Coordination and Other Variables of Mentally Retarded Adolescents.* Unpublished master's thesis, Florida State University, 1980.

Flodmark, A.: Augmented auditory feedback as an aid in gait training of the cerebral-palsied child. *Developmental Medicine & Child Neurology*, 1986, **28**, pp. 147-155.

Flowers, Sister E.: Musical sound perception in normal children and children with Down's syndrome. *JMT*, 1984, **21**(3), pp. 146-154.

Folio, M.R.: *Physical Education Programming for Exceptional Learners.* Gaithersburg, MD: Aspen Systems, 1986.

Force, B.: The effects of mainstreaming on the learning of nonretarded children in an elementary music classroom. *JMT*, 1983, **20**(1), pp. 2-13.

Ford, S.C.: Music therapy for cerebral palsied children. *Music Therapy Perspectives*, 1984, **1**(3), pp. 8-13.

Forsythe, J.L. & Jellison, J.A.: It's the law. *MEJ*, 1977, **65**(3),pp. 30-35.

Foster, B.: *Training Songs for Special People.* Boulder, CO: Myklas Music Press, 1979.

Frances, R., Thermitte, F.S. & Verdy, M.F.: Music deficiency among aphasics. *International Review of Applied Psychology*, 1973, **22**(2), pp. 117-136.

Furman, C., & Furman A.: Music therapy research with mental retardation. In: C.E. Furman (Ed.), *Effectiveness of Music Therapy Procedures: Documentation of Research and Clinical Practice.* Washington, DC: NAMT, 1988, pp. 285-299.

Furman, C. & Steele, A.: Teaching the special student: A survey of independent music teachers with implications for music therapists. *JMT*, 1982, **19**(2), p. 66-73.

Gallagher, P.: *Educational Games for Visually Handicapped Children.* Denver, CO: Love Publishing Co., 1982.

Galloway, H.F.: A comprehensive bibliography of music referential to communicative development, processing, disorders, and remediation. *JMT*, 1975, **12**, pp. 164-196.

Galloway, H.F.: Stuttering and the myth of therapeutic singing. *JMT*, 1974, **11**(4), p. 202.

Galloway, H.F. & Bean, M.F.: Effects of action songs on the development of body image and body part identification in hearing-impaired preschool children. *JMT*, 1974, **11**(2), pp. 125-134.

Galloway, H.F. & Berry, A.: A survey of communicative disorders in college vocal performance and pedagogy majors. *JMT*, 1981, **18**(1), pp. 25-40.

Gardiner, B.L.: *Improving the Peer Acceptance of Educable Mentally Handicapped Students in a Mainstreamed Setting: Aerobics Music Therapy Program in a Physical Education Class.* Unpublished master's thesis, Florida State University, 1984.

Gardiner, E.C.: *The Effect of Music on Retention in a Paired-Associate Task with EMR Children.* Unpublished master's thesis, Florida State University, 1978.

Gaston, E.T. (Ed.): *Music in Therapy.* New York: Macmillan, 1968.

Gfeller, K.: Music mnemonics as an aid to retention with normal and learning disabled students. *JMT*, 1983, **20**(4), pp. 179-189.

Gfeller, K.: Prominent theories in learning disabilities and implications for music therapy methodology. *Music Therapy Perspectives*, 1984, **2**(1), pp. 9-13.

Giacobbe, G.A.: Rhythm builds order in brain-damaged children. *MEJ*, 1972, **58**(4), pp. 40-43.

Giacobbe, G. A. & Graham, R.M.: The response of aggressive emotionally disturbed and normal boys to selected musical stimuli. JMT, 1978, **15**(3), pp. 118-135.

Gibbons, A.C.: Rhythm responses in emotionally disturbed children with differing needs for external structure. *Music Therapy*, 1983, **3**(1), pp. 94-102.

Gilbert, J.P.: Mainstreaming in your classroom: What to expect. *MEJ*, 1977, **63**(6), pp. 64-68.

Gilbert, J.P.: A comparison of the motor music skills of nonhandicapped and learning disabled children. *Journal of Research in Music Education*, 1983, **31**(2), pp. 147-155.

Gilbert, J., Gampel, D. & Budoff, M.: Classroom behavior of retarded children before and after integration into regular classes. *Journal of Special Education*, 1975, **9**, pp. 307-315.

Gilliland, E.: Prescriptions set to music – musical instruments in orthopedic therapy. *Exceptional Children*, 1957, **18**, p. 68.

Giovanni, S.: Music as an aid in teaching the deaf. *Music Therapy Proceedings*, NAMT, 1959, pp. 88-90.

Gollnitz, G.: Fundamentals of rhythmic-psychomotor music therapy. *Acta Paedopsychiatrica*, 1975, **41**(4-5), pp. 130-134.

Goodnow, C.C.: The use of dance in therapy with retarded children. *JMT*, 1968, **5**(4), pp. 98-102.

Goodenough, F. & Goodenough, D.: The importance of music in the life of a visually handicapped child. *Education of Visually Handicapped*, 1970, **2**(1), pp. 28-32.

Goolsby, T.M., Frary, R.B. & Rogers, M.M.: Observational techniques in determination of the effects of background music upon verbalizations of disadvantaged kindergarten children. *JMT*, 1974, **11**(1), pp. 21-32.

Gordon, E.: *Music Aptitude Profile*. Boston: Houghton Mifflin, 1965.

Gordon, E.: The use of the musical aptitude profile with exceptional children. *JMT*, 1968, **5**(2), pp. 38-40.

Graham, R.M.: Seven million plus need special attention. Who are they? *MEJ*, 1972, **58**(4), pp. 22-25, 134.

Graham, R.M. (Ed.): *Music for the Exceptional Child*. Reston, VA: MENC, 1975.

Graham, R.M. & Beer, A.: *Teaching Music to the Exceptional Child*. Englewood Cliffs, NJ: Prentice-Hall, 1980.

Grant, R.E. & LeCroy, S.: Effects of sensory mode input on the performance of rhythmic perception tasks by mentally retarded subjects. *JMT*, 1986, **23**(1), pp. 2-9.

Grant, R.E. & Share, M.R.: Relationship of pitch discrimination skills and vocal ranges of mentally retarded subjects. *JMT*, 1985, **22**(2), pp. 99-103.

Grayson, J.: A playground of musical sculpture. *MEJ*, 1972, **58**(4), pp. 51-54.

Greaves, E.R. & Anderson, L.P.: *101 Activities for Exceptional Children*. Palo Alto, CA: Peek Publications, 1981.

Greene, B.: Opening locked doors with music. *Children's House*, 1974, **7**(4), pp. 6-10.

Greenwald, M.A.: The effectiveness of distorted music versus interrupted music to decrease self-stimulatory behaviors in profoundly retarded adolescents. *JMT*, 1978, **15**(2), pp. 58-66.

Greer, R.D., Randall, A. & Timberlake, C.: The discriminate use of music listening as a contingency for improvement in vocal pitch acuity and attending behavior. *Council for Research in Music Education*, 1971, **26**, pp. 10-18.

Griffin, J.E.: Administration of a music therapy department in an institution for the mentally retarded – with suggested activities. *JMT*, 1966, **3**(3), pp. 99-105.

Gregoire, M.A.: Music as a prior condition to task performance. *JMT*, 1984, **21**(3), pp. 133-145.

Grossman, S.: An investigation of Crocker's music projective techniques for emotionally disturbed children. *JMT*, 1978, **15**(4), pp. 179-184.

Guenzler, S.L.: *Observation of Interpersonal Relationships Between Handicapped and Normal Children and Their Teacher in Music*. Unpublished master's thesis, Florida State University, 1980.

Gunning, S.V. & Homes, T.H.: Dance therapy with psychotic children. *Archives of General Psychiatry*, 1973, **28**, p. 707.

Hair, H.I.: A comparison of verbal descriptions used by TMR students and music therapists. *JMT*, 1983, **20**(2), pp. 59-68.

Hall, J.C.: The effect of background music on the reading comprehension of 278 eighth and ninth grade students. *Journal of Educational Research*, 1952, **45**, pp. 451-458.

Halliday, G.W. & Evans, J.H.: Somatosensory enrichment of a deaf, blind, retarded adolescent through vibration. *Perceptual and Motor Skills*, 1974, **38**, p. 880.

Hanser, S.B.: Group-contingent music listening with emotionally disturbed boys. *JMT*, Winter 1974, **11**(4), pp. 220-225.

Harbert, W.: *Opening Doors Through Music*. Springfield, IL: Charles C. Thomas, 1974.

Hardesty, K.: *Silver Burdett Music for Special Education*. Morristown, NJ: Silver Burdett Co., 1979.

Hardesty, K.W.: *Music for Special Education*. St. Louis, MO: MMB Music, Inc., 1982.

Harding, C. & Ballard, K.: The effectiveness of music as a stimulus and as a contingent reward in promoting the spontaneous speech of three physically handicapped preschoolers. *JMT*, 1982, **19**(2), pp. 88-101.

Haring, N. & Bricker, D.: *Teaching the Severely Handicapped*. Seattle, WA: American Association for the Education of the Severely/Profoundly Handicapped, 1978.

Harris, P.: *Learning, Poco-a-Poco*. Hanford, CA: Learning, Poco-a-Poco Company, 1982.

Harrison, W., Lacrone, H., Temerlin, M.K. & Trousdale, W.W.: The effect of music and exercise upon the self-help skills of non-verbal retardates. *American Journal of Mental Deficiencies*, 1966, 71, pp. 279-282.

Hastings, P. & Hayes, B.: *Encouraging Language Development*. London, UK: Croom Helm, 1981.

Hauck, L.P. & Martin, P.L.: Music as a reinforcer in patient-controlled duration of time-out. *JMT*, 1970, 7(2), pp. 43-53.

Henderson, L.M.: *A Music Therapy Assessment for the Mentally Retarded: Field Testing the Instrument*. Unpublished master's thesis, Florida State University, 1977.

Henderson, S.M.: Effects of a music therapy program upon awareness of mood in music, group cohesion, and self-esteem among hospitalized adolescent patients. *JMT*, 1983, 20(1), pp. 14-20.

Henson, F.O., Parks, A.L. & Cotter, V.: A technique for analyzing rhythmic drum responses. *Behavioral Engineering*, 1977, 4, pp. 29-32.

Herlein, D.: Music reading of the sightless-Braille notation. *MEJ*, 1975, 62(1), pp. 42-45.

Herron, C.J.: Some effects of instrumental music training on cerebral palsied children. *JMT*, 1970, 7, p. 55.

Hoem, J.C.: Don't dump the students who "can't do." *MEJ*, 1972, 58(4), pp. 29-30.

Hollander, F.M. & Juhrs, P.D.: Orff-Schulwerk, an effective treatment tool with autistic children. *JMT*, 1974, 11(1), pp. 1-12.

Holloway, M.S.: A comparison of passive and active music reinforcement to increase preacademic and motor skills in severely retarded children and adolescents. *JMT*, 1980, 17(2), pp. 58-69.

Hoper, C.J., Kutzleb, U., Stobbe, A. & Weber, B.: *Awareness Games: Personal Growth Through Group Interaction*. New York: St. Martin's Press, 1975.

Hoshizaki, M.K.: *Teaching Mentally Retarded Children Through Music*. Springfield, IL: Charles, C. Thomas, 1983.

Houchins, R.: Pitch discrimination in learning-impaired children. *The Volta Review*, 1971, 64, p. 424.

Hummel, C.J.M.: The value of music in teaching deaf students. *The Volta Review*, 1971, 73(4), pp. 224-228.

Humphrey, T.: The effect of music ear training upon the auditory discrimination abilities of trainable mentally retarded adolescents. *JMT*, 1980, 17(2), pp. 70-74.

Hurwitz, I., Wolff, P., Bortnick, B. & Kokas, K.: Nonmusical effects of the Kodaly music curriculum in primary grade children. *Journal of Learning Disabilities*, 1975, 8(3), pp. 167-174.

Implementation of Part B of the Education of the Handicapped Act. *Federal Register*, 42474-42518, August 23, 1977.

Irwin, C.E.: *The Use of Music in a Speech and Language Development Program with Mentally Retarded Children with Emphasis on the Down's Syndrome Child*. Unpublished thesis, Florida State University, 1971.

Isern, B.: Summary, conclusion, and implications: The influence of music upon the memory of mentally retarded children. In: E.H. Schneider (Ed.), *Annual Book of Proceedings NAMT, 1960*. Lawrence, KS: The Allen Press, 1961.

James, M., Weaver, A., Clemens, P. & Plaster, G.: Influence of paired auditory and vestibular stimulation on levels of motor skill development in a mentally retarded population. JMT, 1985, 22(1), pp. 22-34.

James, M.R.: Neurophysical treatment of cerebral palsy: A case study. *Music Therapy Perspectives*, 1986, 3, pp. 5-8.

Janiak, W.: *Songs for Music Therapy*. Long Branch, NJ: Kimbo Educational, 1978.

Jellison, J.A.: Music instructional programs for the severely handicapped. In: E. Sontag (Ed.), *Educational Programming for the Severely/Profoundly Handicapped*. Reston, VA: The Council for Exceptional Children, 1977.

Jellison, J.A.: The music therapist in the educational setting: Developing and implementing curriculum for the handicapped. *JMT*, 1979, 16(3), pp. 128-137.

Jellison, J.A.: Structuring small groups and music reinforcement to facilitate positive interactions and acceptance of severely handicapped students in the regular music classroom. *Journal of Research in Music Education*, 1984, 32(4), pp. 243-364.

Jellison, J.A.: A content analysis of music research with handicapped children (1975-1986): Application in special education. In: C.E. Furman (Ed.), *Effectiveness of Music Therapy Procedures: Documentation of Research and Clinical Practice*. Washington, DC: NAMT, 1988, pp. 223-281.

Johnson, J.M. & Zinner, C.C.: Stimulus fading and schedule learning in generalizing and maintaining behaviors. *JMT*, 1974, 11(2), pp. 84-96.

Jones, M.E.: *A Comparison of Play Therapy Versus Play/Music Therapy with Three Emotionally Disturbed Children.* Unpublished master's thesis, Florida State University, 1982.

Jorgenson, H.: Effects of contingent preferred music in reducing two stereotyped behaviors of a profoundly retarded child. *JMT*, 1971, **8**(4), pp. 139-145.

Jorgenson, H.: The use of a contingent music activity to modify behaviors which interfere with learning. *JMT*, 1974, **11**(1), pp. 41-46.

Jorgenson, H. & Parnell, M.K.: Modifying social behaviors of mentally retarded children in music activities. *JMT*, 1970, **7**(3), pp. 83-87.

Josepha, S.M.: Music therapy with certain physically handicapped children. In: *Music Therapy.* Lawrence, KS: Allen Press, 1969, p. 90.

Kaplan, M.: Music therapy in the speech program. *Exceptional Children*, 1955, **20**, p. 112.

Karras, B.: *Down Memory Lane: Topics and Ideas for Reminiscence Groups.* Wheaton, MD: Circle Press, 1985.

Kaslow, F.W.: Movement, music, and art therapy techniques adapted for special education. In: R. Hyatt & N. Rolnick (Eds.), *Teaching the Mentally Handicapped Child.* New York: Behavior Publications, 1974.

Kaufman, F.M. & Sheckart, G.R.: The effects of tempo variation and white noise on the general activity level of profoundly retarded adults. *JMT*, 1985, **22**(4), pp. 207-217.

Keith, R.W.: *Central Auditory and Language Disorders in Children.* San Diego, CA: College-Hill Press, 1981.

Kennedy, R.: *Bach to Rock.* New Orleans, LA: Rosemary Corp., 1983 (4th ed. 1987).

Kerr, N., Myerson, L. & Michael, J.: A procedure for shaping vocalizations in a mute child. In: Ullman & Krasner (Eds.), *Case Studies in Behavior Modification.* New York: Holt, Rinehart, and Winston, Inc., 1965, pp. 366-370.

Kivland, M.J.: The use of music to increase self-esteem in a conduct disordered adolescent. *JMT*, 1986, **23**(1), pp. 25-29.

Klinger, H. & Peter, D.: Techniques in group singing for aphasics. In: E.H. Schneider (Ed.), *Music Therapy.* Lawrence, KS: Allen Press, 1963, pp. 108-112.

Knolle, L.: Sioux City's special brass band: An instrumental program for the mentally retarded. *MEJ*, 1973, **60**(2), pp. 47-48.

Korduba, O.: Duplicated rhythmic patterns between deaf and normal hearing children. *JMT*, 1975, **12**(3), pp. 136-146.

Kral, C.: Musical instruments for upper-limb amputees. *Inter-Clinic Information Bulletin*, 1972, **12**(3), pp. 13-26.

Kramer, S.A.: The effects of music as a cue in maintaining handwashing in preschool children. *JMT*, 1978, **15**(3), pp. 136-144.

Krauss, T. & Galloway, H.: Melodic intonation therapy with language delayed apraxic children. *JMT*, 1982, **19**(2), pp. 102-113.

Kratz, L.E.: *Movement Without Sight.* Palo Alto, CA: Peek Publications, 1973.

Krout, R.: *Teaching Basic Guitar Skills to Special Learners.* St. Louis, MO: MMB Music, Inc., 1983.

Krout, R.E.: Use of a group token contingency with school-aged special education students to improve a music listening skill. *Music Therapy Perspectives*, 1986, **3**, pp. 13-16.

Kuper, E.C.: Speech training through musical ear-training for pitch deficient children having articulatory defects. *Journal of Auditory Research*, 1972, **12**(2), pp. 168-172.

Laffley, N.A.: *Music Therapy Intervention in the Deinstitutionalization and Community Integration of the Mentally Retarded.* Unpublished master's thesis, Florida State University, 1984.

Lam, R.C. & Wang, C.: Integrating blind and sighted through music. *MEJ*, 1982, **68**(8), pp. 44-45.

Larson, B.A.: A comparison of singing ranges of mentally retarded and normal children with published songbooks used in singing activities. *JMT*, 1977, **14**(3), pp. 139-143.

Larson, B.A.: Auditory and visual rhythmic pattern recognition by emotionally disturbed and normal adolescents. *JMT*, 1981, **18**(3), pp. 128-136.

Lathom, W.: The effect of certain action songs on body concept. In: E.H. Schneider (Ed.), *Annual Book of Proceedings NAMT, 1962.* Lawrence, KS: The Allen Press, 1963, pp. 115-121.

Lathom, W.: Music therapy as a means of changing the adaptive behavior level of retarded children. *JMT*, 1964, **1**(4), p. 132.

Lathom, W.: Application of Kodaly concepts in music therapy. *JMT*, 1974, **11**, pp. 13-20.

Lathom, W.B.: & Eagle, C.T. (Eds.): *Music Therapy for Handicapped Children: Project Monograph Series.* NAMT, 1982.

Lehr, J.K.: Teaching training programs for exceptional classes. *MEJ*, 1982, **68**(8), pp. 46-48.

Lehr, J.K.: Investigation of music in the education of mentally and physically handicapped children in the United Kingdom with particular reference to the course Music for Slow Learners at Dartington College of Arts. *Contributions to Music Education*, 1983, **9**, pp. 60-69.

Levin, H.D. & Levin, G.M.: Instrumental music: A great ally in promoting self image. *MEJ*, 1972, **58**(4), pp. 31-34.

Levin, H., & Levin, G.: *Learning Songs*. Bryn Mawr, PA: Theodore Presser, 1981.

Levin, H. & Levin, G.: *Garden of Bell Flowers*. Bryn Mawr, PA: Theodore Presser, 1977.

Levin, G., Levin, H. & Safer, N.: *Learning Through Songs*. New York: Teaching Resources, New York Times, Co., 1971.

Levin, G., Levin, H. & Safer, N.: *Learning Through Music*. New York: Teaching Resources, New York Times, Co., 1975.

Levine, S.J.: The recorded aid for braille music. *JMT*, 1968, **5**(1), pp. 1-2.

Levine, S.J.: A recorded aid for braille music. Paper No. 3, The Prospectus Series. Michigan State University, East Lansing. Regional Instructional Materials Center for Handicapped Children and Youth. Washington, DC: Bureau of Education for the Handicapped, 1968.

Levinson, S. & Bruscia, K.: Putting blind students in touch with music. *MEJ*, October 1985, p. 49.

Lewis, M.F.: A handbell choir for blind students. *The New Outlook for the Blind*, 1974, **68**(7), pp. 297-299.

Liebman, J. & Liebman, A.: On stage everybody. *MEJ*, 1973, **60**(2), pp. 45-46.

Liehmohn, W.: Rhythm and motor ability in developmentally disabled boys. *American Corrective Therapy Journal*, 1976, **30**, pp. 12-14.

Lienhard, M.E.: Factors relevant to the rhythmic perception of a group of mentally retarded children. *JMT*, 1976, **13**(2), pp. 58-65.

Lipman, M.H.: Blinded at 63, I can still learn. *MEJ*, 1972, **58**(8), p. 60.

Loeb, R. & Sarigiani, P.: The impact of hearing impairment on self-perceptions of children. *The Volta Review*, February-March, 1986, pp. 89-99.

Lunt, I.: Rhythm and the slow learner. *Special Education*, 1973, **62**(4), pp. 21-23.

Madsen, C.K.: *Music Therapy: A Behavioral Guide for the Mentally Retarded*. Lawrence, KS: NAMT, Inc., 1981.

Madsen, C.K. & Alley, J.M.: The effect of reinforcement on attentiveness: A comparison of behaviorally trained music therapists and other professionals with implications for competency-based academic preparation. *JMT*, 1979, **16**(2), pp. 70-82.

Madsen, C.K., Cotter, V.W. & Madsen, C.H. Jr.: A behavioral approach to music therapy. *JMT*, 1968, **5**(3), pp. 69-71.

Madsen, C.K., Dorow, L.G., Moore R.S. & Womble, J.U.: The effect of music via television as reinforcement for correct mathematics. *Journal of Research in Music Education*, 1976, **24**(2), pp. 51-59.

Madsen, C.K. & Forsythe, J.L.: Effect of contingent music listening on increases of mathematical responses. In: C.K. Madsen, R.D. Greer & C.H. Madsen, Jr. (Eds.), *Research in Music Behavior in the Classroom*. New York: Columbia University, Teachers College Press, 1975.

Madsen, C.K. & Geringer, J.M.: Choice of televised music lessons versus free play in relationship to academic improvement. *JMT*, 1976, **13**(4), pp. 154-162.

Madsen, C.K., Madsen, C.H., Jr. & Greer, R.D. (Eds.): *Research in Music Behavior in the Classroom*. New York: Columbia University, Teachers College Press, 1975.

Madsen, C.K. & Kuhn, T.L.: *Contemporary Music Education*. Arlington Heights, Il: AHM, 1978.

Madsen, C.K. & Madsen, C.H., Jr.: Music as a behavior modification technique with a juvenile delinquent. *JMT*, 1968, **5**, pp. 72-76.

Madsen, C.K. & Madsen, C.H., Jr.: *Teaching/Discipline: A Positive Approach for Educational Development*, 3rd ed. Boston: Allyn & Bacon, Inc., 1980.

Madsen, C.K. & Madsen, C.H., Jr. & Michel, D.: The use of music stimuli in teaching language discrimination. In: C.K. Madsen, R.D. Greer & C.H. Madsen, Jr. (Eds.), *Research in Music Behavior in the Classroom*. New York: Columbia University, Teachers College Press, 1975.

Madsen, C.K., Moore, R.S., Wagner, M.J. & Yarbrough, C.A.: Comparison of music as reinforcement for correct mathematical responses versus music as reinforcement for attentiveness. *JMT*, 1975, **12**, pp. 84-95.

Mahlberg, M.: Music therapy in the treatment of an autistic child. *JMT*, 1973, **10**(4), pp. 189-193.

Marsh, J. & Fitch, J.: The effect of singing on the speech articulation of Negro disadvantaged children. *JMT*, 1970, **7**, p. 88.

Matteson, C.A.: Finding the self in space: More than one handicap doesn't make less than one child. *MEJ*, 1972, **58**(4), pp. 63-65; 135.

McCann, B.J.: Assume every child will succeed. *MEJ*, 1985, **71**(6), pp. 18-21.

McCarty, B.C., McElfresh, C.T., Rice, S.V. & Wilson, S.J.: The effect of contingent background music on inappropriate bus behavior. *JMT*, 1978, **15**(3), pp. 150-156.

McCarthy, H.: Use of the Draw-a-Person test to evaluate a dance therapy program. *JMT*, 1973, **10**(3), pp. 141-155.

McClelland, E.: Music for the trainable mentally retarded. *Deficiente Mentale: Mental Retardation*, 1970, **20**(1), pp. 18-20.

McCollom, M.A.: Piano-tuning: A new look at an old skill. *The New Outlook for the Blind*, 1969, **63**(8), p. 152.

McCoy, M.: In the mainstream: Selected music activities. *MEJ*, 1982, **68**(8), p. 51.

McRae, S.W.: The Orff connection. . . Reaching the special child. *MEJ*, 1982, **68**(8), pp. 32-34.

Merrill, T.: *Activities with the Aged and Infirmed: A Handbook for the Untrained Worker.* Springfield, IL: Charles C. Thomas, 1976.

Metzler, R.K.: Music therapy at the Behavioral Learning Center, St. Paul schools. *JMT*, 1973, **10**(4), pp. 177-183.

Metzler, R.K.: The use of music as a reinforcer to increase imitative behavior in severely and profoundly retarded female residents. *JMT*, 1974, **11**(2), pp. 97-110.

Michel, D.E.: Self-esteem and academic achievement in black junior high school students: Effects of automated guitar instruction. *Council for Research in Music Education*, 1971, **24**, pp. 15-23.

Michel, D.E.: *Music Therapy: An Introduction to Therapy and Special Education Through Music.* Springfield, IL: Charles C. Thomas, 1976.

Michel, D.E., *et al.*: Music therapy and remedial reading: Six studies testing specialized hemispheric processing. *JMT*, 1982, **19**(4), pp. 219-229.

Michel, D.E. & Martin, D.: Music and self-esteem research with disadvantaged problem boys in an elementary school. *JMT*, 1970, **7**(4), pp. 124-127.

Michel, D.E. & May, N.H.: The development of music therapy procedures with speech and language disorders. *JMT*, 1974, **11**(2), pp. 74-80.

Miller, D.M.: Effects of music listening contingencies on arithmetic performance and music preference of EMR children. *American Journal of Mental Deficiency*, 1977, **8**, pp. 371-378.

Miller, D.M., Dorow, L.G. & Greer, R.D.: The contingent use of music and art in improving arithmetic scores. *JMT*, 1974, **11**, pp. 57-64.

Mills, S.R.: Band for the trainable child. *Education and Training of the Mentally Retarded*, 1975, **10**(4), pp. 268-270.

Moog, H.: On the perception of rhythmic forms by physically handicapped children and those of low intelligence in comparison with non-handicapped children. *Council for Research in Music Education Bulletin*, 1979, **59**, pp. 73-78.

Mooney, M.K.: Blind children need training, not sympathy. *MEJ*, 1972, **58**(4), pp. 56-60.

Moore, R. & Mathenius, L.: The effects of modeling, reinforcement, and tempo on imitative rhythmic responses of moderately retarded adolescents. *JMT*, 1987, **24**(3), pp. 160-169.

Murphy, J. & Slorach, N.: The language development of pre-preschool hearing children of deaf parents. *British Journal of Disorders of Communication*, 1983, **18**(2), pp. 118-126.

Munro, S.: *Music Therapy in Palliative/Hospice Care.* St. Louis, MO: MMB Music, Inc., 1986.

Music and the Physically Handicapped: Report of the Joint Study Conference. London, England, 1970. National Council of Special Service, London England; Disabled Living Foundation.

Music in Special Education. Reston, VA: Music Educators National Conference, 1972. Originally, *MEJ*, 1972, **59**(8).

Music in Special Education. MEJ, 1982, **68**(8), entire issue.

Musselwhite, C.R. & St. Louis, K.W.: *Communication Programming for the Severely Handicapped.* San Diego, CA: College Hill Press, 1982.

Myers, E.G.: The effect of music on retention in a paired-associate task with EMR children. *JMT*, 1979, **16**(4), pp. 190-198.

Myers, K.F.: The relationship between degree of disability and vocal range, vocal range midpoint, and pitchmatching ability of mentally retarded and psychiatric clients. *JMT*, 1985, **22**(1), pp. 35-45.

Nash, G.C.: *Creative Approaches to Child Development with Music, Language and Movement.* Port Washington, NY: Alfred Publishing, Co., 1974.

Nelson, D., Anderson, V. & Gonzales, A.: Music activities as therapy for children with autism and other pervasive developmental disorders. *JMT*, 1984, **21**(3), pp. 100-116.

Nocera, S.D.: *Reaching the Special Learner Through Music.* Morristown, NJ: Silver Burdett, Co., 1979.

Nocera, S.: Special education teachers need a special education. *MEJ*, 1972, **58**(4), pp. 73-74.

Nordoff, P.: *My Mother Goose, I.* Bryn Mawr, PA: Theodore Presser, 1981.
Nordoff, P.: *My Mother Goose, II.* Bryn Mawr, PA: Theodore Presser, 1981.
Nordoff, P.: *Folk Songs for Children to Sing and Play on Resonator Bells.* Bryn Mawr, PA: Theodore Presser, 1982.
Nordoff, P.: *Fanfares and Dances.* Bryn Mawr, PA: Theodore Presser, 1979.
Nordoff, P. & Robbins, C.: *Fun for Four Drums.* Bryn Mawr, PA: Theodore Presser, 1968.
Nordoff, P. & Robbins, C.: *Pif-Paf-Poltrie.* Bryn Mawr, PA: Theodore Presser, 1969.
Nordoff, P. & Robbins, C.: *Songs for Children.* Bryn Mawr, PA: Theodore Presser, 1973.
Nordoff, P. & Robbins, C.: *Spirituals for Children to Sing and Play.* Bryn Mawr, PA: Theodore Presser, 1971.
Nordoff, P. & Robbins, C.: *Children's Play Songs.* Bryn Mawr, PA: Theodore Presser, 1962.
Nordoff, P. & Robbins, C.: *Music Therapy in Special Education.* St. Louis, MO: MMB Music, Inc., 1986.
North, E.F.: Music therapy as an important treatment modality with psychotic children. *JMT*, 1966, 3(1), pp. 22-24.
Obrecht, D.: The wheeling motor facilitation program. *Journal of the Association for the Study of Perception*, 1968, 3(2), pp. 11-17.
Orff, G.: *The Orff Music Therapy.* London: Schott & Co. 1974.
Palmer, H.: *Songbook: Learning Basic Skills Through Music I.* Activity Records, Inc., 1971.
Palmer, H.: *Songbook: Learning Basic Skills Through Music II.* Activity Records, Inc., 1972.
Palmer, H.: *Songbook: Getting to Know Myself.* Activity Records, Inc., 1974.
Peters, M.L.: A comparison of the musical sensitivity of mongoloid and normal children. *JMT*, 1970, 7(4), pp. 113-123.
Peterson, C.A.: Sharing your knowledge of folk guitar with a blind friend. *The New Outlook for the Blind*, 1969, 63(4), pp. 142-146.
Pirtle, M. & Seaton, K.P.: Use of music training to actuate conceptual growth in neurologically handicapped children. *Journal of Research in Music Education*, 1973, 21(4), pp. 292-301.
Plach, T.: *Creative Use of Music in Group Therapy.* Springfield, IL: Charles C. Thomas, 1980.
Podvin, M.G.: The influence of music on the performance of a work task. *JMT*, 1967, 4(2), pp. 52-56.
Poffenberger, N.: *Poffenberger Keyboard Method – for Normal, Exceptional and the Handicapped Population.* Cincinnati, OH: Fun Publishing, 1982.
Ponath, L.H. & Bitcon, C.H.: A behavioral analysis of Orff-Schulwerk. *JMT*, 1972, 9(2), pp. 56-63.
Presti, G.M.: A levels system approach to music therapy with severely handicapped children in the public school. *JMT*, 1984, 21(3), pp. 117-125.
Price, R., Rast, L. & Winterfeldt, C.: Out of pandemonium – music! *MEJ*, 1972, 58(4), pp. 35-36.
Purvis, J. & Samet, S. (Eds.): *Music in Developmental Therapy: A Curriculum Guide.* Baltimore: University Park Press, 1976.
Ramsey, J.: For Peggy, a chance to excel. *MEJ*, 1982, 68(8), pp. 28-29.
Reardon, D.M. & Bell, G.: Effects of sedative and stimulative music on activity levels of severely retarded boys. *American Journal of Mental Deficiency*, 1970, 75(2), pp. 156-159.
Reeves, H.: *Song and Dance Activities for Elementary Children.* West Nyack, NY: Parker Pub. Co., 1985.
Reid, D.H., Hill, B.K., Rawers, R.J. & Montegar, C.A.: The use of contingent music in teaching social skills to a nonverbal hyperactive boy. *JMT*, 1975, 12(1), pp. 2-18.
Rejto, A.: Music as an aid to the remediation of learning disabilities. *Journal of Learning Disabilities*, 1973, 6, pp. 286-295.
Resnick, R.: Creative movement classes for visually handicapped children in a public school setting. *The New Outlook for the Blind*, 1973, 67(10), pp. 442-447.
Rice, T.A.: *Music as Auditory Stimuli to Facilitate Visual Memory in Learning Disabled Children.* Unpublished master's thesis, Florida State University, 1978.
Richman, J.S.: Background music for repetitive task performance of severely retarded individuals. *American Journal of Mental Deficiency*, 1976, 81(3), pp. 251-255.
Rieber, M.: The effect of music on the activity level of children. *Psychonomic Science*, 1965, 3, pp. 325-326.
Rigrodsky, S., Hanley, T.D. & Steer, M.D.: *Application of Mowrers Autistic Theory to the Speech Habilitation of the Mentally Retarded Pupils.* Lafayette, IN: Purdue University, 1959.
Ritschl, C., Mongrella, J. & Presbie, R.: Group time out from rock-and-roll music and out-of-seat behavior of handicapped children while riding a school bus. *Psychological Reports*, 1972, 31, pp. 967-973.

Robbins, C. & Robbins, C.: *Music with the Hearing Impaired.* St. Louis, MO: MMB Music, Inc., 1982.

Robins, F & Robins, J.: *Education Rhythmics for Mentally and Physically Handicapped Children.* New York: Association Press, 1968.

Robinson, D.: Is there a correlation between rhythmic response and emotional disturbance? *JMT*, 1970, **7**(2), p. 54.

Rosene, P.E.: Including the handicapped in junior high general music classes. *MEJ*, May 1981, pp. 56-57.

Rosene, P.E.: Instrumental music. . . A success opportunity. *MEJ*, 1982, **68**(8), pp. 37-39.

Roskam, K.: Music as a remediation tool for learning disabled children. *JMT*, 1976, **16**, pp. 31-42.

Roskam, K.: Music as a remediation tool for learning disabled children. *Sounding Board*, May 1976, p. 20.

Roskam, K.: Music therapy as an aid for increasing auditory awareness and improving reading skill. *JMT*, 1979, **16**(1), pp. 31-42.

Ross, D.M., Ross, S.A. & Kuchenbecker, S.L.: Rhythmic training for educable mentally retarded children. *Mental Retardation*, 1973, **11**, pp. 20-23.

Ruud, E.: *Music Therapy and its Relationship to Current Treatment Theories.* St. Louis, MO: MMB Music, Inc., 1986.

Salsburg, R.S. & Greenwald, M.A.: Effects of a token system on attentiveness and punctuality in two string instrument classes. *JMT*, 1977, **14**(1), pp. 27-38.

Saperston, B.: The use of music in establishing communication with an autistic mentally retarded child. *JMT*, 1973, **10**(4), pp. 184-188.

Saperston, B., Chan, R., Morphew, C. & Carsrud, K.: Music listening versus juice as a reinforcement for learning in profoundly mentally retarded individuals. *JMT*, 1980, **17**(4), pp. 174-183.

Scartelli, J.: The effect of sedative music on electromyographic biofeedback assisted relaxation of spastic cerebral palsied adults. *JMT*, 1982, **19**(4), pp. 210-218.

Schlanger, B.: Speech measurement of handicapped children. *American Journal of Mental Deficiency*, 1953, **58**, pp. 114-120.

Schloss, P.J., Smith, M.A., Goldsmith, L. & Selinger, J.: Identifying current and relevant curricular sequences for multiply involved hearing-impaired learners. *American Annals of the Deaf*, September 1984, pp. 370-374.

Schulberg, C.H.: *The Music Therapy Sourcebook.* New York: Human Sciences Press, 1982.

Seybold, C.D.: The value and use of music activities in the treatment of speech delayed children. *JMT*, 1971, **8**(3), pp. 102-110.

Shames, G.H. & Rubin, H. (Eds.): *Stuttering: Then and Now.* Columbus, OH: Charles E. Merrill, 1985.

Shames, G.H. & Wiig, E.H. (Eds.): *Human Communication Disorders: An Introduction.* Columbus, OH: Charles E. Merrill, 1985.

Shehan, P.K.: A comparison of mediation strategies in paired-associate learning for children with learning disabilities. *JMT*, 1981, **18**(3), pp. 120-127.

Shepherd, L.T. Jr., & Simons, G.M.: Music training for the visually handicapped. *MEJ*, 1970, **57**(6), pp. 80-81.

Sheridan, W.: *The Oregon Plan for Mainstreaming in Music.* Salem, OR: State Department of Education, 1977.

Sherwin, A.C.: Reactions to music of autistic (schizophrenic) children. *American Journal of Psychiatry*, 1953, **109**, pp. 823-831.

Slyoff, M.R.: *Music for Special Education.* Fort Worth, TX: Harris Music, 1979.

Smith, R.B. & Flohr, J.W.: *Music Dramas for Children with Special Needs.* Denton, TX: Troostwyk Press, 1984

Sontag, E., Smith, S. & Certo, N. (Eds.): *Educational Programming for the Severely and Profoundly Handicapped.* Reston, VA: Council for Exceptional Children, 1977.

Soraci, S., Deckner, C., McDaniel, C. & Blanton, R.: The relationship between rate of rhythmicity and the stereotypic behaviors of abnormal children. *JMT*, 1982, **19**(1), pp. 46-54.

Sparks, R.W. & Holland, A.: Melodic intonation therapy for aphasia. *JMT*, 1976, **4**(41), pp. 287-297.

Spitzer, M.: A survey of the use of music in schools for the hearing impaired. *The Volta Review*, December 1984, pp. 362-363.

Stainback, S.B., Stainback, W.C. & Hallahan, D.P.: Effect of background music on learning. *Exceptional Children*, 1973, **40**(2), pp. 109-110.

Staum, M.J.: Music and rhythmic stimuli in the rehabilitation of gait disorders. *JMT*, 1983, **20**(2), pp. 69-87.

Staum, M.J.: Music notation to improve the speech prosody of hearing impaired children. *JMT*, 1987, **24**(3), pp. 146-159.

Staum, M. J. & Flowers, P J.: The use of simulated training and music lessons in teaching appropriate shopping skills to an autistic child. *Music Therapy Perspectives*, 1984, **1**(3), pp. 14-17.

Steele, A.L.: Effects of social reinforcement on the musical preference of mentally retarded children. *JMT*, 1967, **4**(2), pp. 57-62.

Steele, A.L.: Programmed use of music to alter uncooperative problem behavior. *JMT*, 1968, **5**(4), pp. 103-107.

Steele, A.L.: Music Therapy for the learning disabled: Intervention and Instruction. *Music Therapy Perspectives*, 1984, **1**(3), pp. 2-7.

Steele, A.L.: In: Zolinger, R. & Klein, N. (Eds.), *Learning Disabilities: An Interdisciplinary Perspective*. Case Western Reserve, Department of Education, 1975.

Steele, A.L. & Jorgenson, H.A.: Music therapy: An effective solution to problems in related disciplines. *JMT*, 1971, **8**(4), pp. 131-145.

Steele, A.L., Vaughan, M. & Dolan, C.: The school support program: Music therapy for adjustment problems in elementary schools. *JMT*, 1976, **13**, pp. 87-100.

Stern, V.: They shall have music. *The Volta Review*, 1975, **77**(8), pp. 495-500.

Sterlicht, M., Deutsch, M.R. & Siegel, I.: Influence of musical stimulation upon the functioning of institutionalized retardates. *Psychiatric Quarterly Supplement*, 1967, **41**(2), p. 323.

Stevens, E.: Music therapy in the treatment of autistic children. *JMT*, 1969, **6**(4), p. 98.

Stevens, E.A.: Some effects of tempo changes on stereotyped rocking movements of low-level mentally retarded subjects. *American Journal of Mental Deficiency*, 1971, **76**(1), pp. 76-81.

Stoesz, G.: *A Suggested Guide to Piano Literature for the Partially Seeing*. New York: National Society for the Prevention of Blindness, 1966.

Stubbs, B.: A study of the effectiveness of an integrated, personified approach to learning with trainable mental retardates. *JMT*, 1970, **7**(3), pp. 77-82.

Swaiko, N.: The role and value of an eurhythmics program in a curriculum for deaf children. *American Annals of the Deaf*, 1974, **119**(3), pp. 321-324.

Talkington, L.W. & Hall, S.M.: A musical application of Premack's hypothesis to low verbal retardates. *JMT*, 1970, **7**(3), pp. 95-99.

Thaut, M.H.: The use of auditory rhythm and rhythmic speech to aid temporal muscular control in children with gross motor dysfunction. *JMT*, 1985, **22**(3), pp. 108-128.

Thompson, K.: Music for every child: Education of handicapped learners. *MEJ*, 1982, **68**(8), pp. 25-28.

Tomat, J.H. & Krutzky, C.D.: *Learning Through Music for Special Children and Their Teachers*. South Waterford, MA: Merriam-Eddy, 1975.

Tomatis, A.: *Education and Dyslexia*. Dallas, TX: Sound of Light, 1986.

Topics in Language Disorders. Case studies of phonological disorders. 1983, **3**(2). (Gaithersberg, MD: Aspen Systems).

Topics in Language Disorders. Nonbiased assessment of language difference. 1983, **3**(3). (Gaithersberg, MD: Aspen Systems).

Topics in Language Disorders. Aphasia: Selected contemporary consideration. 1983, **3**(4). (Gaithersberg, MD: Aspen Systems).

Topics in Language Disorders. Pragmatics in language-disordered children. 1983, **4**(1). (Gaithersberg, MD: Aspen Systems).

Topics in Language Disorders. Adolescent language learning disorders. 1984, **4**(2). (Gaithersberg, MD: Aspen Systems).

Topics in Language Disorders. Neurolinguistic approaches to language disorders. 1984, **4**(3). (Gaithersberg, MD: Aspen Systems).

Topics in Language Disorders. Language development and disorders in the social context. 1984, **4**(4). (Gaithersberg, MD: Aspen Systems).

Topics in Language Disorders. Language intervention with the mentally retarded child. 1984, **5**(1). (Gaithersberg, MD: Aspen Systems).

Topics in Language Disorders. Discourse and language impaired children: Clinical issues. 1985, **5**(2). (Gaithersberg, MD: Aspen Systems).

Topics in Language Disorders. The years between 10 and 18. 1985, **5**(3). (Gaithersberg, MD: Aspen Systems).

Topics in Language Disorders. Implications for L1 and L2 learning. 1985, **5**(4). (Gaithersberg, MD: Aspen Systems).

Topics in Language Disorders. High technology and language disorders. 1985, **6**(1). (Gaithersberg, MD: Aspen Systems).

Topics in Language Disorders. Discourse disorders. 1986, **6**(2). (Gaithersberg, MD: Aspen Systems).

Traub, C.: The relation of music to speech of low verbalizing subjects in a music listening activity. *JMT*, 1969, **6**(4), pp. 105-107.

Underhill, K.K. & Harris, L.M.: The effect of contingent music on establishing imitation in behaviorally disturbed retarded children. *JMT*, 1974, **11**(3), pp. 156-166.

Vaughn, M.M.: Music for our gifted children: A bridge to consciousness. *MEJ*, 1972, **58**(4), pp. 70-72; 131-132.

Vernazza, M.: What are we doing about music in special education? *MEJ*, 1967, **68**(8), pp. 49-50.

Vettese, J.: Instrumental lessons for deaf children. *The Volta Review*, 1974, **76**(4), pp. 219-222.

Walker, J.B.: The use of music as an aid in developing functional speech in the institutionalized mentally retarded. *JMT*, 1972, **9**(1), pp. 1-12.

Walker, D.: When it comes to music they see the light. *The Pointer*, 1974, **19**(2), p. 127.

Ward, D.: *Hearts and Hands and Voices: Music in the Education of Slow Learners.* London: Oxford University Press, 1976.

Ward, D.: *Sing a Rainbow: Musical Activities with Mentally Handicapped Children.* London: Oxford University Press, 1979.

Wasserman, N., Plutchik, R., Deutsch, R. & Taketomo, Y.: A music therapy evaluation scale and its clinical application to mentally retarded adult patients. *JMT*, 1973, **10**, pp. 64-77.

Wasserman, N., Plutchik, R., Deutsch, R. & Taketomo, Y.: The musical background of a group of mentally retarded psychotic patients: Implications for music therapy. *JMT*, 1973, **10**(2), pp. 78-82.

Weber, R.D.: The use of musical instruments in the education of TMR's. *Council for Research in Music Education*, 1971, **25**, pp. 79-88.

Weigl, V.: Functional music, a therapeutic tool in working with the mentally retarded. *American Journal of Mental Deficiency*, 1959, **63**, pp. 672-678.

Weigl, V.: Music for the retarded. *Music Journal*, 1969, **27**, pp. 56-57.

Weiner, P.S.: Auditory discrimination and articulation. *Journal of Speech and Hearing Disorders*, 1967, **32**, pp. 19-28.

Weisbrod, J.: Shaping a body image through movement therapy. *MEJ*, 1972, **58**(4), pp. 66-69.

Welsbacher, B.T.: The neurologically handicapped child: More than a package of bizarre behaviors. *MEJ*, 1972, **58**(4), pp. 26-28.

Werbner, N.: The practice of music therapy with psychotic children. *JMT*, 1966, **3**(1), pp. 25-31.

White, L.D.: How to adapt for special students. *MEJ*, 1982, **68**(8), pp. 49-50.

Williams, L.D.: A band that exceeds all expectations. *MEJ*, 1985, **71**(6), pp. 26-29.

Wilson, B.L.: *The Effects of Music and Verbal Mediation on the Learning of Paired-Associates by Institutionalized Retardates.* Unpublished master's thesis, Florida State University, 1971.

Wilson, C.V.: The use of rock music as a reward in behavior therapy with children. *JMT*, 1976, **13**(1), pp. 39-48.

Wingert, M.L.: Effects of a music enrichment program in the education of the mentally retarded. *JMT*, 1972, **9**(1), pp. 13-22.

Winson, M.T.: *Arts and Crafts for Special Education.* Belmont CA: Fearon Teacher-Aids, 1972.

Wolfe, D.E.: The effect of automated interrupted music on head posturing of cerebral palsied individuals. *JMT*, 1980, **17**(4), pp. 184-206.

Wolfgram, B.J.: Music therapy for retarded adults with psychotic overlay: A day treatment approach. *JMT*, 1978, **15**(4), pp. 199-207.

Wolpow, R.L.: The independent effects of contingent social and academic approval upon the musical on-task performance behaviors of profoundly retarded adults. *JMT*, 1976, **13**(1), pp. 29-38.

Wylie, M.E.: Eliciting vocal responses in severely and profoundly mentally retarded handicapped subjects. *JMT*, 1983, **20**(4), pp. 190-200.

Yarbrough, C., Charboneau, M. & Wapnick, J.: Music as reinforcement for correct math and attending in ability assigned math classes. *JMT*, 1977, **14**(2), pp. 77-78.

Zimmer, L.J.: *Music Handbook for the Child in Special Education.* Hackensack, NJ: Jos. Boonin, 1976.